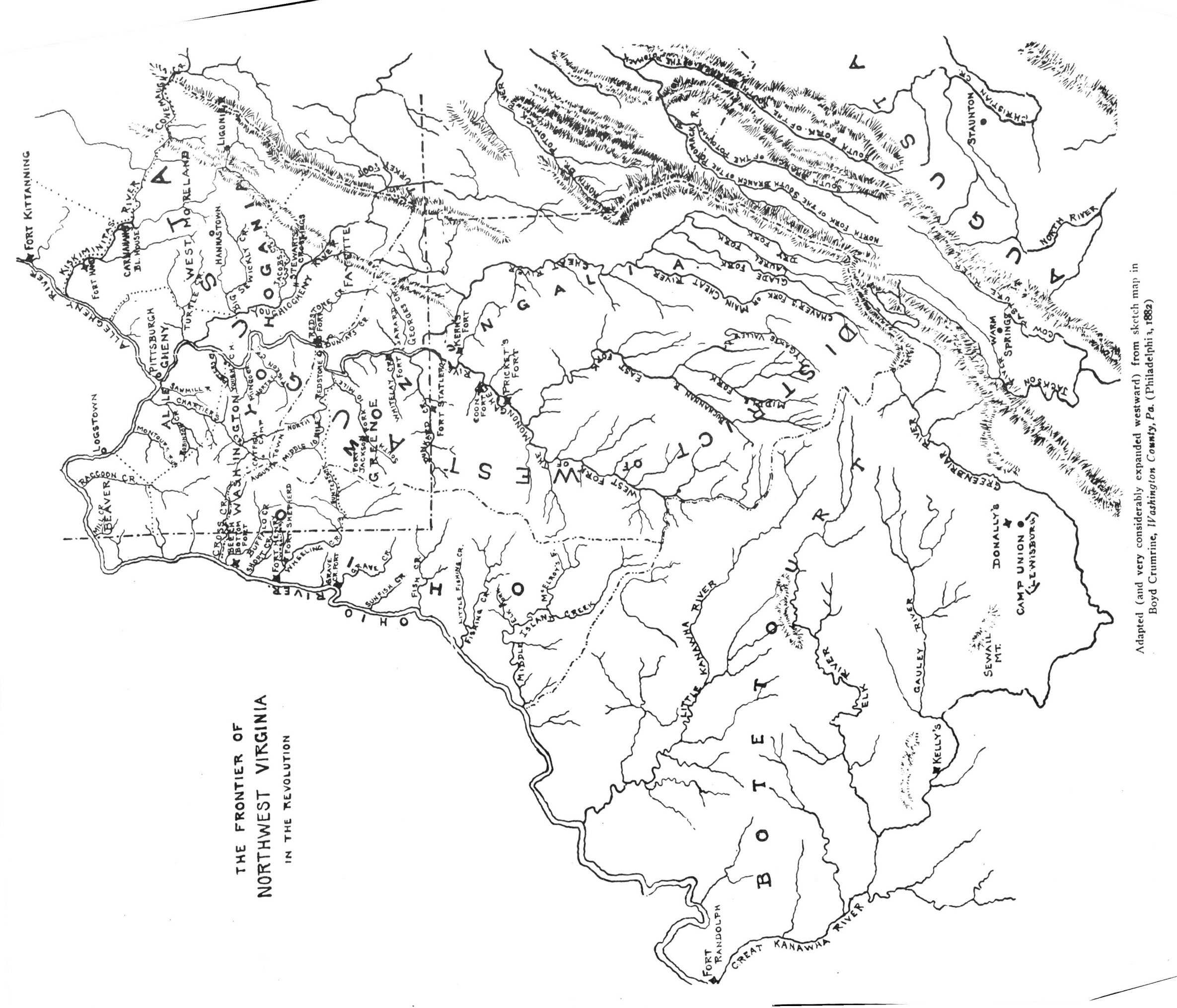

FRONTIER DEFENSE ON THE
UPPER OHIO, 1777-1778

DRAPER SERIES, VOLUME III

FRONTIER DEFENSE

ON THE

Upper Ohio, 1777-1778

Compiled from the Draper Manuscripts in the
Library of the Wisconsin Historical Society
and published at the charge of the Wisconsin
Society of the Sons of the American Revolution

EDITED BY

REUBEN GOLD THWAITES, LL. D.

Superintendent of the Society

AND

LOUISE PHELPS KELLOGG, Ph. D.

Editorial Assistant on the Society's Staff

MADISON
WISCONSIN HISTORICAL SOCIETY
1912
R 77-12270 7 7
KRAUS REPRINT CO.
Millwood, New York
1977

Copyright, 1912
BY THE STATE HISTORICAL SOCIETY OF WISCONSIN

Thwaites, Reuben Gold, 1853-1913, ed.
  Frontier defense on the Upper Ohio, 1777-1778.
  Original ed. issued as v. 3 of Draper series.
  "Compiled from the Draper manuscripts in the library of the Wisconsin Historical Society and published at the charge of the Wisconsin Society of the Sons of the American Revolution."
  1. Ohio Valley—History—Revolution. 2. United States—Revolution—Campaigns and battles. I. Kellogg, Louise Phelps, d. 1942, joint ed. II. Wisconsin. State Historical Society. III. Sons of the American Revolution. Wisconsin Society. IV. Title.
  E230.5.O3T5   1973   973.3'33   72-14277

ISBN 0-527-89980-1

KRAUS REPRINT CO.
A U.S. Division of Kraus-Thomson Organization Limited

Printed in U.S.A.

CONTENTS

Page

Introduction. *The Editors*
Explanation

Documents

Hand at Fort Pitt	1, 188
Frontier posts on the Ohio	3
News from Fort' Pitt	5, 14, 128
Affairs at Detroit	7, 14, 230, 280
Defense of the Virginia frontier	16, 21, 69, 205, 209, 223
General Hand warned	18
Friendly Indian warnings	25
Suggestions from Governor Henry	30
Provisioning and strengthening the forts	33, 46
Sundry raids and skirmishes	33, 36, 78, 93, 138, 151, 248, 273, 294
Expeditions planned	42, 48, 74, 100, 133, 145, 154, 193, 197, 202, 278
The Tory conspiracy	51
The siege of Fort Henry	54, 72
Situation at Fort Henry	50, 76, 83, 129, 138, 245
Kittanning evacuated	82
Indians murdered by frontiersmen	85
Relations with the Delawares	86, 93, 112, 164, 228, 241, 244, 269
Fort Hand built	97
Word from the Muskingum	100
Foreman's defeat	106
Aftermath of Foreman's defeat	118
Reinforcements for Fort Randolph	122

CONTENTS

	Page
Troops for the Continental Army	132
Good news from the East	136
Tory drowned; Zackwell Morgan arrested	142
Fort Randolph reinforced; Cornstalk detained	149
The murder of Cornstalk	157, 168, 175, 240
News from Fort Randolph	171, 194, 246
Indians of the Allegheny	172, 188
Temper of Western Indians	178
The Kentucky settlements	181
Loyalists at Fort Pitt	184
Plans for Clark's expedition	196, 226, 263, 271
The Squaw Campaign	201, 215
Oaths of allegiance	203
Conciliating the Shawnee	234, 258
Report of Commissioners	238
Loyalists escape	249, 274
Boat building	256, 276
Defense of the Southwestern frontier	262, 265
Relations with Spaniards	289
Congress plans for the West	293
News of the French alliance	297
Muster rolls	300
INDEX	307

ILLUSTRATIONS

	Page
Map of the Frontier of Northwest Virginia in the Revolution	*Frontispiece*
Portrait of Gen. Edward Hand	1
Facsimile of portion of Gen. Henry Hamilton's report of Council at Detroit	8
Fort Henry (Wheeling, W. Va.) in 1777	50
Portrait of Mrs. Lydia (Boggs-Shepherd) Cruger	66
Blockhouse, Fort Pitt	128
Monument to Cornstalk, at Point Pleasant, W. Va.	160
Portrait of Col. Moses Shepherd	222
Portrait of Gen. James O'Hara	278
Facsimile of portion of letter by John Campbell to George Rogers Clark	298

INTRODUCTION

The Draper Series, of which this is Volume III, is devoted to the publication of original documentary material obtained in the main from the Draper Manuscript Collection, now in the Society's possession. The task of selection and annotation, and of putting the volumes through the press, has fallen to the present Editors; but the cost of printing has generously been borne by the Wisconsin Society of the Sons of the American Revolution. The first volume, a *Documentary History of Dunmore's War, 1774*, was published in May, 1905; the second, *Revolution on the Upper Ohio, 1775-1777*, appeared in February, 1908. The present is a continuation of Volume II, and will, it is expected, be followed by others, extending the subject to the close of the Revolutionary War.

Volume II closed with news of the coming to Fort Pitt of Gen. Edward Hand. For the frontiersmen of the Upper Ohio, this was an event of much importance. He had served in its garrison during the British regime, and was well-known and popular throughout the district. His appointment was a welcome assurance to the borderers that the commander-in-chief and the Continental Congress proposed, so far as seemed then possible, to assist in their protection.

But the barbaric enemy facing the frontier differed greatly from the well-equipped, well-drilled professional army from Europe that confronted the armed men of the tidewater. The stealthy foes of the border aimed their heaviest blows at the homes, wives, and children of the settlers; no life was safe from them, no person secure. Through long and bitter experience, the backwoodsmen had come to understand the art of defense by concentration within neighborhood blockhouses and log forts. But a new danger presented itself. The Indians were now guided and stimulated by the nation's white enemies, so that to their native cunning were added the superior intelligence and more astute methods of the English. The situation soon became desperate.

The British authorities at Detroit were especially active in urging the Indians to war against the Americans. Permissory orders to that effect were received by Lieutenant-Governor Hamilton early in June, 1777. With consummate skill he roused the barbarians to frenzy; under his stimulus they prepared to hurl themselves upon the American frontier. The invading parties were provided by Hamilton with proclamations prepared both by Governor Carleton and himself, calling on the Western inhabitants to submit to King George and take refuge within the British posts, where a land bounty would be given them for loyal service. This project was adroitly devised to mingle terror and mercy, in the hope that the colonists' rebellion would speedily be crushed on the Western borders; and that the Easterners, finding themselves between two fires, would be obliged to yield. The effect of these proclamations, scattered by Indian raiders throughout the American backwoods settlements, was considerable. In some cases they were suppressed by American officers, but the Loyalist disaffection in the trans-Alleghany is largely attributable to this source.

The herculean task confronting Hand on his arrival at Fort Pitt was to defend the vast frontier (stretching from Kittanning on the north to the Great Kanawha on the south) from the inroads of Indian parties, and to overawe disaffection and active Loyalist measures within the settlements. To accomplish this result, Congress had given him a mere handful of regular troops, and left him to recruit militiamen and commandeer the supplies sufficient for his needs. Four principal forts were placed at strategic points—Kittanning, Pitt, Henry, and Randolph. In addition there were numerous local blockhouses, for every small community "forted" while danger hovered near; but during a lull in hostilities, the men ventured to attend to their home duties in the widely scattered farmsteads and fields. To add to his difficulties, Hand was much embarrassed by the active and often virulent boundary controversy between Pennsylvania and Virginia, both states claiming jurisdiction of the region around Fort Pitt.

Fortunately for the final event, the tribesmen who had declared war against the border were those known to the frontiersmen as the "far Indians," with habitats about Detroit and along the Sandusky, Maumee, and Wabash rivers, where they were closely under British tutelage. The Shawnee and Delawares of the nearer wilderness had not yet forgotten the battle of Point Pleasant (1774), and for the time adhered to their treaty with the Americans made in 1775 at Pittsburgh—not only maintaining neutrality, but proving their friendliness by giving timely warnings of the approach of war parties. The Delawares in particular acted as a buffer between the Americans and the Indian allies of the British. Their chiefs went frequently and freely to Fort Pitt, and the Moravian missionaries among them were useful agents for the colonial cause.

Had the frontiersmen but carefully distinguished between Indian friends and foes, and kept the faith as loyally as the former, much trouble might have been avoided. There was, however, a savage spirit among the rank and file of the borderers, that did no honor to the American cause. Hand was obliged continually to intervene to protect the lives of the friendly Delawares, for he had reason to fear their massacre by the inhabitants around Fort Pitt. This disposition culminated in the dastardly murder of Chief Cornstalk, with three of his tribe, in the autumn of 1777, while they were detained as hostages within the walls of Fort Randolph. This same indiscriminately revengeful disposition broke out against the Loyalists, one of whose leaders, Hickson, was drowned while a prisoner, apparently by the connivance of the militia officer in charge. With Cornstalk's death vanished the hope of neutrality for the Shawnee, and both the Kentucky settlements and the Virginia frontier suffered repeatedly from the avenging fury of this tribe.

As a rule, Indian war-parties against the American frontier were small. They sought to elude the garrisons, penetrate into the settlements before discovery, strike a quick blow, and then retire. During 1777, however, considerable forces of the aboriginal enemy twice appeared on the border, prepared for hostile operations on a larger scale than usual. September 1, two hundred or more Indians invested Fort Henry, determined, as White Eyes picturesquely put it, "to carry Wheeling home" to the native towns. Although forewarned by the friendly Delawares, the militia officers had grown careless, dismissed the levies that had come to their assistance, and on the morning of the attack had less than a hundred men within the stockade. The siege continued during two exciting days, at the close of which the persistent enemy withdrew, after slaying all outlying cattle and other domestic animals.

The attack on Wheeling aroused the county militia of both Pennsylvania and Virginia, and company after company poured into Fort Pitt to do garrison duty for the outlying posts. Among the reinforcements sent to Fort Henry was a band of men from the interior county of Hampshire,[1] whose inhabitants had for a generation been free from Indian ravages. These newcomers found the inaction at Wheeling irksome. Toward the last of September, forty-six of them, headed by their officers, started on a scouting expedition down the Ohio, when twenty-one of the party lost their lives in a native ambush at McMechen's Narrows—the event known in border history as the Foreman Massacre. For some time after this unfortunate affair, savage raids on the Western border were

---

[1] Now in West Virginia.

less frequent. This seems to have been due to the defeat of St. Leger's expedition, and the terror inspired in the Western tribesmen by Burgoyne's surrender, together with the possibility of final colonial triumph.

In the frontiersman's calendar, winter stood for peace. But the vengeance to be feared for Cornstalk's murder made the winter of 1777-78 a time of busy preparations for defense. Hand even hoped to conduct an offensive raid, to seize some stores at Sandusky, and thus inflict a blow on the British fur-traders and their tribal customers. Collecting a small force from the western counties of Pennsylvania, he set forth in February on the first regular expedition into Indian territory since the outbreak of the Revolution. A sudden rise of the waters defeated his plans. He penetrated no farther than Beaver Creek, where he raided two Indian camps, inhabited chiefly by squaws. This expedition was thenceforth derisively known as the "Squaw Campaign."

During the winter, Pittsburgh and its vicinity was a hive of activity, induced by preparations for three important Western expeditions. Documents descriptive of the voyage of Gibson and Linn to New Orleans, to secure powder, were presented in Volume II of this series. Encouraged by the success of that undertaking, and by the strong sympathy with the Americans evinced by the Spanish authorities at New Orleans, two expeditions outfitted in Pittsburgh to proceed to the lower reaches of the Mississippi. One originating in Virginia, was led by Col. David Rogers and had for its object the procuring of supplies. The one authorized by Congress was in the care of Capt. James Willing; this was bolder in scope, and embraced a plan to seize West Florida and hold that region for the patriot cause. The third was under Col. George Rogers Clark, a pioneer of Kentucky; but the destination of this expedition was as yet unrevealed. Colonel Clark himself arrived at the neighborhood of Fort Pitt early in February, and at once began the work of recruiting, boat-building, and provisioning. Considerable opposition was manifested by the inhabitants to detaching men from this exposed frontier at so critical a juncture; but General Hand was admitted to the secret of Clark's intention to capture the British-French garrisons in the Illinois, and quietly aided him with such supplies and support as he could furnish. Not until Clark was well on his way down the river did the news of the French-American alliance reach Pittsburgh. This important fact was communicated to him with all speed, and no doubt contributed materially to his success among the French of the Illinois.

Meanwhile communications were maintained with the Spanish of Louisiana. In February a message from the governor of New Orleans was received at Fort Pitt; but as no one there was able to translate this document, it was taken to Congress by Col. George Morgan. Even in this body no satisfactory translator could be found; consequently, Morgan's response, forwarded by Captain Willing, was necessarily couched in vague terms of friendship, with a recapitulation of the colonial victories and successes.

Hand had in view for the spring of 1778 another invasion of Indian territory; he was convinced that nothing else would prove efficacious in subduing the tribesmen. At first, success seemed wholly probable. But among the men surrounding the general was Col. Alexander McKee, formerly an Indian agent, but long suspected of Loyalist tendencies. He was necessarily well-informed of Hand's plans. On the night of March 28, McKee broke the parole which he had given, and taking with him several confederates and servants, escaped to the Indian towns, on his way to place and preferment under the British flag.

Hand had by now found his position intolerable. Eager to serve his country, he was satisfied that, without success, he had done all that any man might in the circumstances, and that he could henceforth be more useful in the Eastern army. A new commandant, better supported than he had been, might, he thought, win laurels on the Western frontier. His petition for a recall was seconded by three commissioners then at Fort Pitt investigating the situation and the Loyalists' movements, and received the assent of Congress. Gen. Lachlan McIntosh was thereupon appointed to the West, and being better equipped was able to take the offensive from Fort Pitt and strike an effective blow in the enemy's country.

Hand, however, had ably performed a difficult service. At a critical period he saved the frontier from being pushed back upon the colonies. His watchful care, his careful husbanding of resources, his aid to far Western expeditions, and his successful maintenance of local garrisons, mark his administration as one of vigor and efficiency. His command at Fort Pitt is memorable in the annals of the American Revolution. Our volume closes with his recall to the Eastern field.

In addition to the material found in the Draper Manuscripts we include a few documents from other sources—some letters from Col. George Morgan's letter-book, the transcripts of which have kindly been furnished to us by Mr. Harrison W. Craver, librarian of the Carnegie Library, Pittsburgh; three documents obtained through the courteous offices of Dr. Arthur G. Doughty, from the Canadian Archives at Ottawa; and portions of the Hand letters to Yeates, of which accurate transcripts were obligingly sent to us by Dr. John Billings, director of the New York Public Library. Our acknowledgments are also due to Dr. Victor Hugo Paltsits, late New York State Historian, for information concerning the Oswego Treaty of 1777.

The transcriptions from the Draper Manuscript Collection are largely the careful work of Miss Daisy G. Beecroft, of the Society's Library staff; the proofreading has been under the expert supervision of Miss Annie A. Nunns, secretary to the senior Editor; and the excellent map has been prepared by Miss Mary Stuart Foster, also of the Society's staff.

R. G. T.
L. P. K.

EXPLANATORY

Following the names of the writer and recipient of each document is given its press-mark in the Draper Manuscript Collection, by which the original can readily be identified if its further consultation is desired. The capital letter or letters refer to the series to which the document belongs; the volume number precedes the series letter, the folio or page number follows. E. g., the press-mark 1SS57 means Vol. 1 of the Shepherd Papers, p. 57; the press-mark 49J13 is equivalent to Vol. 49 of the George Rogers Clark MSS, p. 13.

Immediately after the press-mark, the nature of the document is indicated by the descriptive initials customarily employed in describing manuscripts:

A. L.—autograph letter unsigned (usually a draft in the author's handwriting).

A. L. S.—autograph letter signed.

L. S.—letter signed (text being in another's handwriting).

D. S.—document signed.

GENERAL EDWARD HAND
From *Pennsylvania Archives*, 2d series, x, p. 14

FRONTIER DEFENSE ON THE UPPER OHIO, 1777-1778

HAND TAKES COMMAND AT FORT PITT

[Gen. Edward Hand to Col. David Shepherd. 1SS57— A. L. S.]

Whereas the Honourable the Continental Congress have thought proper to appoint me to take the Command on the Frontiers of Virginia and Pennsylvania[1] & to embody such of the Militia as I shall think adequate to the Defence of the Country. And whereas the late Murders committed by the Savages, encouraged & supported by our cruel Enemies evidently point out the absolute Necessity of a perfect union and Harmony amongst the Frontier Inhabitants in Defence of their Lives, Liberties & Properties

I do hereby declare, that in Execution of the Trust reposed in me, I shall consider those persons as dangerous & disaffected to the American Cause, who abet or in any wise foment the present unhappy disputes between the states of Virginia & Pennsylvania to the

---

[1] Concerning General Hand and his appointment to command at Fort Pitt, see Thwaites and Kellogg, *Revolution on the Upper Ohio* (Madison, 1908), p. 256. He arrived June 1, escorted by a troop of Westmoreland lighthorse militia.—ED.

public injury.² The Love of our Country will I trust, teach us to forget all Invidious distinctions & to pay the proper attention to merit, unconfined to Party. we shall do the most essential Service to the Common weal by Carefully avoiding the giving any just cause of offence to the Indians. Should a General war with the savages be inevitable, I have the highest Confidence in the fortitude of the Militia & their Zeal for the public Service, which Comprehends their dearest Interests. The knowledge I have formed of the Country & its Inhabitants by a long residence at Fort Pitt, renders my present Command highly pleasing to me.³ Happy should I be if I can Conduce by my Labours to the Safety of the Frontier. Congress hath directed the removal of the Continental Troops from this Quarter except the 300 Men to be stationed at Forts Pitt, Randolph & the Kittanning⁴ as these Companies are not yet Compleated; I expect you will be pleased to

---

² For the boundary dispute between Virginia and Pennsylvania, each claiming the site of Pittsburgh, see *Ibid*, pp. 18, 19.—ED.

³ General Hand came to America in 1767 with the 18th (or Royal Irish) regiment, two companies of which were stationed at Fort Pitt 1768-72. There Hand purchased a commission as ensign in the regiment, which he resigned two years later to settle in Lancaster, Pa.—ED.

⁴ Fort Pitt was built not far from the site of the French Fort Duquesne not long after the evacuation of the former, and was garrisoned by British troops until 1772, when it was abandoned by them. In January, 1774, it was restored by Virginia authority and rechristened Fort Dunmore, after the governor of that colony. At the close of Dunmore's War it was again evacuated, until garrisoned by American troops under Col. John Neville in the summer of 1775.

For Fort Randolph, see Thwaites and Kellogg, *Dunmore's War* (Madison, 1905), p. 310, note 27; for Kittanning, *Rev. Upper Ohio*, p. 200, note 39.—ED.

take the most effectual methods in your Power to have the posts directed to be occupied on the Frontiers by the late Board of Officers, kept up untill some more advantageous regulation can take place. If in the mean Time any pressing Occasion should demand an additional number of the Militia I hope they will be in readiness to march on the shortest Notice.

I rely greatly on your activity & public Zeal & have the Honour to be Y^r. most obed^t. & most Hble. Servt.

EWD^d HAND B. G.

FORT PITT June 3^d. 1777.
On public Service to Col. David Shepherd at the Mouth of Wheeling Ohio County Virginia.[5]

FRONTIER POSTS ON THE OHIO

[Memorandum, unsigned. 1U54.]

FORT PITT June ye 3^d 1777

Memorandum for General Hand of the Difrent Post[s] from Wheeling to the Great Kanhaway

The Kittaning 50 Mile from this Post Garrison^d. by on[e] Company of the Western Battallion of Continentall Troops and a Comp^y ordered from the Westmoreland Militia to Releve them[6]

A small Guard of men Consisting of nine at a Stockaid Built at Munters bottom by the Adgecent [adjacent] inhabitants,

---

[5] For David Shepherd, at this time county-lieutenant for the newly-erected Ohio County, see *Ibid*, p. 196, note 30.—ED.

[6] The 8th Pennsylvania regiment marched from Kittanning in December, 1776, leaving one company to garrison the fort at that place. This was an independent company under command of Capt. Samuel Moorhead. See a letter dated June 4, 1777, from General Hand to Colonel Lochry, concerning supplies for this post, in Mrs. Mary C. Darlington, *Fort Pitt and Letters from the Frontier* (Pittsburgh, 1892), p. 223.—ED.

at a place Call^d. Rordons bottom about 40 Miles below this post an Officer and 15 men

at the Mouth of Yellow Creek[7] fifteen Miles below the Last mentioned Place Built by the inhabitants an officer and 20 men

at the Mingo Bottom[8] 20 below Yellow Creek a Lieut. of the Regelers and 18 men, to be releved if not alredy don by Milititia

at Wheeling[9] a Company of Boutt [Botetourt?] Militia

at the Mouth of Grave Creek twelve Miles below Wheeling a Company of Ohio County Militia[10]

---

[7] Yellow Creek was the scene of the massacre of Logan's family, three years before the building of this fort. See *Dunmore's War,* pp. 17-19.—ED.

[8] Mingo Bottom was on the west side of the Ohio, where the town of Mingo Junction now is. Probably the fort was opposite, on the Virginia side of the river, which may likewise have been called Mingo Bottom. The locality took its name from a town of Mingo Indians established there during the French and Indian War. Croghan in 1765 speaks of it as a "Seneca village" on a high bank on the north shore. When Washington passed in 1770 there were twenty cabins and about seventy inhabitants. Rev. David Jones in 1772 says the people of this town were wont to plunder canoes, and that he was happy enough to pass in the night undiscovered. The raiding of this band of robbers was one of the inciting causes of Dunmore's War. Before that war they had abandoned their town near Cross Creek, and retreated to the headwaters of the Scioto. There Wood visited them the following year—see Rev. *Upper Ohio,* p. 48, note 77; also p. 217. The locality of their former town on the Ohio retained its name. It was the rendezvous both for the Moravian expedition and that of Crawford in the latter part of the Revolution. An important Indian trail led thence to the Muskingum towns; hence the necessity of the garrison here noted.—ED.

[9] For the garrison at Wheeling, see Rev. *Upper Ohio,* pp. 232, 242-244.—ED.

[10] For this garrison, commanded by Capt. William Harrod, see *Ibid,* index. It was abandoned in July, 1777, the troops being concentrated at Wheeling.—ED.

at the Great Kanhaway 2 Comp^y. of Regalors one hundred Each to releve by Militia[11]

NEWS FROM FORT PITT

[Gen. Edward Hand to Jasper Yeates. Original MS. in New York Public Library; Hand Papers[12]—A. L. S.]

FORT PITT 10th. of June 1777

DEAR YEATES—Since I wrote to Kitty[13] by Col: Morgan[14] nothing has happened in this part of the World worth notice except the murder of One man on the evening of the 7th. Instant at wheeling[15], I suppose by a part of the Pluggys town Gang[16]. the

---

[11] For a sketch of Fort Randolph, at the mouth of the Great Kanawha River, see *Ibid*, p. 185, note 18. Of the two companies one was from Virginia, under Capt. Matthew Arbuckle; one from Pennsylvania, under Capt. John Robinson. *Ibid*, pp. 230, 231, 239-241.—ED.

[12] A portion of the Hand Papers which are among the Draper MSS. are in the form of transcripts made in 1852 by Dr. Draper. The originals of a number of these, however, are now in the New York Public Library, whose director, Dr. John S. Billings, has kindly furnished us with fresh transcripts thereof, and these are followed in the present volume.

For a brief sketch of Jasper Yeates, who was commissioner for the treaty of 1775, see *Rev. Upper Ohio*, p. 191, note 25.—ED.

[13] Kitty (Catherine Ewing) was Mrs. Edward Hand. She was a niece of Jasper Yeates, whose sister Sarah was her mother. General Hand was married in 1775; his wife died in 1805, aged fifty-four years.—ED.

[14] George Morgan, Indian agent, who had gone to Philadelphia to consult with Congress on the Indian situation. For a sketch, see *Rev. Upper Ohio*, p. 31, note 59.—ED.

[15] The man whose murder is here mentioned was Thomas McCleary, a member of Captain Van Meter's company, who with one comrade had gone fishing up Wheeling Creek. For details, see *Pennsylvania Archives*, 1st series, v, p. 445.—ED.

[16] For the hostilities committed by this band of Indians and the expedition against their town planned and then abandoned, see *Rev. Upper Ohio, passim.*—ED.

Chiefs of the wiandots & Mingos are expect[ed] to Assemble here towards the end of next month. hope that nest may be removed. I have seen an Address from some of the Principle Inhabitants of Philad[a] to the Inhabitants of Westmoreland, inclosing A Coppy of one to the Board of War & Assembly of Pennsylvania, & the Boards Ans[r] when I saw it there was but two Signers. I am tomorrow to Attend A Gen[l]. Meeting of Militia Officers at Catfish's Camp[17]. it is not unprobable that the Congress will send Commissioners to meet the indians at the Approaching Treaty I beg my love to every body & am D[r]. Yeates most Affectionately yours

Edw[d]. Hand

Jasper Yeates Esq[r].

A great Part of the most Valuable stores are Arived the rem[r]. to be at Hanna's Town[18] to day. the Gar-

---

[17] Catfish's Camp was the early name for the white settlement on the site of the present town of Washington, Pa. The land was taken up as early as 1768, and a small settlement developed, which was augmented during the Indian troubles by removals from the Ohio. The name is said to have been given in honor of Catfish, a Delaware Indian who had his village in this vicinity. At the council of war held at this place, it was decided that 200 men, properly armed and officered, should be drafted to relieve the militia then on duty. June 27, the Monongalia officers held a council to make preparations to carry out this draft. Draper MSS., 1U60.—Ed.

[18] Hannastown was an important station on the road to Pittsburgh, being located at the junction of Forbes's road with an Indian trail to the Kiskiminitas. In 1773 it was made the seat of the newly-erected county of Westmoreland, and was the first seat of justice west of the Alleghanies. During 1774-78 it rivalled Pittsburgh in importance. In 1782 the town was captured and completely destroyed by a marauding band of Indians. Although partially rebuilt, and remaining the county seat until 1786, it never regained its earlier importance.—Ed.

rison not Better Supplied with provision than you found it.

Give me leave to introduce Col: Russell the Commandant of the West Augusta Battalion a very worthy man[19]. Jessy is Well & Desires his love[20].

ED. H.

COUNCIL AT DETROIT

[Official report of Hamilton. 49J13—D. S.[21]]

Extract from the Council held at Detroit by the following Nations—Ottawas, Hurons, Chippewas, Pouteouattamis, Miamis, Shawanese, Delawares, Ottawas from Ouashtanon, Pouteouattamis of S^t. Joseph[22] &c^a.

DETROIT 17th June 1777

Governor Hamilton opened the Council in the usual form; and then inform'd the different nations of his

---

[19] For a brief biographical sketch of Col. William Russell, see *Dunmore's War*, p. 6, note 9.—ED.

[20] Jasper (called Jesse) Ewing was a brother of Mrs. Edward Hand, and was born in 1753 at Lancaster. In 1776, he joined the Continental army, and being commissioned a second-lieutenant, took part in the battle of Long Island. When General Hand went to Pittsburgh, he took with him as aide-de-camp his brother-in-law, who had been promoted to be brigade-major. After the Revolution, Major Ewing removed to Northumberland County, where he served as prothonotary, and died in 1800.—ED.

[21] This manuscript report of the council was prepared at the instigation of Gov. Henry Hamilton (for whom see *Rev. Upper Ohio*, p. 135, note 36), signed by himself, and captured when Vincennes was taken by Col. George Rogers Clark (Feb. 24, 1779). Clark kept the paper, which passed with his collection to the keeping of the Wisconsin Historical Society. Hamilton's brief letter on this subject, to his superior at Quebec, is printed in *Wis. Hist. Colls.*, xii, p. 45.—ED.

[22] For these tribes, formerly allies of the French, but now of the British government of Canada, see *Rev. Upper Ohio*, index.—ED.

intent in calling them together; which he s^d. was principally to strengthen the alliance he form'd with them last year[23], to inform them of what had come to his knowledge regarding them, to know their sentiments and lastly to be of any service to them that lay in his power.

The Kings Health was then drank by all present. Then some Belts from the Six Nations address'd to the Western Confederacy were shewn & explained. Chiefly exhortations to their Brethren to fullfill the many promises they had made & the Engagements they had enterd into to support His Majesty & Government.[24] Govr. Hamilton then gave them an account of the great Success of His Majestys Arms over his rebellious Subjects in many places, & of their obstinate disobedience, of their threats regarding the Indians, & lastly that their Brethren from Michilimackinac,[25] & the Six Nations &^c. were permitted & had taken up the Hatchet. and finish'd by telling them he would next day inform them of his real Sentiments. The Indians thank'd him for what he in-

---

[23] See *Rev. Upper Ohio*, p. 202.—ED.

[24] The Six Nations (Iroquois) were at the beginning of the Revolution inclined to remain neutral. Several chiefs attended the treaty at Pittsburgh in 1775 (*Ibid*, pp. 25-135, 159-167), and the Seneca in particular were favorable to the American cause. The British agents from Canada, however, exerted their influence to good effect. Col. Guy Johnson wrote that in April, 1777, the Six Nations had called in and assembled all of their people in order to make a diversion on the frontiers of New York and Pennsylvania, agreeable to the messages he had sent. See *N. Y. Colonial Documents*, viii, pp. 711, 712.—ED.

[25] For the Indians at Mackinac and their gathering for assistance to the British, see *Wis. Hist. Colls.*, xviii, pp. 357, 358, and references there cited.—ED.

Extract from the Council held at Detroit by the following Nations
Ottawas, Hurons, Chippewas, Pottawatamies, Miamis, Shawnese, Delawares, Mingoes
for assistance (Mohawatamis? & Joseph &c.

Detroit 17 June 1777

Governor Hamilton found the Councils in the usual form; and then
informed the different Nations of his intent in calling them together; And as a
means principally to bring them the alliance we have had with them last year, to infuse
him of what had come to his knowledge regarding them, & know their sentiments
will testify to be of very service to them that day in his honour —

The Kings health was then severally & fervently —

Then some Belts from the Six Nations adressed to the Nottawissa (spokesman were

AN INDIAN COUNCIL

formd them of & said when they heard his sentiments next day, he should know theirs.

18 June Being assembled as before, G[overnor] H[amilton] Told the English & french Gentlemen, that he was authorised to put the Hatchet into the Hands of the Indians, and expected an implicit obedience to the orders of His Majesty.[26] He then informd the Indians of what he thought they should do upon the occasion, shewed them the Hatchet then Sung the War Song—as did Mr Hay, Depu^y agent,[27] the officers of the Garrison, all the Nations present, & some of the French & English. G[overnor] Hamilton then thanked them for their Zeal and Unanimity, & adjournd to the open Field, to a feast prepared for the purpose, and appointed next morning to meet three or four Chiefs of each Nation to meet him at his own House.

19th Being assembled according to adjournment, Govr. Hamilton gave some things & Belts of Wam[pum] to cover & bury in oblivion the Murder of an Ottawa, killd here last winter by a Chippawa, to

---

[26] Hamilton's orders from headquarters must have arrived between the 15th and 18th of June. On the former date he wrote Carleton that the Indians had come to council and he should retain them as long as possible, pending orders; see *Wis. Hist. Colls.*, xii, p. 46. These orders were sent from Quebec, May 21st; see letter of Carleton, with enclosure from Lord George Germaine, *Id*, xi, pp. 175, 176, giving explicit directions to urge the Western nations upon the warpath. As this was in response to a request from Hamilton to be permitted to do so, it may be considered that the project originated at Detroit, and this partially accounts for the frontier hatred of Hamilton, who was called "hair-buyer," because of his custom of paying for American scalps.—ED.

[27] For Jehu Hay, see *Rev. Upper Ohio*, p. 130, note 27.—ED.

prevent any animosity from existing after they had so unanimously joined to take up the Hatchet. Then informed them of a Message the Chiefs of the Miamees rec^d. the night before; Shewing the perfidy of the Virginians, & the threats they had made use of against the Indian Nations in general and the Kings Troops at this place ending with a declaration of their not wanting to be at peace with the one or the other. The Miamee Chiefs declared this to be the purport of the Message sent them by their Nation. The Huron Nation was then pitched upon by all the rest to be the guardians of the Hatchet;[28] all declaring they had taken it up with an intent to hold it fast, untill desired to lay it down. Equeshawey[29] then expressed his happiness at seeing all his Brethren the Indians so unanimous—that he had just arrived from the Wabach where he had been to conduct his Father G[overnor] Abbott[30] that he had not seen anything bad on his voy-

---

[28] Americans called the Huron Indians, Wyandot. See *Ibid*, p. 36, note 62.—ED.

[29] An Ottawa chief, head of the tribe residing near Detroit. He was a faithful adherent of the British, attended all of their councils, and accompanied Hamilton to Vincennes in 1778. He was in the town when Clark arrived there, but escaped with Isadore Chene. In 1794, he was wounded at Fort Recovery, but was able to take part in the battle against Wayne. The following year he signed the treaty of Greenville. The last mention noted was in 1808, so that he probably died before the battle of Tippecanoe.—ED.

[30] Edward Abbott was a British artillery officer. He came early to the Northwest, being in Detroit soon after the close of the French regime. In 1775 he was commissioned Indian agent for the Crown on the Ohio; and in the spring of 1777 was sent to command at Vincennes, where he was the first and only British governor. He remained there less than a year, being summoned to Detroit in February, 1778. While at Vincennes he built Fort Sackville, which was captured in

AN INDIAN COUNCIL 11

age; on the contrary all the Nations shew'd an inclination to obey the will of their Father. G[overnor] H[amilton] thankd them all & particularly the Hurons as Guardians of the Ax & appointed

20 G[overnor] H[amilton] told the diff^t. Nations the Method he thought they should proceed in in making war and informd them of the diff^t. armeys that were to attack the Rebells this Summer which he desired them to consider of & let him know the Chiefs & Warriors ready to go, & also to name a Chief or two & some young Men to go to Niagara where they would see their Bre^n. the Six Nations &^{c}. &^{c}. were acting the same part—adjour^d. till next day.

21st According to adjournment, the above Nations came & named their War Chief & young men then ready for war, and an ax was presented for each Nation to be deliv^d. when they all should meet in a day or two Lt Caldwell[31] was named to accop^n. the few that

---

1779 by Clark. In July, 1778, Abbott was recalled from the West and sent by General Haldimand to the West Indies. His name appears in the army lists until 1788. At the time he commanded at Vincennes, Abbott was captain-lieutenant. He seems to have been a brave and humane officer. His protest to Haldimand against the employment of Indians on the frontiers does him credit. See *Mich. Pion. & Hist. Colls.*, ix, pp. 488, 489. His letters from Vincennes are printed in *Ill. Hist. Colls.*, i, pp. 313-318.—ED.

[31] William Caldwell was an Irishman and came to Pennsylvania before the Revolution. Having taken part in Dunmore's War, he was, after the outbreak of the Revolution, employed by Lord Dunmore to carry dispatches; and succeeded in escaping from the Americans and reaching Niagara. There he raised a company for Butler's Rangers, which was sent in 1776 to Detroit. The following year (probably at the time indicated in this document), Caldwell was sent back to Niagara, where he participated in the siege of Fort Stanwix and the raids against Wyoming and Cherry Valley. In 1781

were going to Niagara Jehu Hay D^{ty}. [deputy] agent to conduct the whole when they acted in a body, & many others who had offerd to serve his Majesty upon this occasion, to accompany them when in small parties. G[overnor] H[amilton] then as upon several other occasions recommended it to all the Nations to remember they were men, & were desired to make war against men, and not against women or Children, and to forbear to dip their hands in the blood of the two latter—adjourn'd to Monday 23^d. but it being bad weather & some other Indians being arrived did not meet till 24th

G[overnor] H[amilton] Returned thanks to the Chiefs & young men for their orderly behaviour since

---

he returned to Detroit, and in the summer of the next year was commander of the force that defeated Col. William Crawford at Sandusky, wherein Caldwell was himself wounded. After recovering he went out with the army that in 1782 penetrated Kentucky, besieged Bryant's Station, and defeated the Americans at Blue Licks. After the close of the war Caldwell was retained in the British Indian department, and is said to have been in the army that was defeated in 1794 by Wayne. Upon the American occupation of Detroit, Caldwell removed to Malden and laid out a town near the mouth of the river. Here he was justice of the peace and colonel of the militia. In 1812 he was quartermaster general and associated with General Brock in the capture of Detroit. In 1814, upon the retirement of Matthew Elliott, Caldwell was made superintendent of the British Indian department, from which office he retired two years later, after a disagreement with the military commandant. Caldwell was popular with the Indians, and his half-breed son, Billy Caldwell, became a Potawatomi chief. His other sons (William, James, and Thomas) served under the British in the War of 1812-15. Two of them were still living in 1863, and related to Dr. Draper incidents from their father's career (Draper MSS., 17 S). The elder Caldwell died in 1822 at his Canadian home, aged seventy-five years. He was one of the most noted border partisans of the West.—ED.

the commencement of the Council—then shewed them English & french Gentlemen who had offered to serve as Officers & private men upon this occasion. Then deliv^d. a War Hatchet to each Nation which they receivd & Sung the War Song then some Merchandize was shewn them destined to Cover their old men women & Children, & G[overnor] H[amilton] told them they should be furnish'd with ammunition &^{c}. necessary for their Y^g. Men G[overnor] H[amilton] delivered them his thanks for their unanimity & professions of friendship, and as soon as the division of pres^{ts} was over G[overnor] H[amilton] told them he would give each nation a Bullock to make a feast & would visit them turn about beginning with the Ottawas then closed the Council.

Since[32] the closing the council, I have been at the War feast of each nation, and the greatest decency and alacrity has appeared. 30th. of June most of the Nations had brought in their Sticks for the number of Warriors,[33] and in a Month I dont question one thousand Warriors going against the Frontiers. at the same time I have exhorted them to act vigorously, I have endeavored to teach them to spare Old Age Women and Children

HENRY HAMILTON

Endorsed: Extract of a Council held at DETROIT 17 June 1777.

---

[32] The following paragraph was written by Hamilton, and closes with his autograph signature.—ED.

[33] This was the Indian method of making an official count. At treaties, councils, or where presents or annuities were to be paid, one stick was presented to the agent for each member of an Indian family. Hamilton means at this point that the chiefs gave him an enumeration of the number of warriors ready to take the field.—ED.

HAMILTON'S PROCLAMATION

[Hamilton to American frontiersmen.   45J62—D. S.]

DETROIT 24th June, 1777.

By virtue of the power and authority to me given by his Excellency Sir Guy Carleton Knight of the Bath, Governor of the province of Quebec, General and Commandant in chief, &c. &c. &c.

I do assure all such as are inclined to withdraw themselves from the Tyranny and oppression of the rebel Committees, & take refuge in this Settlement, or any of the Posts commanded by his Majesty's Officers, shall be humanely treated, shall be lodged and victualled, and such as come off in arms & shall use them in defence of his Majesty against Rebels and Traytors, 'till the extinction of this rebellion, shall receive pay adequate to their former Stations in the rebel service, and all common men who shall serve during that period, shall receive his Majesty's bounty of two hundred acres of Land.

Given under my hand & Seal   God save the King

HENRY HAMILTON,

Lieut^t. Govr: and Superintendent[34]

EVENTS NEAR FORT PITT

[Calendar of letters and documents. 1U56, 58, 59; 3NN46, June 19-30.]

June 19. David Shepherd writes from Wheeling that "the Indians has not come to see us Since our

---

[34] A number of these proclamations were prepared by Hamilton, and given to the custody of the Indian bands attacking the frontiers of the colonies. They left them on doorsteps, and beside the bodies of their victims. See letters *post*.—ED.

DEPREDATIONS CONTINUE 15

Meeting at the Council [at Catfish Camp], and hope they Never May until we are Ready to Return them the Compliment."

The same day, Samuel Moorhead writes from the fort at Kittanning that he finds the garrison badly off for stores and shelter, and that the fort is commanded by a hill two or three hundred feet distant.

June 21. Pluggy's Town gang, led by that Indian's son, of whose approach the Delaware Chief Killbuck[35] had warned General Hand, killed two men on Allegheny River about twenty miles above Pittsburgh. Hand thinks no remedy will be efficacious but a counter stroke upon their town.

June 22. William Zane[36] writes from Fort Henry that being more than sixty years old, with a constitution much shattered by five years' captivity in Braddock's war, the loss of his negro carried off by the Indians deprives him of means of support. He re-

---

[35] For a brief biography of this chief, see *Rev. Upper Ohio*, p. 38, note 64. Throughout the early years of the war, he was a staunch friend of the American colonists, and frequently warned them of the approach of hostile Indian bands.—ED.

[36] William Zane was probably the father of the well-known Zane brothers, the first settlers of Wheeling. William was a descendant of Robert Zane, who emigrated to America in 1673 and settled at Newton, N. J. It is supposed that the latter's first wife, grandmother of William, was of Indian origin. William was born in 1712. Breaking with the sect of Quakers to which his ancestors belonged, he removed to the South branch of the Potomac, in the present Berkeley County, West Virginia. His son Isaac was captured at this place, possibly at the time of the captivity of which his father speaks. The other sons, Ebenezer, Silas, Jonathan, and Andrew, were early upon the Ohio, and all settled near Wheeling.—ED.

quests General Hand to secure the return of this man if the Indians make peace.

June 30. General Hand writes to his wife: "Nothing bad has yet happened since the affair of the 21st. A number of Chippewas & Thawa [Ottawa] Indians have been here to profess much friendship; they also offered their mediation to remove the banditti that infests our frontier, which I accepted with pleasure."

VIRGINIA MILITIA ORDERED OUT
[Gov. Patrick Henry to Gen. Edward Hand. 15ZZ7—L. S.]

WILLIAMSBURG July 3'd 1777.

SIR—By the constitution of this Commonwealth no Militia can be embody'd but by orders from the Executive Power, except in Case of Invasion or Insurrection; and when embody'd such Militia is under the sole Direction of the Governour. I do not make this observation with any View to counteract you, very far otherwise. I shall be made happy in forwarding your Designs to protect and secure the Frontiers from those dangerous Incursions by means of which our People suffer so much, and so great Diversion is made of our best Men from the main Object. But I am constrained by my Duty, by the Oath of my Office, to claim the supreme command of all the Militia which are or may be embody'd in the State. Altho' I do this on the present Occasion, and shall certainly do the like on every similar one, yet I beg leave to assure you, Sir, that I shall most gladly contribute all in my Power to render effectual every Plan calculated to promote the general Good; and I do hereby empower you to call for the number of Men necessary for defending the Frontiers

MILITIA CALLED OUT

from the County of Yohogany, Monongalia, Ohio, Hampshire, Botetourt, Augusta, Dunmore and Frederick until further Orders.

The Resolution of Congress respecting the Lead, never came to Hand 'til yesterday. Orders will be sent for its Delivery without loss of Time. Several Tons were long since ordered for the militia in your Parts. The Resolution for the artillery going to Fort Pitt, is not yet received.

Col°. Aylett,[37] who lives in this Town, is appointed Commissary to supply the Western Garrisons with Provisions. His Appointment came to my Hands from the War-office yesterday, and is communicated to him. I doubt some time will pass before M^r. Aylett can take the necessary Steps for furnishing Provisions, and in the mean Time M^r. Morgan perhaps can supply them. There seems no other chance to get them.

You will please to direct the Militia already embody'd to continue in Service so long as you think there is occasion for them, and make such other necessary Draughts from the above Counties as Exigencies may require, giving me notice thereof from Time to Time, and of the reasons that induce you to make them.

---

[37] Col. William Aylett belonged to a distinguished Virginia family, intermarried with the Washingtons, Lees, Dandridges, etc. Born in 1743, he was a member of the House of Burgesses (1772-74), and delegate from King William County to the conventions of 1775 and 1776. He resigned from the latter May 22, having been chosen deputy commissary-general by the Continental Congress. He served in this capacity until his sudden death in April, 1780. His home was at "Fairfield," and here he frequently entertained Washington and the Lees on their way to Williamsburgh.—ED.

The chastising of Pluggy's Town seems to me absolutely necessary, but is submitted to you, as being better enabled to judge on the Spot.

I have the Honor to be Sir Y^r. mo. ob^t. & very hble serv^t P. HENRY.

To Brigadier General Edward Hand at Pittsburgh

[Gov. Patrick Henry to Col. David Shepherd. 1SS61—A. L. S.]

SIR—You are hereby required to raise so many of the Militia of your County as General Hand may demand for the Protection of the Frontiers of this State. I am Sir Your mo. Hble Servt. P. HENRY.
W^{ms}·BURGH July 3. 1777.
County Lieutenant of Ohio

[Col. Zackwell Morgan[38] to Gen. Edward Hand. Calendar of 1U63—A. L. S.]

Letter dated Monongalia July 8, 1777, says that the militia of his county will be drafted in a few days. He has placed Maj. James Chew[39] in command. Spies are ranging, and one company is apprehending deserters.

GENERAL HAND WARNED

[David Zeisberger to Col. George Morgan. Calendar of 3NN11-13—Transcript by Draper.]

Letter dated Cuchachunk[40] July 7, 1777, says that

---

[38] For Col. Zackwell Morgan, see *Rev. Upper Ohio*, p. 230, note 71.—ED.

[39] Maj. James Chew is noted *Ibid*, p. 246, note 88.—ED.

[40] For Zeisberger see *Ibid*, p. 45, note 71. The town was on the site of that now known as Coshocton, for which see *Ibid*, p. 46, note 73.—ED.

the messengers sent to Pluggy's Town and Sandusky met a hostile band of Mingo, Wyandot, and Mohican bound towards Wheeling. They did not go to war of their own wish, but because ordered to do so by the governor at Detroit. Later the messengers met John Montour,[41] who described the Detroit treaty, where the governor was painted and dressed like an Indian, and presented a large black belt painted red, sent by the Six Nations. Colonel Morgan is urged to come to Cuchachunk, for the Wyandot will not go to the treaty at Pittsburgh; they will, however, come to the former place.[42]

[Gen. Edward Hand to Jasper Yeates. MS. in New York Public Library; Hand Papers—A. L. S.]

FORT PITT 12th. July 1777

DEAR YEATES—I can not for my life find out the Intention of the Indians, but believe they will be gouverned by the Success of the British arms against us. if they turn out too strong for us the Indians will join them, if the Contrary, they will sit still. we cant furnish the Articles necessary for trade Consequently the Indians will not Attempt anything Against the English. I inclose you a Coppy of a letter I this day rec^d. from Cushakunk,[43] you will See how busie the British Agents are to engage the Savages to depopulate the Frontiers. there is a Treaty now holding at

---

[41] For John Montour and his presence at Detroit in 1776, see *Ibid*, pp. 28, 202.—ED.

[42] Morgan, who was Indian agent at Pittsburgh, had gone to Philadelphia to report to Congress.—ED.

[43] See preceding document for letter referred to.—ED.

Oswego, to which Col: Butler has Cal'd the Indians.[44] they say they dont know what he intends by it, but think if the English Attempt Our Frontiers it will be by the way of the Susquehana. two Tribes of the Shawanese declare for us, two are against us,[45] the Wiandats also are evidently our Enemies. All other nations that I have heard from declare they will be at peace.

I wish much to hear from Lancaster, and to learn how the Armies in the field proceed. I have not now time to ans^r. Jacky Ewings letter would be glad to Ans^r two together, Col: Morg[an's] Absence gives me infinite trouble. there are now here upwards of 50 Indians of Diff^t. Tribes. Jessy Ewing Joyns me in Duty, Love & Comp^{ts}. to All I am D^r. Yeates most Affectionately Yours   Edwd. Hand
Jasper Yeates Esqr.

---

[44] The treaty of Oswego was held preliminary to St. Leger's operations against Fort Stanwix. It was called early in July by Col. John Butler (for whom see *Rev. Upper Ohio*, p. 152, note 67), and was attended by Sir John Johnson and several Loyalist officers. See British accounts in *N. Y. Colon. Docs.*, viii, pp. 719, 724. These corroborate the account of the Seneca chief Blacksnake (Draper MSS., 16F115-117) that the Seneca particularly were averse to going to war, but were urged thereto by the Mohawk chief Joseph Brant. See also *Journals of the Provincial Congress* [etc. of New York] (Albany, 1842), i, pp. 1006, 1007, 1025, for reports of this council at Oswego, given by Oneida Indians and the commandant of Fort Schuyler. The attitude of the Six Nations had a powerful influence on the Western tribes.—Ed.

[45] The four tribes or clans of the Shawnee were the Kiscapoo (Kishapocoke), Piqua, Chillicothe, and Mequochoke. Of these the two first-named were hostile, being located farthest from the colonial frontier, and nearest the sphere of British influence.—Ed.

A PUNITIVE EXPEDITION 21

WAR PARTIES STRIKE THE FRONTIER
[Calendar of letters. 1U64-67, 71, 72, July 14-20.]

July 14. At 8 o'clock Capt. John Minor writes from Fort Stradler[46] to Col. Zackwell Morgan that three men have just come in who escaped from a party of Indians, twenty at least; that Jacob Farmer's house was fired, he and Nathan Wirly [Worley] killed, and three children captured. "We shall march after them in Less than an hour."

July 15. Col. Zackwell Morgan sends the above letter by express to General Hand, giving account of mischief done on Dunkards Creek. "Is not this Cruel, While those Savage Nations are coming to treat with your Excellency Pray for God sake Send me full Instructions."

July 17. Capt. Samuel Mason writes from Fort Henry of an attack on the 13th at Grave Creek. Lieutenant Tomlinson[47] sallied out with twenty odd men and followed the Indians, who had driven off many horses; the pursuing party took canoes and dropped down to Sunfish Creek,[48] where they found the trail.

---

[46] This was properly Fort Statler, so called from a family of that name. It was a blockhouse located on the waters of Dunkard Creek, a western tributary of the Monongahela. Statler's Fort was in the present Monongalia County, W. Va., just south of the Pennsylvania border.
For Capt. John Minor, see *Rev. Upper Ohio*, p. 235, note 70.—ED.

[47] This was Lieut. Samuel Tomlinson, brother of Joseph (whose children were interviewed by Draper in 1846—3S164-166). He came to the Grave Creek neighborhood about 1771, served as lieutenant in Captain Mason's company, and was killed in the attack on Fort Henry, Sept. 1, 1777.—ED.

[48] Sunfish Creek is five miles below Fish Creek, in Monroe County, Ohio, and comes into the Ohio from the west. The

Coming upon their camp-fires after dark, one of their guns went off by accident, whereupon fearful of being surrounded, the party of whites retreated to Grave Creek Fort, and sent word to Col. David Shepherd. The latter sent Mason with fifty men in pursuit. On the 15th they went to where the former party had found the Indian Camp, but seeing it had been deserted two days, thought it needless to continue the pursuit. Returning by canoe they were surprised by three separate volleys from Indians concealed on the left bank. After reaching the Indian shore, random shots and some conversation ensued. The Indians called out that they were Delaware and some Shawnee; apparently they were twenty-five or thirty in number. After dark the whites pushed up stream, crossed, and lay on their arms all night. Seeing moccasin tracks, they followed them toward Grave Creek, only to find that these signs were of Captain Pigman[49] with a party of fifteen returning from a scout to Little Kanawha. "The Boys seem'd very anxious to Action for further particulars you may be inform'd exactly by the Bearer M^r. Hoseae Cam S^r." As Captain Van Metre[50] talks of being removed, it would be well if

---

earlier settlers called the right bank of the Ohio the "Indian shore," since by the Treaty of Fort Stanwix it formed the southern boundary of their unceded territory.—ED.

[49] For Capt. Jesse Pigman, see *Rev. Upper Ohio*, p. 235.—ED.

[50] Capt. John Van Meter, son of Henry, an early settler west of the mountains, was born about 1738. In 1771 he owned 300 acres at the site of the present town of Waynesburg, Greene County, Pa. Early in the Revolution he commanded a company of rangers from Westmoreland. Later he settled in Brooke County, Va., and there died about 1803. During the Indian wars his home was raided, his wife and daughter being killed, and one son (John) carried captive.

A PUNITIVE EXPEDITION 23

Mason should be stationed at Fort Henry ready to lead out a pursuing party at short notice.

In an undated letter Morgan Jones writes to his parents from Grave Creek full particulars of the actions described in the preceding letter. The cattle and horses carried off by the savages belonged to Joseph Tomlinson, John Harness, Samuel Harries, Zephaniah Blackford, Mr. Rogers, and Yates Conwell. The battle on Sunfish Creek was on a hill where the whites were nearly surrounded. "So I hope you wont fail to Come Down with five or six horses with all speed to help us up to y^r. parts &c. the Sign of Indians is very Numerous over the Ohio, having Numbers of Camps & one Large Bark Camp Below fish Creek. I was in Both the Actions & saw the Signs myself."

July 19. James Chew took the testimony of two spies, Richard Ashcraft and Thomas Carr, who on oath declared that they saw tracks supposed to be those of a party of seven or eight Indians, on the headwaters of Buffalo Creek, making towards Monongahela River.

July 20. William Cross writes to Col. Zackwell Morgan from Fort Gerrard,[51] which he was guarding with twelve men, for reinforcements and ammunition.

John Corbly[52] writes an undated note to Col. Zack-

The son never returned to civilization, but in habits and feeling became partially an Indian. The elder John afterwards married Mrs. Jemima Bukey, mother of the famous spy, Hezekiah Bukey. Their home was on Short Creek.—ED.

[51] Garard Fort was situated on Big Whiteley Creek, in Greene Township, in the Pennsylvania county of the same name.—ED.

[52] John Corbly was a Baptist minister who in 1776 was pastor at the Goshen Church, near Garard Fort. He was de-

well Morgan, that the men will not go scouting without flour, and asks for an order on Wilson's or Hardin's mills.

July 20. Col. Zackwell Morgan sends to General Hand the four preceding papers, and adds that according to the spies' report he sent an express to warn Prickett's Fort.[53] They had already been alarmed, and were all forted. Morgan hopes that the enemy will be disappointed. "I shall send Major Chew with a party on Tuesday next to Scour that part of the Country. The Bussy Time of Harvest prevents my doing it sooner." Captain Minor pursued the party who did mischief on Dunkard's Creek, but could do no more than recover a drove of cattle.

[Gen. Edward Hand to President Wharton[54]. Summary of letter dated Fort Pitt, July 24th, 1777—printed in *Pennsylvania Colonial Records*, v, pp. 443, 444.]

Sends an account of the late murders and ravages. Every day's experience proves that nothing but penetrating the country and destroying the settlements of these perfidious miscreants will prevent the depopula-

---

voted to the cause of the colonies, and preached vigorous and warlike sermons that much heartened the frontiersmen who came from many miles around to be his auditors. In May, 1782, while Corbly and his family were on their way to meeting, Indians fell upon them and massacred his wife and five children. See Thwaites (ed.), *Withers's Chronicles of Border Warfare* (Cincinnati, 1895), pp. 345, 346.—ED.

[54] Thomas Wharton Jr. was president of the executive council of Pennsylvania, and chief officer of that state. For another letter of Hand about this date, see Darlington, *Fort Pitt*, pp. 224, 225.—ED.

[53] For the location of Prickett's Fort, see *Rev. Upper Ohio*, p. 235, note 79.—ED.

tion of the frontiers. Has determined to do this as soon as he can obtain provisions and men enough to ensure success. Needs the militia of Westmoreland and Bedford counties.[55] The Indians are now going to a treaty at Oswego, and have lately had one at Niagara. Is apprehensive of an attack via the Susquehanna or toward Albany.

FRIENDLY INDIAN WARNINGS

[Capt. Matthew Arbuckle to Col. William Fleming. 1U68—
A. L. S.]

FORT RANDOLPH July 26th 1777

SIR—Having yesterday received Inteligence from the Shawnee Towns by some Indians who I'm Convinced are as yet our friends, that there has lately been a Treaty at Detroit, where all Nations have unanimously agreed to Distress the frontiers as much as in their Power. they accepted of the War Belt & Tomahawk and are so near as the Shawnee Towns, where they are indeavouring to draw over what Shawnees were resolved to remain Neuter they are Invited & Encouraged by a French Man & a Wyndott Chief who accompanys them. there was a Part of Shawnies ready to Come to this Garrison, who upon receiving the News from Detroit Postponed their Journey & repaired to the Council.[56] their first Intentions are to

---

[55] The two most westerly counties of Pennsylvania. Bedford was erected in 1771 out of Cumberland; and Westmoreland in 1773, out of that portion of Bedford west of Laurel Hill—the eleventh and last provincial county.—ED.

[56] In Draper MSS., 3NN71-73, is a letter from Arbuckle to Hand, containing practically the same information as this letter to Fleming. In it he says that the Shawnee council was being held "at the New Town where the Chillicothe Indians

De[s]troy this & Whelen Garrisons & then Proceed to the frontier Inhabitants. They are resolved if Possible to Secure this Place to them selves either by Storming the Garrison or Starving us out, from the Author of the above information[57] I understand there are some Partys now on their way to this Place & they suppose their General Attact will be very Shortly their method to reduce this Garrison is as follows there will a few Indians way lay some of our People a hunting Cows or Horses upon which we will Detatch a Pretty large Party to Drive them, when they get our Party a Sufficient Distance from the Garrison Their Main Body will Surround & Destroy them, by

---

now live." In an accompanying note, Dr. Draper locates this Indian village on the Little Miami, three miles above the present site of Xenia. This was later known as Old Town, or Old Chillicothe, and had a famous history. Thither Daniel Boone was carried captive in 1778 and lived as the adopted son of the Chief Blackfish. This was also the town that Col. John Bowman marched against, in 1779, and the one burned by the Indians on the approach in 1780 of Clark's forces. After this last-named date it was practically abandoned.—ED.

[57] The author of the information was an Indian woman known to the whites as the Grenadier Squaw, from her unusual height. Her tribal name was Non-hel-e-ma; she had also been baptized Catherine (hence was called Katy). She was a sister of Cornstalk and a woman of note, having a village in the Pickaway Plains. See *Dunmore's War*, p. 301. She was attached to the Americans, and frequently brought them valuable information. After the death of Cornstalk, she abandoned her people, and with forty-eight head of cattle and some horses and other property made her way to Fort Randolph and dwelt with the garrison, by whom she was frequently employed as an interpreter. Later she removed to the neighborhood of Pittsburgh, where in 1785 she petitioned the Indian commissioners for relief and for a grant of land on the Scioto, where her family had lived and her mother was buried. This petition was referred to Congress, but apparently was never acted upon. Draper MSS., 3D39.—ED.

REPORT FROM ZEISBERGER 27

which Scheme this Garrison is to Become an easy Prey. upon the Strength of this information I have Detained M[r]. Wallace with the remainder of his C[o].[58] untill farther Orders; or Relieved by the Militia. I have Sent the within mentioned Particulars to General Hand at Fort Pitt from whom I expect my first Instructions.[59]

I desire if you think Proper that the Governor & Council be made acquainted with the Particulars being certain it can be conveyed much more expeditiously by you than by the General I am S[r]. with esteem your very Humble Serv[t]

MATTHEW ARBUCKLE.

[David Zeisberger to Gen. Edward Hand. 1U69—A. L. S.]
CUCHACHUNK July 29th 1777.

HONOUR'D SIR—I receiv'd your favor of the 9th Instant with the Message to the Counsellers at Cuchachunk which I explained to them. They are allways glad to hear from their friends & Brethren at the Fort

---
[58] Andrew Wallace, son of Peter Jr., and his wife Martha Woods, belonged to a well-known Augusta County family. He was in 1774 a private in Capt. Murray's company of volunteers. At the opening of the Revolution he, with several of his brothers, enlisted and was lieutenant of the 8th Virginia, and later captain of a company in this regiment. In 1776 he was recruiting for Captain Arbuckle; see *Rev. Upper Ohio,* index. He arrived at Fort Randolph early in the summer of 1777, with orders from his colonel to march his men, who had re-enlisted in the Continental army, into the settlements. About twenty had gone, and the rest were detained awaiting the return of the pack-horses, as here narrated. Lieut. Andrew Wallace joined the Eastern army later, and was killed in 1781 at the battle of Guilford.—ED.

[59] In Arbuckle's letter to Hand, he states that should Lieut. Andrew Wallace leave, the garrison would then consist of but eighty-seven rank and file.—ED.

& it giveth them new Encouragement to hold fast to friendship. I wish therefore that you & Col. Morgan might let them hear from you at this critical time as often as you can. On the 20th this Month the Half King of the Wyondats[60] with 19 of his Men arrived at Cuchachunk where they had a great Council & after they had delivered several Speeches the Half King drew out the War Belt with the Tomhawk, told the Delawares, that all the Nations on the other Side & this Side the Lake had join'd & taken hold of it, that the Delawares only had not yet taken hold of & deliver'd the Belt to them. After they had consulted about it they returned it back to the Half King & told him that they would mind nothing but sit still & hold fast to peace & friendship, that they had promised at a Treaty when Peace was concluded after last War that they would never fight no more against the white people as long as the Sun shineth & the Rivers run & that they would keep. The Half King not being pleased with this Answer returned the War Belt & compelled the Delawares to take it who are yet firm in their Mind & stand fast. After the Wyondats were gone, they gathered all their Men & Women & admonished them not to have any thoughts of going to War nor to join any of the Warriors when they pass by. We now expect nothing else but that after these Wyondats got home their Warriors will march into the Settlements very fast. They desired them to let their Warriors not come by the Delaware Towns that they should march another Way, but they did not consent

---

[60] For this chief, see *Rev. Upper Ohio*, p. 91, note 14.—ED.

to it & said they will march by Cuchachunk. Capt. White Eye will inform you of every thing that has passed & how Matters are. No doubt but you will encourage them to be strong & to stand fast, for if they should give out, we with our Indians could not maintain ourselfs here any longer. We wish that an Army might soon come out, this would in my Opinion be the only Method to get a Peace settled among the Nations.

23 Warriors returned lately from the Settlements I heard from Red stone with 3 Prisoners & 3 Scalps & 7 or 8 horses Last Night we got Intelligence by an Indian who came from Sandusky that a Party of 30 Wyondats & French among them, were not far of[f] on their March to the Settlements & will come to Cuchachunk perhaps to Day.

The Delawares flatter themselves that an Army will soon come out which is their only Hope yet, but should that fail I am afraid they cannot stand, & than [then] surely all the Nations, that have not yet joined & taken the War Belt, will join them.[61] I beg the favour of forwarding the enclosed Letter & you will much oblige your sincere friend & humble Servt.

D. ZISEBERGER.

To His Excellency Edwd Hand
   Genl. at Pittsburgh

---

[61] Governor Hamilton wrote July 17, 1777, that there had already gone out fifteen parties, composed of 289 warriors, with thirty white officers. See *Wis. Hist. Colls.*, xi, p. 98, note.—ED.

SUGGESTIONS FROM GOVERNOR HENRY

[Gov. Patrick Henry to Gen. Edward Hand. 18J26—L. S.]

W^{ms}.BURGH July 27th. 1777

SIR—I have this Day rec^d. your Despatches by M^r. Kelly. I was favor'd with yours a copy of which you transmitted by this Express. Col°. Croghan[62] was here & about to go up. By him I wrote you an answer & together with that sent Letters to the Lieutenants of sundry Countys most convenient directing them to furnish from Time to Time, Such Requisitions of men as you may think the safety of our Frontier, will make it necessary for you to call for. In the Letter to you, I observed that by the Constitution of Virginia, none but the Governor with the Advice of Council had a Right to embody the Militia; & that when embodyed, the sole Direction of them is given to the Governor. And I beg Leave here again to repeat, that I do not claim this Power with any Intention to retard your Views, but I shall on every Occasion think myself happy to forward them & give you every possible Aid & Furtherance. Least any of the Letters sent by Col°. Croghan should miscarry I herewith send others to the Coty Lieutenants in the N°. West, desiring their Co-operation with you.

I am very sorry for the Mischief done by the Indians. I was ever of opinion, that the severest Vengeance should be taken on Pluggys People. The Terror of their Fate, may serve as a usefull Lesson to the neighbouring Tribes. Savages must be managed by working on their Fears. No doubt but much address

---

[62] For a brief sketch, see *Dunmore's War*, p. 7, note 12.—ED.

will be necessary in keeping the other Indians quiet & unoffended. I pretend not to point out the proper means to effect this, & rely on your Skill & Ability to do it.

Accounts from Kentucki tell me of the most distressing & deplorable condition of the surviving Inhabitants in that Quarter. Your Movements I trust will prove the best Defence to them. Two hundred men are ordered to their Assistance.[63] But it seems to me, that offensive operations can alone produce Defence ag^t. Indians.

Are not the Six Nations wavering? perhaps the progress of the Enemy about Lake George may incline them against us.

With Respect to any particular Orders respecting the Draft or march of any of the Militia, I cannot give them. I must submit the whole Matter to you Sir, & I have Confidence that whilst you exert yourself in defending the Frontier & chastising the Enemy, you will not forget the Domestic concerns of the people composing the Militia. Indeed they will do well to consider, that the Enemy stands between them, & that State of Safety & Repose which I hope awaits them.

I'm very sorry to find the recruiting Business goes

---

[63] The latter part of May the three forts of Harrodsburg, Boonesborough, and Logan's Station were simultaneously attacked, and messages of appeal for aid were sent to Virginia and Fort Pitt. The relief ordered by Governor Henry was two companies of militia, commanded by Col. John Bowman, who arrived at Boonesborough August 1. While there were only about a hundred men in the two companies, their arrival brought great hope and comfort to the harassed Kentuckians.—ED.

on so slowly. I shall write Col°. Campbell[64] on the Subject. The Beef & Flour you will want for y^r. Expedition, no Doubt will be considerable. But I can't p[r]event the Sale to the Drovers you Speak of. The Lead you spoke of I ordered. The Relief for Fort Henry will be ordered by you. I have to desire you will favor me with an Acco^t. of the State of the Frontier as occasions happen, & of every Draught of the Militia & the Reason & Design of making it as soon as possible, the great Distance making it impossible to wait for Orders from hence. The Disposition of Capt. Arbuckles men I submit to you.

You will now find Sir The Choice of Militia given you over a great Extent of Country, from which may be drawn the most formidable men in the State. I confide the dearest Interests of these people to your Conduct. Pardon me Sir, for observing the Magnitude of the Trust, which (tho' I have not the pleasure of a personal Acquaintance with you) I doubt not will be so managed as to redound to your Honor & the Happiness of the Frontiers. I need not mention that you will take the men from such Countys whose Situation & Circumstances will best enable them to Spare the proper Soldiers for the Service. I am Sir y^r. mo. ob^t. hble Serv.

P. HENRY.

P. S. Culpepper County has furnished so many men I Should be glad you'd Spare them if possible.

P. H.

Brigadier General Edward Hand, Pittsburgh

---

[64] Probably John Campbell, for whom, see *Rev. Upper Ohio*, p. 231, note 74.—ED.

CAPTURE OF A FAMILY 33

I yesterday recd Letters from Gov. Henry he desires me to act as I think proper with regard to the Men at your Post but their being ordered to remain where they are prevent the Necessity of any further directions at present.[65]

PROVISIONING THE FORTS

[George Morgan to David Shepherd. Calendar of 1SS63— A. L. S.]

From Fort Pitt, July 29, 1777, George Morgan writes that he has just returned from Philadelphia and desires Colonel Shepherd to provision the garrison at Wheeling and keep accurate accounts therefor. Since flour is not to be had in that neighborhood, Morgan will supply all that is ordered. Wishes Shepherd to supply all of the stations in Ohio County. Herd the cattle until they are needed for the expedition, when salt will be sent. Particulars about accounting and issuing. Congress has ordered particular care to be taken of the hides and tallow.

BEAVER CREEK RAID

[Col. John Gibson to Gen. Edward Hand. 1U70—A. L. S.]

DEAR GENERAL—This Moment two men came in here they had Been a Reaping near the Mouth of Beaver Creek, they informed me that on going to George Bakers[66] house they found every thing de-

---

[65] This last paragraph was written on the bottom of the letter by General Hand, who transmitted it either to Col. David Shepherd at Wheeling, or Capt. Matthew Arbuckle at Point Pleasant.—ED.

[66] George Baker was of German birth, and coming to America in 1750 married an English girl. About 1772 they removed

stroyed and the people Missing, that one of them tracked where the Indians went with the Children almost to the River, they found three Letters laying Before the door, which they say were wrote at Detroit, that upon this they were making the Best of their way to this place, when about a Mile from here they saw two Indians who Ran of[f] as soon as they Discovered them. one of the men has the letters having in the hurry forgot to Leave them as he went out to pilot the party who turned out after them. there is a number of the people out from the Fort, probably they may have done more mischief. As soon as I Learn the particulars shall inform you more fully Bakers family Consisted of himself, his Wife and five Children and Lived about four miles from here on the Dividing Ridge between the Ohio and Racoon. This moment a party of 6 men who went to the mouth of Racoon on a Scout, returned they saw Six Indians crossing in a Cannoe near the mouth of Beaver Creek to the Indian Side, and they were at the place where the[y] tied Bakers family with Bark and saw where the[y] Crossed the River. Fifteen men will pursue in a few minutes, and as there hardly ten men will be left here, if a Large party of Indians should be out they will be Scarcely able to Defend the Fort. I have been taken ill with a Fever last night which Still Con-

---

to the Western country and built their cabin as herein described. The entire family were carried captive to Detroit, and well-treated while in captivity. Upon their release they lived awhile on the south branch of Potomac, and finally came back to their home on Raccoon Creek, where Baker died in 1802. See Joseph H. Bausman, *History of Beaver County* (N. Y., 1904), i, p. 149.—ED.

AN EXPECTED ATTACK

tinues, I am not able to pursue with the party. I am Dear General with much Respect your most obedient humble Servt.

J^{No}. GIBSON[67]

LOGSTOWN July 31st. 1777 3 oClock P. M.
To Brigadier General Hand, Fort Pitt, per Express.

[Col. John Gibson to Gen. Edward Hand. 1U73—A. L. S.]

DEAR GENERAL—About an hour agoe a party of Indians fired on a Serj^t, 2 men and 2 Boys about 2 miles up the River the[y] killed the Sergeant and took one of the Boys prisoner, the men Escaped. By two Delawares who came from Coshachking I wrote you a letter, By them which least it should Miscarry I have sent you this. The Delawares say that 30 Wiandots and some french will be here in a Day or two to Attack this Settlement and that a both[sic] number of English and french and Indians are on their way to Attack Fort Pitt. if White Eyes[68] passes this way he will Be in danger of Being killed, it was with the utmost Difficulty I prevented one of the men who Escaped from killing the Delawares. I think if the Accts are true this Small Garrison will Suffer. from the present Temper of the Inhabitants they intend to fly. I wish a party cou'd be Spared to Bring of[f] the Women and Children. I shall Remain here until tomorrow morning, if any person comes they had better come this night, they militia all threaten to Leave this Immediately.

---

[67] For a sketch of John Gibson, see *Dunmore's War*, p. 11, note 19. He was at this time forted at Logstown, for which, see *Rev. Upper Ohio*, p. 26, note 52.—ED.

[68] For White Eyes, see *Dunmore's War*, p. 29, note 48.—ED.

I am Dear Gen¹. your most humble Servᵗ.

Jnº. Gibson

August 1ˢᵗ 4 ºClock P. M. 1777
To Brigadier General Hand per Express

SUNDRY RAIDS AND SKIRMISHES

[Calendar of letters. 1U74-79, 81, 82; 4ZZ10; 3NN146; 3S76-78; and Darlington's *Fort Pitt*, p. 226, Aug. 2-13]

At the beginning of August, reports began to pour in to General Hand at Fort Pitt, of simultaneous raids in widely-scattered places.

Aug. 2. Joseph Ogle[69] writes from Beech Bottom Fort[70] that spies having discovered Indians about eight miles below this post, his lieutenant and five men went in pursuit, met a party of five, within three miles of Wheeling, and had a skirmish in which they killed and scalped one Indian. This party of aborigines had slightly wounded two negroes within three hundred yards of Wheeling Fort, whence they were pursued but not discovered. The booty was "A good Rifle Gun and his Accuterments and a famous Neet-made Ware Club his scalp was Ellegantly Adornd with Three fine Rows of Tassels and Feathers."

---

[69] A family of Ogles were among the earliest settlers of Ohio County; of these, Joseph appears to have been the most prominent. As captain of a militia company he took part in the siege of Fort Henry—see *post*. In 1781 he commanded a company in Brodhead's Coshocton expedition. An autograph letter of his (1785) is among the Draper MSS., 4NN101. The same year he emigrated to Illinois, where for the remainder of the Indian wars he maintained his reputation as an Indian fighter. He died Feb. 24, 1821, in St. Clair County, Ill.—Ed.

[70] For Beech Bottom Fort, see *Rev. Upper Ohio*, p. 243.—Ed.

RAIDS AND SKIRMISHES

Aug. 2. James Booth[71] writes from Koon Fort to Capt. Zedick Springer[72] at Prickett's Fort, that Charles Grigsby's wife and child were killed and scalped and one person missing on the 31st of July from the waters of Elk Creek.[73] A party of thirteen or fourteen intend to pursue the raiders.

Aug. 4. Col. David Shepherd writes to General Hand from Ohio County of the skirmish of the preceding Friday, when six scouts attacked and killed one of five Indians and put the rest to flight. The people are alarmed and may remove from the frontier.

Aug. 5. Capt. Samuel Moorhead writes from Kittanning to General Hand, thanks him for his warnings, and reports the visit of a Delaware whom he suspects is a spy. The latter reported having seen the writer's brother and Mr. McFarlane[74] at Niagara twenty days ago.

---

[71] James Booth was one of the early settlers of the Monongahela region, making his improvement on Booth Creek in 1771, not far from the present site of Morgantown. He was killed by Indians, in the summer of 1778, and his loss was a blow to the young community—see Thwaites, *Withers's Border Warfare*, p. 247. Coon Fort was on the land of Joseph and Philip Coon in Marion County, W. Va.; for the exact location, see Henry Haymond, *Harrison County, W. Va.* (Morgantown, 1910), p. 64. This fort was kept up until some time in 1789 or 1790, when it was abandoned.—ED.

[72] Zadoc Springer belonged to a German family who emigrated in early days from New Jersey to the Monongahela. In 1782 he was a magistrate in Westmoreland County, and his sister was the wife of Col. Zackwell Morgan.—ED.

[73] For a more extended account of the raid upon the Grigsby homestead, see *Border Warfare*, pp. 217, 218. It was situated on a branch of Elk Creek in Harrison County, W. Va. For the exact location, see Haymond, *Harrison County*, p. 63. The date has usually been given from tradition as June, 1777; this document gives the exact time.—ED.

[74] For their capture, see *Rev. Upper Ohio*, pp. 245, 246.—ED.

38   FRONTIER DEFENSE ON UPPER OHIO

Aug. 7. Dorsey Pentecost, at Greenway,[75] sends an express to General Hand to inquire concerning a rumor that a man taken captive last autumn has lately escaped from Detroit, and reported to Hand that an army of 10,000 to 16,000 Canadians, Indians, and British are marching toward Pittsburgh. The panic is great, and the writer wishes the rumor either confirmed or denied.

Aug. 8. Samuel Moorhead from Kittanning reports the desertion of the Indian mentioned in his letter of the 5th, after stealing a gun and other articles, and setting their canoes adrift. If attacked, no information can be sent by water. Urges Hand to send him more men. On the same date, Hand appointed a meeting of militia officers at Ligonier for Monday, Aug. 18.

Aug. 11. Arthur Campbell writes from Washington County to Col. William Fleming[76] that Peter and Daniel Harmon, fifty miles down Sandy River,[77] were fired at by an Indian party, thought to be forty or fifty in number, from four large canoes drawn up in a small creek. The Harmons escaped and warned the inhabitants. One settler was killed and scalped last Friday, near Blackmore's on the Clinch River;[78] traces of the enemy are found along other parts of the Clinch. The

---

[75] For Dorsey Pentecost see *Dunmore's War*, p. 101, note 47. "Greenway" was probably somewhere on Youghiogheny River, whither Pentecost removed his family during the panic of 1777.—ED.

[76] For Arthur Campbell and Col. William Fleming see *Ibid*, p. 39, note 70, and pp. 428, 429, respectively.—ED.

[77] For the Harmon family and their previous scouts in this vicinity, see *Ibid*, p. 70.—ED.

[78] For this location, see *Ibid*, p. 85, note 33.—ED.

RAIDS AND SKIRMISHES

people are closely forted, and in more distressing circumstances than last summer. They need men, provisions, and salt, and can with difficulty get lead, although so near the mines. It is rumored that Point Pleasant has been evacuated. Can no plan be made to chastise these ravagers? Can nothing be done at Fort Pitt? Are they to look to Congress or their own state for relief? As Fleming is the only representative in whom they have confidence, they expect him to make some plan to save this back country from total devastation.

Aug. 12. Samuel Mason writes General Hand that Colonel Shepherd has set men to work, strengthening the fort. He found a package of ten proclamations from Detroit, but kept them a profound secret, for fear that spreading them would be hurtful to the cause.

Aug. 12. Archibald Lochry writes from Twelve Mile Run[79] to General Hand that he finds it difficult

---

[79] Archibald Lochry (Laughrey, Lockrey, Loughrey) was of Scotch-Irish parentage, and born on the frontiers of Pennsylvania. He was justice of the peace for Bedford County, and on the organization of Westmoreland (1773) was chosen county lieutenant, in which office he acted acceptably until his departure for his ill-fated expedition (1781). His home was in Unity township, between Greensburgh and Ligonier, on a small stream designated in his letters as "Twelve Mile Run"; it is, however, no longer so called. In 1781 Lochry raised a volunteer expedition to join Gen. George Rogers Clark in his operations in the West. Leaving the rendezvous not far from Hannastown on July 24, he set out expecting to join Clark at Wheeling. Upon reaching this latter place he found Clark had gone in advance, and set forth to overtake him. Having landed about ten miles below Miami River, to refresh his party, Lochry and his men were overpowered by a superior force of Indians and obliged to surrender. The commandant was one of the first to be killed by a Shawnee tomahawk.

to spirit up the people of his county. He has only enlisted twenty-five. A substitute has orders to range from Laurel Hill to the mouth of Kiskiminitas Creek.[80]

Aug. 13. The inhabitants of a small fort on Buffalo Creek write to General Hand requesting "your Excellency to take our distressed case into your serious consideration. we have at the risk of our lives preserved our Crops untill now and last night we heard of a party of Indians preparing to cross the river about a mile above the Beech bottom Station and we have out of what few men we have in the fort amounting in the whole to about 20 men, sent 7 to assist in pursuing them." Beg to be excused from a draft. "Signed by Tho⁵. McGuire, Edward Perins[81] and the fort people in general."

His widow afterwards married Capt. Jack Guthrie. Two of Lochry's children petitioned Congress for bounty land, and in 1859 a committee reported favorably upon their claim; see 35th Cong., 1st sess. *House Reports*, no. 289.—ED.

[80] Laurel Hill was the eastern boundary of Westmoreland County. Kiskiminitas Creek was on the northwestern border, and peculiarly exposed to Indian attacks. Along this route came the savages who burned and captured Hannastown (1782), and during the later Indian wars (1789-95) this region was under special stress. A small blockhouse known as Reed's Station was erected near the Kiskiminitas during the latter period; at the time of this letter there was no protection nearer than Fort Kittanning, some ten miles farther up the Allegheny.—ED.

[81] Thomas McGuire was an Irish emigrant who settled first on the South Branch of Potomac; thence he removed in 1772 to Washington County, Pa., where he settled near the upper waters of Buffalo Creek. He was the father of Maj. Francis McGuire, later noted in border history. The site of his fort is not precisely known, but it was probably on or near Buffalo Creek, some miles above its mouth.

Edward Perrin came West from Antietam, Md., and settled

RAIDS AND SKIRMISHES 41

James Chambers of Westmoreland County told Dr. Draper that in August, 1777, he and six or seven other men were reaping oats near Adam Carnahan's blockhouse.[82] On receiving notice of skulking Indians, they went to John McKibben's, where Fort Hand was built the next winter.[83] The Indians plundered several cabins and finally attacked Carnahan's blockhouse. On

---

about seven miles east of Wellsburg, probably near Buffalo Creek. Oct. 15, 1779, while hunting with two companions, he was shot and killed by Indians on a stream fourteen miles above the mouth of Short Creek, since known as Perrin's Run. He was about fifty years of age when killed, and left a widow and several children. See interview with his granddaughter in Draper MSS., 16S262, 263.—ED.

[82] James Chambers was born in Ireland in May, 1749, emigrated to America about 1768, and in the autumn of 1773 settled on Kiskiminitas Creek, in Washington township, Westmoreland County. There Dr. Draper in 1846 interviewed the aged pioneer. He described his capture by Indians in 1781 while on a scout near Sewickley Creek, his sojourn at Detroit, and at Prison Island near Montreal, whence he escaped in 1782. His memory was very retentive, and he gave Dr. Draper many facts about Indian warfare.

Adam Carnahan was a neighbor of Chambers. His blockhouse was located about a mile south of the Kiskiminitas and six miles below the mouth of Conemaugh Creek. Carnahan's son James enlisted in the Continental service, and was an officer of repute. This blockhouse was the rendezvous for Lochry's forces in his expedition of 1781.—ED.

[83] Fort Hand was built in the autumn of 1777 after Fort Kittanning was evacuated (see *post*), and the garrison of the latter transferred thither. It was the only fort in that region, on the Continental establishment. In the latter part of July, 1778, Capt. Samuel Miller with nine soldiers of the 8th Pennsylvania were waylaid without the fort, when the captain and seven men were killed. See *Penna. Archives*, vi, p. 673. In March of the following year, Fort Hand was again attacked and ably defended by Capt. Samuel Moorhead for twenty-four hours, when the besiegers finally withdrew. Fort Hand was evacuated shortly after this; but again occupied during the Indian wars, and kept up until 1791 or 1792. It was located in Washington township of Westmoreland County, about a mile south of the Kiskiminitas ford.—ED.

stepping to the door, John Carnahan was instantly shot dead. The firing continued briskly until dark, when the Indians decamped, carrying their wounded on litters. One Indian, left dead, had about him articles plundered from Chambers's cabin.

RETALIATORY EXPEDITION PLANNED
[Gen. Edward Hand to Col. William Fleming. 1U80— A. L. S.]

REDSTONE[84] 12th. Augt. 1777

SIR—The Murders lately committed by the Savages on our Frontiers have occasioned much distress and uneasiness in the minds of the Inhabitants, and as a General Confederacy of the Western tribes has taken place at the Instigation of the British Emisaries in their Country it will no doubt be productive of Multiplied Greivances to us except we can penetrate their Country and take on them the Vengence due to their perfidy

I therefore in Consequence of his Excellency the Governor of Virginia's permission desire you will be pleased to furnish me with 200 Men properly officered and Equiped for an Expedition into the Indian Country, and willing to serve Six Months from the first of September next unless sooner discharged. The Counties of Monongalia youghogania & Ohio have proposed to furnish their proportions by Volanteers, you Sir will be the best Judge how to proceed in your own Country as soon as the Men are ready (which I wish to be as soon as possible) order them to March to Fort Randolph at the mouth of the Great Kanha-

---
[84] For Redstone see *Dunmore's War*, p. 12, note 22.—ED.

RETALIATION 43

way. if in the meantime I find any other place of General Rendevous more convenient will take the earliest opportunity of Acquainting you. Least the Garrison at Fort Randolph may not have the proper supply of Provision beg you may contrive to send flour & live Cattle to supply your detachment for some time after their Arrival. Col. Aylett of Williamsburgh is appointed Commissary for the Westren Posts and will give you the necessary assistance.[85] I am Sir your most Obed^t. & Most Hbb. Servt.

Edwd. Hand

To County Lieutenant of Bottetourt

P. S. Please to forward the Inclosed to Augusta by Express.

[Col. Zackwell Morgan to Capt. William Harrod.[86] 4NN58— A. L. S.]

Sir—You are to Proceed to Recruit all the able Bodied Volenteers as Soon as Possible. enlist them to go on an Expedition to the Indian Towns, and have

---

[85] Upon receipt of this letter Colonel Fleming called a court martial whose resolutions (passed Aug. 29, 1777) are in Draper MSS., 1U88. There were present William Fleming, county lieutenant, Col. George Skillern, Maj. George Poage, Capt. Thomas Rowland, Capt. John Armstrong, Capt. Martin McFarren, Capt. Patrick Lockhart, Capt. George Givens, and Capt. James Hall. On considering the letter of General Hand it was determined to send an express to the governor of Virginia to know how far they were authorized to obey this requisition. They are sensible that the frontier would profit by such an expedition, but the county has been drained of men, and they are apprehensive of the consequences, as winter is approaching. As to supplies, Eastern parties are buying cattle in their vicinity at extravagant rates, and they request a stop thereto.—Ed.

[86] For a sketch of Capt. William Harrod, see *Dunmore's War*, p. 68, note 14.—Ed.

them in Readiness as Soon as Possible. The place of Rendevouse at Carns Fort,[87] where you are to Order your men as Soon as Recruited, pray use Every Method in Your Power to Dispatch this Business. I wish you Success and am Sir your Hble Ser^t.

Zack^{ll}. Morgan

Aug. 15, 1777

N. B. inlist the men for Six Months from 1st Sep^t. tho they are to be under pay as Soon as Listed and all plunder is to be Divided Equal.

To Capt William Harrod.

[Maj. Henry Taylor to Gen. Edward Hand. 1U83—A. L. S.]

Rerdons Bottom[88] 17th. Augst. 1777

Dear General—I received yours of the 9th. of Augst. Deated at Pittsburgh, and Must confess your condesending to leave the place of fixing the post to the people to be as satisfactory as the[y] Could Desire and as the Chief of the old posts was below Logs-Town I marched the Men down to this post, and went down myself to the Lower posts taking the minds of the people, and I found that every one was for having it at the place where the[y] were. I found that the people at Large could not fix it, I then ordred the Officers to meet at this post and there to Agree on the place. the[y] promised to do so, but has not yet come. Owing I beleave to an alarm of some Indians being in the settlement the Inhabatants is in the Ut-

---

[87] Probably intended for Kern's Fort, in the present Monongalia County, W. Va., on Decker's Creek See S. T. Wiley, *Monongalia County* (Kingwood, W. Va., 1883), p. 649.—Ed.

[88] Reardon's Run is on the southeast side of Raccoon Creek, in Independence township, Beaver County, Pa.—Ed.

RETALIATION

most confusion yet it is as bad as Deth to think of moving. the Inhabatants of Holladay's cove[89] Declared the[y] would stay & Difend themselves as long as the[y] could. & secured all the Ammonition and Guns, telling me that the[y] would Acc^t. w^t. the publick for all the[y] would Use of them Indeed I must confess the[y] did not Use me w^t. any indeacency. Capt. perce and his Vollounteers is here only 8 which was left to Assist M^r. Baker and his family to this place.[80] the Militia is Cheefly all Gon & going home therefor I will have only Capt Hogland[91] and Capt Perces Vollounteers, Unless New Draughts is sent

I long to here what was concluded on at the council at Redstone Fôrt. I have no News but what you have had I have kept out constant scouts to tray to meet them Indians that was in the Inhabatants but can not make Any Discoverys, there is about 50 Voll^s and 10 Militia Draughts here which will be free in a few Days the people in General seems keen for an Expedition but how the[y] will Turn out I am at a loss to Gess I am w^t Respect y^r. Hubl Servt

         HENRY TAYLOR MAJ^r.[92]

To Brigadeer Genl. Hand, Fort Pitt

---

[89] Holliday's Cove settlement was formed in 1776 and lay in what is now Hancock County, W. Va., about three miles back from Ohio River. There is at present on the site a postoffice by this name.—ED.

[90] Probably the family of Joshua Baker, who lived opposite the mouth of Yellow Creek in the present Hancock County, W. Va. See *Dunmore's War*, pp. 15-18.—ED.

[91] Capt. Henry Hoagland lived on Pigeon Creek, in the Monongahela district. He served with McDonald in the Wakatomica campaign of 1774; and went out as captain in 1782 under Crawford. After the latter's defeat he was never again heard from.—ED.

[92] For a sketch of Maj. Henry Taylor, see *Rev. Upper Ohio*, p. 233, note 76.—ED.

FORTS STRENGTHENED

[Capt. Samuel Moorhead to Gen. Edward Hand. 1U84— A. L. S.]

KITTANING 19th. Augt. 1777

SIR—This evning sent Out A party of men to drive up the Cattle, A little ways from the fort was fird on by a Considerable Party of indeans, as it Appears by their tracks. Killed and Scalpt three of the men, and left with them two papers, equal in Substance, one of which I inclose to you for your Consideration[93] Am Sir Your Obdt Hum^l. Servt

SAM^l. MOORHEAD

Have but three small Beef Cattle at Present

To Genl. E. Hand Commander in Chieff Fourt Pitt

[Col. David Shepherd to Gen. Edward Hand. 1U85—A. L. S.]

FORT HENRY August the 22^d 1777

SIR—In obedience to your order I have Caled in all the men to this place that is under pay and have Removed my famely Likewise, but there Seems a Great Confusion in the County Concerning it. I have ordered Capt Ogle to keep up a Scout Between this fort and the Beach Bottom Likewise Capt Mason to send a party to Scout Betwen this and Grave Creek and Shall order Such Scouts and Spies over the River as our Strength will admit of, Captains Shannon,[94]

---

[93] See Hamilton's proclamation of June 24, *ante*, p. 14.—ED.
[94] Probably Capt. Samuel Shannon from Ligonier, Westmoreland County, where he took up land in 1773. He was head of a ranging company from 1777-81. In the latter year he accompanied the ill-fated Lochry expedition (see *ante*, p. 39, note 79), as one of its officers. Sent in advance by Colonel Lochry with a note to General Clark, he was captured by the Indian party lying in wait, and induced to advise sur-

STRENGTHENING FORTS

Leach and Marchant[95] Arived here on the 20th Inst and Seems Very well Behaved and Oblidging our Captons is making up their Companeys as fast as posible. But the Men Complains Greatly that they are not paid of as they want the money for their former Service to aquip them for a Campain it would be well if this Could be Done and a pay Master Sent Down or some way ordred that the Men are paid But I make no Doubt But we Shall Get the Men Required of our County as they are Recruiting fast Col Morgan has not yet arived here Neither have we heard from him we are Repairing the fort as fast as posible and Shall Soon have it Indian proof Except they Scale the Stockades' the Indians has Been with [us] Once Since I Saw you they Crossed the River in the Night near the mouth of Buffelow Creek when Capt Ogle with a party of his men followed their tracks next morning and over took them they Changed Several Shot but none kiled or Cripled on Either Side. our people Got Eleven Blankets and plunder that Sold for 24 Pounds the Indians made their Escape a Cross the River the next night by the plunder got it is

---

render to Lochry's force. He was carried captive to Lower Sandusky, whence he managed to escape, and had reached the hill opposite Wheeling when retaken by a marauding Indian on his return from the settlements and tomahawked. See Draper MSS., 6NN146, 175, 176.—ED.

[95] These companies had been recruited in Westmoreland County for the relief of the Ohio River forts. A Swiss family named Marchand lived in 1770 on Little Sewickley Creek in Hempfield township of that county, and had several distinguished descendants. Capt. David Marchand with a company of thirty-four men and Capt. James Leetch with thirteen men served on the Ohio frontier. 3NN10.—ED.

thought that they was a party that had been at fort Pitt[96]   I am Sir with Respect Y^r Humble Servt
DAVID SHEPHERD
To His Honour General Hand   at Fort Pitt

TROOPS FOR EXPEDITION
[Gen. Edward Hand to Jasper Yeates. MS. in New York Public Library; Hand Papers—A. L. S.]

FORT PITT 25th. August 1777.

DEAR YEATES—Your favour of the 7th. Instant I rec^d. the 16th. by M^r. Steel.   by a person just returned from Williamsburg I learn that the British fleet has Appeared in Chesapeak Bay.   this will cause a new & fatigueing movement in our Army,   I am as Apprehensive as yourself of S^t. Clairs fate.   Indian Affairs remain as when I last wrote to you.   I have demanded 2000 men from the Several frontier Counties of Virginia & Pennsylvania   if I get them cant have a doubt of reducing the Wyandots & Pluggys Town Confederacy, at present our most Troublesome Neighbours. this County is in great confusion & Distress at present. the prospects of fixing a permanent boundary between Virginia & Pennsylvania, gives the people much satisfaction.   next to Chastising the Indians, they desire that may take place.   the situation of the Delawares embarraces me much.   I wish to preserve their friendship, how to do this & keep small parties in the Indian Country, (A measure I wish to Adopt,) & steer Clear

---

[96] Aug. 15, General Hand wrote to his wife, "The Delaware Indians have left hostages as a pledge of their friendship." 3NN47.—ED.

of the Delawares I cant tell. I wish you & all our friends Felicity & am D^r.Yeats. very Affectionately y^{rs}.

EDW^d HAND

To Jasper Yeates Esqr. Lancaster
Endorsed: Fort Pitt Augt. 25. 1777. Genl. Hand. (Answ^d. Septr. 13. 1777 p^r Col. Steel)

[Col. Zackwell Morgan to Gen. Edward Hand. 3NN 154, 155—Transcript.]

25th. Aug. 1777.

Captn. Pigman[97] marches this day for Wheeling with his company, & takes the flour he talked of; I shall follow him myself with Maj^r. Chew on Sunday next with about 100 men, & as soon as I get to Wheeling shall return by the way of Fort Pitt to consult with your excellency the future operations of the troops, by which time I am fully convinced that the remainder of the men for the intended expedition will be ready to march, that nothing may retard us any longer.

[Gen. Edward Hand to Mrs. Hand. 3NN47, 48—Transcript.]

FORT PITT, Aug. 25th 1777.

The safety of the country depends on our being able to penetrate the Indian country; but whether I can accomplish it, I don't yet know. Certain it is, that with a proper force (without which it will not be attempted), a measure of that nature be executed without greater danger than this garrison is exposed to. * * * The 16th. instant a party of Indians

---

[97] Captain Pigman did not march as intended; see Shepherd's letter of Aug. 28, and Zackwell Morgan's of Aug. 29, *post.*—ED.

attacked a house about forty miles from here, at a place called Beaver Run in Westmoreland County, where near 40 women & children had taken shelter with 7 men; the Indians were beaten off, two of them left dead on the spot; one white man was also killed.[98] A Delaware Indian who arrived here yesterday met the party—they were Wyandotts—went out with 14 men & were returning with 10—one of them was shot through the body & had his arm broken. The 17th. a party of Chippewas fired on 6 men of the garrison at Kittanning, killed three of them & got off clear. Twenty men from this garrison are now out on the Indian [side] in search of some skulking rascals who fired on & slightly wounded a man near M^r. Croghan's[99] place yesterday. As they are guided by an Indian, I hope they will ferret them out.

QUIET AT FORT HENRY

[Col. David Shepherd to Gen. Edward Hand. 1U87—A. L. S.]

FORT HENRY [Augt.] 28th 1777

SIR—we have not seen any signs of the Indians since I wrote to you Last and we keep out Scouts and Spies Every Day. Col Morgan has not ar[i]ved here from the Monongahale County nor Aney Men from that County neither Do we hear from him Cap' Shannons men was Seemed unesy to go home and as I saw no apperance of the Indians I Let them go they Behaveed them Selves very well During their Stay,

---

[98] This refers to the affair at Carnahan's blockhouse, when John Carnahan was killed. See *ante,* p. 41.—ED.

[99] Col. George Croghan lived on the east side of the Allegheny, about four miles from the intersection of the rivers. The site is now within the limits of Pittsburgh.—ED.

FORT HENRY (Wheeling, W. Va.) IN 1777

From W. De Hass, *Early Settlement and Wars of Western Virginia* (Wheeling, 1851)

A TORY PLOT

we have got the fort in Some Better posture of Defence than it was Before, I ordred the men from the Beach Bottom But the Inhabetants would not Remove I therefore ordred that party to Keep up a Scout on the other Side of the River So as to Cover the Inhabitants as wel as possible. I Shall Come to fort pit in a few Days if Nothing happens. Sir I am with Respect yr Huml. Servt.

DAVID SHEPHERD

To His Honor General Edward Hand

THE TORY CONSPIRACY

[Col. Thomas Gaddis to Lieut.-Col. Thomas Brown[1] at Redstone Old Fort. 3NN156, 157—Transcript.]

DEAR SIR—A certain person was at my house on Monday the 25th inst, and he made oath to me that the Tories have joined themselves together for to cut off the inhabitants, and we know not what hour they will rise. Therefore it would be proper that you would take a particular care and keep a strong guard over the Magazine[2] for a few days, till we can use some means with them. This day I am starting with a party of men for to succor the people and suppress the Tories. I would desire that you would do your utmost endeavor and warn the friends of our country to be upon their watch. Sir, I remain respectfully your friend

THOs. GADDIS

August 26th. 1777.

---

[1] For these officers of Monongalia and Yohogania counties, see *Rev. Upper Ohio*, pp. 233, 234, notes 76 and 78 respectively.—ED.

[2] At Redstone was situated the powder magazine for the Virginia counties west of the mountains.—ED.

[Thomas Brown to General Hand. 3NN155, 156—Transcript.]

REDSTONE FORT, Augt 29th 1777

D^r. SIR—Enclosed you have Col. Gaddis' letter to me directed, from which you may find in what circumstances our country lies under. Agreeable to Col^o. Gaddis' instructions, I have called a guard of fifteen men for the safety of the magazine, which I hope will meet with your approbation. Any instructions from your excellency shall be obeyed if in my power. Col^o Gaddis and Capt. Enochs[3] with about 100 men are in pursuit of the Tories, but their success I have not yet heard; but from different accounts it appears the Tories are determined to stand battle. I expect to hear from Col. Gaddis every hour, and shall transmit a full account as soon as possible. I have the honor to be &c.

THOMAS BROWN.

N. B. From sundry acct^s. the Tories are determined to take the Magazine if in their power.

Genl. Hand.
Endorsed: Col. Thos. Brown.

[Col. Zackwell Morgan to General Hand. 3NN65, 66—Transcript.]

August 29th. 1777

May it please y^r. Exc^y.—It is with the utmost anxiety that I now inform you that our march is retarded for some time against the natural enemies of our country. A few days ago the most horrid conspiracy appeared. Numbers of the inhabitants of this country have joined in a plot and were assembled together to join the English and Indians. This forces me to raise

---

[3] For Capt. Henry Enoch see *Rev. Upper Ohio*, pp. 207, 235.—ED.

what men were enlisted as well as others, to put a stop to this unnatural unheard of frantick scene of mischief that was in the very heart of our country. We have taken numbers who confess that they have sworn allegiance to the King of Great Britain, & that some of the leading men at Fort Pitt are to be their rulers & heads. The parties I have out are bringing in numbers of those wretches & they (those that confess) all agree in their confession that the English, French & Indians will be with you in a few days, when they were with numbers of others to embody themselves, & Fort Pitt was to be given up with but little opposition; some are taken that really astonish me out of measure. Good heavens! that mankind should be so lost to every virtue & sense of their country. I am this moment informed that Gideon Long & Jeremiah Long, two deserters are gone to Fort Pitt to deliver themselves up; should this be the case, & as they have been very active in this conspiracy, I hope your Exc^y. will punish them as they deserve. I am now at Minor's Fort[4] with about 500 men, & am determined to purge the country before I disband, as it would give me much satisfaction to have this matter settled. I shall wait y^r. Excellency's instructions & am with respect your most obed^t. humble serv^t.

ZACK: MORGAN.

---

[4] This was either at Statler's Fort, which Minor commanded (see *ante,* p. 21, note 46), or a blockhouse upon his property in the present Monongalia township of Greene County, Pa. See sketch in *Rev. Upper Ohio,* p. 235, note 79.—ED.

THE SIEGE OF FORT HENRY

[Reminiscences by Dr. Joseph Doddridge.[5] 6NN123-126— A. D.]

Fort Henry, at Wheeling, was built at the expense of the English Government, by the order of the Earl of Dunmore, while on his campaign against the Indians in the summer of 1774, who, when he descended the river in pursuit of the Indians on the Scioto, left Colonel William Crawford and Angus McDonald, with a detatchment of men to build and garrison the fort.[6]

The fort was substantially built of squared timbers painted at the top and furnished with bastions and sentry boxes at the angles. The interior of the fort contained an house for the officers and barracks for the men. Its area was something more than half an acre.

---

[5] Joseph Doddridge was born in 1769 in Bedford County, Pa. In 1773 his father removed with his family to what is now Washington County, not far from the present West Virginia line. Doddridge was thus a boy eight years old at the time of this siege, and living in the immediate neighborhood. For several years he was a Methodist preacher, itinerating throughout the entire region. Later he joined the Episcopal church and studied and practiced medicine, dying in 1826 at his home in Wellsburg. Two years before his death he published (at the last-named place) *Notes on the Settlement and Indian Wars of the Western Parts of Virginia and Pennsylvania*, in which he embodied much of his knowledge of pioneer days. There is not, however, in this book any account of the siege at Wheeling. Such a manuscript account was found among his papers, and secured by Dr. Draper from his daughter. Unfortunately the manuscript is incomplete, breaking off abruptly. We have supplemented this account, therefore, with recollections of other pioneers.—ED.

[6] See *Dunmore's War*, p. 86.—ED.

ATTACK ON FORT HENRY

This fort was designed for the refuge and protection of the lower settlements in this district of country, and being next in strength and importance to fort Pitt, soon attracted the notice of the Indians and their English allies, who at three different periods attempted to break up the establishment.

The first attack on fort Henry took place on the first day of September 1777.

Genl Hand had, at that time, the command of the western department. The Moravian Indians who had three villages on the Muskimgum about sixty miles from the Ohio river were in the practice of sending runners to Genl Hand, with information concerning any intended scout or campaign of the Indian warriors against any of the settlements or forts of the white people.

About three weeks before the attack of fort Henry, Genl Hand sent notice to Col^n David Shepherd, the Lieutenant Colonel of Ohio County, that he had received advice that fort Henry would be attacked in short time, by a large Indian force, aided by a body of british rangers from Detroit. This advice was accompanied with an order to the Col^n to leave his own fort which was about six miles distant from fort Henry, and take the command of the latter fort. The Col^n was directed to issue his orders to all the Captains between the Ohio and Monongahala, to rendezvous at fort Henry with all possible dispatch, with the whole number of their men. Accordingly Captains Williamson, Virgin, Crooks, Miller, Hathaway, and Ogle, with some others whose names are not recollected, assembled with their companies at the fort.⁷ Their number was from four to five hundred men.

The Indians not coming on as soon as was expected, some of the Captains, thinking the report of the intended attack of fort Henry a "false alarm" left the place with their companies and returned home. Two companies left the place the day before the attack. Cap⁺ Ogle, and his company were the only distant troops at the place at the time of the engagament. These troops, and those of Cap Mason of the place, amounting in all to about one hundred men,⁸ constituted the whole force which defended fort Henry at its first attack.

About sunrise, on the day of the attack, Andrew Zane,⁹ with a small party, set out from the fort to go to a place about a mile distant to get some horses, to move a family [Dr. McMechan's] from the fort up the country towards the Monongahala. When this party had reached the brow of the hill, back of Wheeling, at the spot where the national turn pike now passes it, they were attacked by several Indians, who, however, did not fire on them, but endeavoured

---

⁷ Dr. Doddridge has mistaken the names of the local commandants. Captains Leach, Marchant, and Shannon were the reinforcing militia officers, all of whom had departed previous to the attack, except the local company of Capt. Samuel Mason, and the supply from Beech Bottom Fort under Capt. Joseph Ogle.—ED.

⁸ An overestimate of the number of men. According to Duke's account book (1SS149), Captain Ogle's company consisted of thirty-eight men. Mason's was probably no larger if as large.—ED.

⁹ Andrew Zane was one of the brothers whose father was noted *ante*, p. 15, note 36. They were the founders and first settlers of Wheeling. Andrew was killed by Indians; not at the siege of Wheeling, but later while scouting.—ED.

ATTACK ON FORT HENRY

to kill, or take them prisoners without giving an alarm. One of the party of the name of Boyd, was caught, after running about Eighty yards, and tomahawked. Zane made his escape by jumping over a cliff of rocks of considerable height. The Indians who were running after him, not choosing to imitate the perilous leap he had taken gave up the pursuit. Zane was much bruised in the fall, and his gun was broken to pieces; but in the course of the day he reached Col^n Shepherds fort.[10] One man and a negro boy of this little party returned to the fort and gave the alarm.

According to the usual folly and rashness of our militia of early times, about twenty turned out of the fort to give battle to Indians; notwithstanding the advice of Genl Hand, that the place would be attacked by at least 200 of the enemy.

The Indians, after finishing their work with the small party, passed over the top of the hill and descended into the bottom, following the bend of the creek, until they came to the flat piece of ground at the south end of Wheeling hill. In this flat they formed an ambuscade in the form of a crescent, with its convexity towards the creek, it[s] points within a short distance of the foot of the hill. A considerable force had also been left among the bushes, on the western side of the hill, some distance in front of the

---

[10] Col. David Shepherd lived at the forks of Wheeling Creek, where Little Wheeling comes in, about six miles above Fort Henry. He purchased this location from Silas Zane in 1773, and there forted during the wars. According to General Hand's orders, Shepherd had removed to Fort Henry, but some of the neighboring families remained in his blockhouse.—ED.

58 FRONTIER DEFENSE ON UPPER OHIO

ambuscade to prevent the escape of any of our men, in case they should pursue the Indians and fall into the ambuscade.

The Indians in their march over the hill, down the bottom and through the centre of the ambuscade, had taken the precaution to make a large trail so that they might be readily pursued so as to draw our men into the snare.

When the party which had left the fort, for the pursuit of the Indians had fallen on their trail, they selected two or three men to follow directly on the tracks. The others divided into two equal parties and marched in single file at the distance of several steps of each other about 70 yards to the right and left of the trail.

When our party had progressed some distance into the flat, in which the ambuscade was formed, a soldier of the name of Thomas Glen, who was marching next to Captain Mason, discovered an Indian on the right flank of the enemy whom he instantly shot down. The first shot from the Indians wounded Capt Mason in the hand and carried off the lock of his gun.

The battle then commenced with a[11]

[Recollections of John Hanks.[12] 12CC138.]

From the Monongahela, we moved to within 5 miles of Wheeling; remaining there until the Indians com-

---

[11] The manuscript is unfinished. Dr. Draper, in an appended note, says that the latter portion was lost before it came into his hands.—ED.

[12] John Hanks was born Nov. 29, 1767, in Loudon County, Md., and removed in 1774 to the neighborhood of Redstone, on the Monongahela; thence, as he says, to the Wheeling

ATTACK ON FORT HENRY

pelled us to move into Wheeling Fort. Before we moved in one McBride was killed out on the waters of Wheeling.[13] * * * We went out and around by and to Silas Zane's;[14] my father being at that time over the Ohio (about a mile from us) after Indians.
* * * * * * * *
From Zane's we went to the fort. While we were there one morning, were out Jacob Coles, John Mills and Dr. McMahon, looking for McMahon's heifer.[15] McMahon was intending to move out of the fort. I was out at the spring, when the firing was heard.

---

neighborhood. Hanks was, therefore, a boy of ten and in the fort during the siege. In 1786 the family removed to Kentucky and settled in Montgomery County, whence Hanks went out as scout and hunter. There, on the Spruce fork of Slate River, he was interviewed by John D. Shane.—ED.

[13] See *Rev. Upper Ohio*, p. 250.—ED.

[14] Silas Zane was among the first settlers in the neighborhood of Wheeling. He was himself not present at the first siege in 1777, being a captain in the 13th Virginia, and on service in the Eastern states. Hanks here refers to Shepherd's blockhouse, at what had been Silas Zane's location. Zane returned to the Ohio before the close of the Revolution, and was at Fort Henry during the siege of 1782. At the close of the Revolution he went with George Green to the Indian country, with goods for a trader from Maryland. On their return, about 1785, the two traders were waylaid and murdered on the Scioto. Silas Zane left an infant son of the same name.—ED.

[15] There were two brothers McMechen (usually pronounced McMahon) in the neighborhood of Wheeling—William, the founder of the pioneer family of that name; and Dr. James, a physician of Scotch origin, who came from Delaware to the Ohio and was for a time clerk of Ohio County. During the Revolution James returned to the East and never came back to the frontier. His brother William settled six miles below Wheeling. His family was at Redstone during the troubles on the frontier, and later returned to their Ohio River home, where they became prominent in early West Virginia annals.—ED.

About twenty men seized their guns and ran out. Jacob Coles and John Mills were killed, and Dr. McMahon wounded.[16] The Indians seemed to have made as much sign as possible. When they got to the mouth of Wheeling to which the trace led, John Saunders said to the Company, "I wish we were over the other side of the River." Some one said they wouldn't wish to be over the other side. They believed there were plenty of Indians that side. Letters were found on the trail, left by the Indians inviting the pursuers to come over and join them that if they would bring a flag they shouldn't be hurt, and should have fine quarters at Detroit. Dreading some evil consequences from these letters, all the members of the party were mutually sworn not to divulge the secret of their contents, for the next six months.

* * * * * * * *

Dr. McMahon sent an Irishman, and his black man Loudon, out in the morning to get the oxen. When they got out, the Indians were in ambush and took after them. The Irishman was overtaken and tomahawked; but the negro, who was too swift for them rushed into the fort, and cried "Indians, Indians." The men in the fort snatched up their guns, and ran, some without their hats.[17] A high mountain puts in just by Wheeling. There the Indians drew the pur-

---

[16] The narrator has mistaken the persons; it was John Boyd who was killed. Dr. McMechen did not leave the fort. The first party consisted of Boyd, Samuel Tomlinson, Andrew Zane, and the negro Loudon.—ED.

[17] This was Mason's party, ordered out by Colonel Shepherd. The number is variously given; probably it was fifteen, all but two of whom were killed.—ED.

suing party to follow them round this mountain, having others prepared to follow them in the rear, till they closed in on both sides, and the whole party but two cut off. These were Sam. Mason (a Captain) and one Caldwell,[18] who did not get started as soon as the others, and so were not surrounded. Mason and his sergeant encountered two Indians, Mason called on the sergeant to shoot. Both shot on both sides. Both the Indians and the sergeant, named Steell, were killed and Mason wounded. He now crept down under the banks of Wheeling Creek, where he lay till night, and then got on to Shepherd's fort, about six miles.[19]

---

[18] John Caldwell was born in Ireland Jan. 22, 1753. While still a boy his parents emigrated to America and settled first at Baltimore. In 1773 Caldwell removed to the vicinity of Wheeling, and was for several years in the Indian wars. In 1774 he was out with Dunmore. In October, 1776, under the command of Capt. William Harrod, Caldwell was one of a party from Grave Creek Fort that went down the river to rescue the wounded and bury the dead of Robert Patterson's party, coming from Kentucky (see *Rev. Upper Ohio*, pp. 207, 210, 213). The next year Caldwell was a volunteer under Capt. Samuel Mason. At first stationed at Shepherd's Fort, he was at Fort Henry during the siege. His son related to Dr. Draper (3S141-144) that Caldwell ran up the hill to escape the ambuscade, tripped and fell, and was wedged in between two trees. Seeing an Indian pursuing him, he wrenched himself loose with great effort, just as the Indian threw his tomahawk, which missed its aim, and Caldwell escaped to Shepherd's Fort six miles up the creek. In 1778 and 1779 Caldwell was a volunteer guard at Wheeling, and in the latter year went on Brodhead's campaign; he also served awhile at Rail's Fort on Buffalo Creek. He lived on Wheeling Creek, about fourteen miles above its mouth, until his death in 1840, and at one time drew a pension for his services. His pension documents are in Draper MSS., 6ZZ60-66.—ED.

[19] Withers, who obtained his information from Noah, son of Ebenezer Zane, tells a story of the close pursuit of Mason, who having been twice wounded was faint from loss of blood.

[Recollections of Mrs. Joseph Stagg.[20] 12CC236, 237.]

Col. Ebenezer Zane's cabin was right where the fort stood. The fort was handsomely stockaded, at King's expense. White Eyes came to Fort Pitt, and told them that the Indians were going to take Wheeling home. White Eyes was sometimes thought to be of both sides. Col°. Shepherd sent to Fort Pitt, and obtained 70 men of the militia; but returned them again on Sunday morning, saying they had eaten too much beef for nothing. Immediately after he had sent them away, he sent to Mingo bottom for 25 others.[21] The first company [Captain Shannon's], it was supposed the Indians had seen go away, and by

---

The Indian came so near that Mason thrust him back with his hand; and then firing, he killed his red antagonist. After this he hid behind a fallen tree, and after nightfall made his escape. See *Border Warfare*, p. 223.—ED.

[20] Mrs. Joseph Stagg was the daughter of Edward Mills, sister of John Mills, who took an important part in the second siege of Wheeling. At the time of the first siege of Fort Henry, she was the wife of Capt. Jacob Drennon, a prominent Kentucky pioneer. Her granddaughter told Dr. Draper (21S168) that when the alarm came she fled to the fort with her infant, but in her flight left an adopted boy in the cabin. Remembering this she hastened from the fort, although the gates were closing, wrapped the boy in a feather bed, and ran back to the fort unharmed, although several bullets from Indian guns lodged within the bed. The Drennons afterwards removed to Kentucky, settling in Mason County, where Captain Drennon was killed. His widow married Joseph Stagg and for many years lived in Fleming County. She died in 1845, aged ninety, at her son-in-law's home in Harrison County, Ky.—ED.

[21] This refers to Captain Mason's company, who had been scouting as far as Beech Bottom Fort. But the narrator errs in stating that they came in after the siege began. See Shepherd's letter of Aug. 28, *ante*, p. 50.—ED.

ATTACK ON FORT HENRY

the time the sun was up, on Monday morning, the Indians attacked the' fort.

* * * * * * * *

One McMahon sent out some young men, to catch his horses; he and Jacob Drennon[22] were going away. Drennon wouldn't venture so to do [send for horses]. When the Doctor's negro came out to a thick wood, he said, "Why this looks as if it might be a good place for the Indians to hide." At that they started up. They had like to have caught the negro, but he got in. John Boyd, a youth was killed with their tomahawks and scalped. Five or six men ran out, tied his hands and feet, got a pole between them, and so got him in. The Indians had gone to another point. Andrew Zane, a brother of the colonel, jumped down a steep, afterwards measured to be 70 feet, without injury. Sammy Tomlinson was out too, and got in; but went out again with 25 and was killed. Capt. Mason commanded the 25 men that came from Mingo bottom, they got in along the port sally gate. The Indians then thought the fort open, and gave wonderful shouts and yells, and rushed to it, and they said they just came, 15 or 20 in a gang, holding each

---

[22] One of his descendants related (12BB) that Jacob Drennon was born in Greenbriar County, Va., educated in England, and commissioned in the English army; that he returned to America with Lord Dunmore, and would take no part either for or against the colonies. It is known that in 1773 he was in Kentucky with McAfee's party, and visited the lick known thereafter as Drennon's. In 1774 he was with Dunmore on the Ohio, and although frequently in Kentucky made his home in the neighborhood of Wheeling. He was shot in 1787 when descending the Ohio. Knowing that he was mortally wounded, he jumped from the boat into the river, that the Indians should not secure his scalp.—ED.

other's hand. The men complained that the women kept so in their way looking out at the portholes, they couldn't do a thing. A great trail was left where the Indians had dragged their dead to the river. Twenty men staid in, 25 went out. * * * The 25 men went out to head them. 15 were killed, I suppose at once and 5 were wounded.[23]

Francis Duke, Col. Shepherd's son-in-law, came from Vanmetre's fort, and couldn't be made to stop (commissary of the fort).[24] Col. Zane had just finished him a good house, all to one window, shingle-roofed. * * * Women ran bullets in frying pans, and two shot. Mrs. Duke cut bullet patches out of a 700 linen piece, like one cutting out shirts. And one Scotchman prayed all day. Rain came up, just after

---

[23] This refers to the whole number killed and wounded during the siege; see Shepherd's letter, *post*. The narrator does not distinguish between the two sorties of Captain Mason and Captain Ogle. A dense fog overhung the place. Those in the fort could hear the sounds of combat, but could not perceive the number of the enemy. Captain Ogle, with a small number, probably not more than twelve, issued out to the aid of Mason's men, but were immediately included in the massacre.—ED.

[24] Francis Duke was born in Ireland Feb. 11, 1751. Thence the family emigrated to the present Berkeley County, W. Va., where in 1773 Duke married Sarah, eldest daughter of Col. David Shepherd. Thence he removed with the latter's family to Wheeling Creek. He had been appointed by his father-in-law deputy commissary, and as such was stationed at Beech Bottom Fort. It was probably from there that he approached Fort Henry some time in the afternoon of Sept. 1, and was shot down near the gate. The entry in the family genealogy is, "September the 1 day 1777. ffrancis Duke was kled by the Sageus [Savages]." His notebook is in Draper MSS.,1SS149, wherein his last entry was Aug. 30. He left an infant son John, and a posthumous son Francis, whose descendants are numerous in Ohio and the West. His widow married Levi Springer.—ED.

ATTACK ON FORT HENRY 65

the town was set on fire. The women brought up water in tubs, and scrubbed [drenched] the roofs. That night the Indians left.

[Portion of reminiscences of Mrs. Lydia Cruger.[25] 2S148-151.]

Mason received a flesh wound in the hip, and hid himself in a fallen tree top, full of green leaves. Indians hunted all around him, he seeing them, in the night he escaped to some neighboring fort. Captain Ogle escaped to the cornfield with a wounded man, and concealed themselves in the high horse weeds; and while there, a wounded Indian, blood running down and crying, and another Indian with him, both sitting on the fence within a hansel[26] of Ogle; and

---

[25] Lydia Boggs was born Feb. 26, 1766, in Berkeley County, W. Va. In 1768 the family removed to the Youghiogheny, and thence in 1771 to Beeler's Fort (now Uniontown). In 1777 they lived on Buffalo Creek, where Capt. John Boggs commanded a militia company. In August, 1781, the Boggs household removed to a spot three miles below Wheeling, but in 1782 retreated to Fort Henry and were present during the second siege. Shortly afterward Lydia married Moses, son of Col. David Shepherd, and lived at his homestead until her husband's death in 1832. The following year she married Gen. Daniel Cruger, but kept her home at the old stone mansion on Wheeling Creek until her death in September, 1867. She was a woman of extraordinary memory, and great intellectual power. Her reminiscences are entitled to much credit, except where warped by personal prejudice. Although not an inmate of the fort when it was besieged in 1777, her close association with the Shepherd family, and her knowledge of the frontier people, make her account thereof approximately accurate and certainly interesting. For a description of a visit to Mrs. Cruger see *West Virginia Historical Magazine*, July, 1903.—ED.

[26] The word seems to be used in the sense of a hand's reach, although no such significance is ordinarily attributed to this term.—ED.

Ogle expecting every moment to be discovered, he lay with gun cocked, intending if discovered to sell his life as dearly as possible. Those Indians remained on the fence, and finally went away. In the night Ogle took the wounded man with him into the fort.

Three of the men, William Shepherd (oldest son of Col. David Shepherd), Hugh McConnell, and Thomas Glenn started from the defeated spot for the fort, and young Shepherd (only nineteen) as he neared the fort, his foot caught in a grapevine and threw him, and before he could recover, the Indians tomahawked and scalped him. Glenn was chased above the fort a little distance up the river, and was overtaken and killed. McConnell reached the fort.[27] John Caldwell escaped to Shepherd's Fort, six miles from Wheeling at the Forks of Wheeling [Creek], where the neighborhood forted; though Colonel Shepherd himself was at Wheeling. Town lots had been sold, and several had built cabins and lived in them, outside of Fort Henry; and at this alarm, unexpected, the people flew to the fort, leaving all their property in their cabins, all which was plundered; and some of the cabins were burned; and others were seized and occupied by the Indians from which to fight. Francis

---

[27] William Shepherd was the oldest son of Col. David Shepherd, and had married Rebecca McConnell, by whom he left one child. In January, 1790, Rebecca Shepherd petitioned the state of Virginia for a pension in recognition of her husband's services (Draper MSS., 7NN20).

The estate of Thomas Glenn was probated in 1778, together with that of Francis Duke. He had been surveying on the Ohio in 1774; see *Dunmore's War*, pp. 7, 116.

Hugh McConnell was ensign in the Ohio County militia in 1778. His sister Rebecca was the wife of William Shepherd.—ED.

Mrs. Lydia (Boggs-Shepherd) Cruger
From *West Virginia Historical Magazine*, iii, p. 203

ATTACK ON FORT HENRY 67

Duke (a son-in-law of Colonel Shepherd, and deputy-commissary) came from the Beech Bottom Station, above, about noon, and came among the Indians, before he was aware of danger, and made a dash for the fort and was shot dead, some seventy-five yards from the fort, so near that the Indians did not venture for his scalp, until after nightfall, when they dragged his body into one of the cabins and scalped and stripped him. The Indians shot down large numbers of cattle, hogs, geese, and took a good many horses. Soon after dark they decamped, thought to have been 300 Indians; probably Girty was not with them.[28]

* * * * * * * *

The first siege of Wheeling was on Monday, 1st September. That was muster day at Cat Fish camp under Capt. John Boggs and Capt. Reasin Virgin,[29]

---

[28] Many legends have grown up about the siege of Fort Henry. None of them is more persistent than that Simon Girty was the leader of the attacking party. But at this time (1777) Girty was in Pittsburgh and had not yet escaped to the British. It seems probable that no white men were with the Indians at this siege. The aboriginals engaged in the attack were chiefly Wyandot and Mingo, with a few Shawnee and Delawares—a total of about two hundred in number. One Wyandot was killed, and nine of the assailants wounded. See Zeisberger's letter of Sept. 22, *post*.—ED.

[29] Capt. John Boggs was born on the Susquehanna in 1736. He was taken when a child to Berkeley County, Va., and in 1768 came out to the Youghiogheny. In 1771 he was at Beeson's Fort (Uniontown, Pa.), and three years later made an improvement on Chartier's Creek, about three miles west of Catfish Camp. He was at this latter station when the siege of Wheeling occurred. In 1781, while living on Buffalo Creek, his oldest son was captured. In August of the same year he built a cabin three miles below Wheeling, and in the spring of the next year removed his family to Fort Henry for safety. Captain Boggs was sent for reinforcements when the siege of 1782 took place, but returned just after the be-

and while mustering, towards evening, an express came that Wheeling was attacked and Boggs and Virgin and their men immediately resolved to start off, and marched all night and reached Wheeling early Tuesday morning, all the Indians had gone, helped to bury the dead; and haul off the swollen dead cattle into the river.[30]

[Court Martial for Ohio County, Oct. 13, 1778. 2SS33.]

Ordred that Captain Samuel Mason be paid Seven Dollars for a Drum Purchased for his Company Use and Lost by the Attact of the Enemy against Fort Henry Sept[r] 1st 1777.

---

siegers had departed. He had expected to remove to Kentucky, which he visited in 1776, but the Revolution kept him occupied on the Ohio frontier. In 1778 he was out with McIntosh in command of a company, and for many years was a militia captain. His final removal was to Pickaway County, Ohio, where he died in February, 1824.

For Capt. Reazin Virgin see *Rev. Upper Ohio*, p. 207, note 49.—ED.

[30] There is a persistent tradition of the arrival of a relief party at Wheeling while the Indians were still about the fort. It is alleged that on this occasion Maj. Samuel McColloch leaped down Wheeling hill on horseback. If any such event occurred during a siege of Wheeling, it must have been that of 1781, for McColloch was killed before the siege of 1782; and there are no evidences of any incident of the kind during the attack of 1777. In all probability McColloch's famous leap was taken during some one of the escapes from a small marauding party of Indians, such as constantly infested the border. No doubt that in the imagination of the frontier narrators, the story grew to proportions far beyond the facts.—ED.

WESTMORELAND FRONTIER

[Capt. Samuel Moorhead to Gen. Edward Hand. 1U89—
A. L. S.]

KITTANING Septr. 2^d. 1777

SIR—Rec^d. your favour of the 21st. Augt. With Pleasure But upon Capt. Millers[31] Arival who brought 20 Beef Cattle Findes there is not a Reinforcement Coming here. Therefore as we are situated and treated, you Cannot be surprisd if you shoud here, shortly, of our being Cut off in Part, or the whole, If it shoud be the case, I hope these will be part of the discharge of my duty, with makeing use of Such means as it Shall Please God to put in my Power In whom I put my whole dependance for the Preservation of these few men As allso his Other mercies, which I truste will be Sofetient, Though the Aspect be bad no Other means being Usd, Having 3 or 4 new recrutes at hannastown M^r. Jack[32] will Call for Arms for them, the Arms here being Out of Oarder, I am with Obediance your Hum Servt. Sir

SAML MOORHEAD

On Public Service Genl. Edwd. Hand Commanding the Westrin Departement Fort pitt favrd by Capt. Miller

---

[31] Capt. Samuel Miller, of the 8th Pennsylvania Continental regiment, had his home on Big Sewickley Creek, not far from Greensburg, in Westmoreland County, and thence he marched in 1776 to join the Eastern army. He was at Valley Forge in January, 1778, and in March was ordered West to Pittsburgh. July 7 of the same year, as he was taking reinforcements to Fort Hand, he was set upon by Indians and he and his entire party were killed.—ED.

[32] Lieut. William Jack, a brother of the more famous Capt. Matthew Jack of the 8th Pennsylvania. The Jack family came from Ireland and settled near the present Greensburg. Pa. William was for several years lieutenant under Moorhead; later he was county judge, and died at his home Feb. 7, 1821. In 1882 his descendants still owned the homestead.—ED.

[Devereux Smith to Gen. Edward Hand. 1U90—A. L. S.]

HANNASTOWN Sep^{tr} 2^d 1777

DEAR SIR—A party Consisting of one Hondered and odd, Set of under the Command of Colonels Procktor Lochry Smith[33] &c in ordor to find Coll Campble & fore othar Men Said to be Kild neer Connemoch,[34] The Came to the hous & found Letters

---

[33] For Col. John Proctor see *Rev. Upper Ohio,* p. 200, note 37.
Col. Archibald Lochry is noted *ante,* p. 39, note 79.
The Colonel Smith here mentioned would seem to be James Smith, the well-known captive of 1755-59. He states in his book, *Account of the Remarkable Occurrences* (Darlington's edition, Cincinnati, 1870), p. 134, that he returned to Westmoreland County in 1778. His editor, however, finds documentary evidence to prove that he was there in the autumn of 1777, and probably he was the person here mentioned. Born in 1737 he was captured at the age of eighteen, returned home in 1760, served in Bouquet's expedition in 1764, and explored Kentucky two years later. Having settled in Westmoreland he was chosen to the Virginia convention of 1776, and a member of the assembly the following year. In 1779 he led an expedition up the Allegheny to destroy Indian towns. In 1788 he removed to Kentucky, where he died in 1812.—ED.
[34] Charles Campbell was a descendant of the Argyle family, one of whom fled to America after the battle of Culloden. Charles settled and built a mill on Blacklick Creek, in the present Indiana County in early days a part of Westmoreland. He and four friends, Randall Laughlin, John Gibson and brother, and one Dickson were out looking for horses. While preparing a meal in Laughlin's cabin they were surprised by a party of Indians, who told them that if they would surrender they should not be harmed. Campbell was allowed (as this letter states) to append a note to a proclamation, telling of their capture. They were taken to Detroit, and afterwards to Canada, where three of them were exchanged, two—Dickson and Gibson—having died in captivity. At the time of his capture, Campbell was lieutenant-colonel of the county, an office again given him after his return. Later he became county lieutenant, and as such was prominent in the West-

Left their to the Same Porport of those Left by the Dead Bodyes at Kattaning Signed Guy Carlton, ouer Peeples Was attacted Whith Coll Lochry at thire Head about 5 or 6 Milles from Wallises Mill[35] Wee Left one Campble Shot Dead on the Spot, he being in the front, the[y] Discovered only a Leven Indians, Wo all Made thire Escape Coll Campbile Wrote at the Bottom of one of Mr Carltons Letters That he & the fore Men that Was With him Was all takon Prisnors & used Well This acct I have from thre of Coll Smiths Party Just Retorning Home

Mrs Hanna[36] informs Me this Morning that Shee Was informed two Days Since at Capt Lochrys, that Mr Kelley Was intended to Mouve Down the Contery in a few Days; & that he Was at a Loss What to Do

---

moreland defense during the Indian wars (1789-95). In 1827 he was an associate judge of the county, and died about ten years later at his original seat on Blacklick Creek, Indiana County; see 7NN159. His brother Richard was on Lochry's expedition, being killed in the affray.—ED.

[35] Richard Wallace had a mill and blockhouse on McGee's Run, a branch of the Conemaugh, which was established as early as 1774. It was a centre for ranging parties, and was often attacked; see *post*. Richard Wallace was with Lochry in 1781, and returned after captivity, only to be killed by Indians four years later on an expedition to choose lands; see on this attack, *Penna. Archives*, v, p. 741.—ED.

[36] Mrs. Hanna was the wife of Robert, proprietor and innkeeper at Hannastown. She was a woman of ability and character, and much revered in her neighborhood. In July, 1782, she was captured at the siege of Hannastown. On that occasion she saved the life of Capt. Matthew Jack, by her resource and quickness in giving warning (6NN189). Taken to Detroit, she won favor with the Indians and British, was sent prisoner to Montreal, and at the Peace of Paris was restored to her home.—ED.

With your Creetters I am Sir your obedeant Humbel Servant

DEVEREUX SMITH[37]

To General Edward Hand
To the Honnorable General Edward Hand Commanding The Forth Department Pittsburgh

SIEGE OF FORT HENRY REPORTED

[Col. David Shepherd to General Hand. 3NN147— Transcript.]

FORT HENRY, Septr. 3^d 1777.

SIR—Whereas I have sent M^r. Robinson[38] to you, who can inform you in particular of what happened us in our late dreadful action with the Indians, you may rely on him for the particulars, as he assisted through the whole of it, better than I can write to you at present. We stand in great need of provision & men, & likewise some cash to pay some of the workmen who have lost every thing they had——& for some other purposes. M^r. Robinson and myself have advanced all that was in our power. Of the number of the dead and wounded, he can inform you. Our whole reliance now, Sir, must be on you for succour. I am, Sir, y^r. humble serv^t.,

DAVID SHEPHERD

Gen!. Hand.

---

[37] Devereux Smith was a prominent settler of Westmoreland County. During the troubles with Connolly in 1774, over the Pennsylvania-Virginia jurisdiction, he maintained the side of the former and was once arrested during the contest, and carried to Stanton. He held some office in the militia during the Revolution, and as late as 1795 was living three miles from Pittsburgh.—ED.

[38] Capt. John Robinson, mentioned in *Rev. Upper Ohio*, pp. 230, 231, note 72.—ED.

ATTACK ON FORT HENRY

[Col. John Gibson to General Hand. 1U91—A. L. S.]

FORT PITT Septr 4th 1777

DEAR SIR—This moment I Recieved your letter, and accordingly have Examined all Major Smallmans papers which we coud find in presence of the persons you directed. we can find none but papers of an old date, I Immagine any others, if any, are out of the Way. Nothing material has happened since you left us, Simon Girty[39] made his Escape on Sunday, But he Returned next night and is now safe. We have a flying Report of Wheeling Being Attacked last Monday by a party of 100 hundred Indians, that Capt. Mason sallied out with some of the Garrison and was wounded in the Hip and Wrist But I am in hopes the news is without foundation. Genl. Howe is landed at Turkey point near Charles town in Maryland, this we have by Capt. Sullivan. I am Dear Sir with much Respect your most Obedient humble Servt.

J$^{N^o}$. GIBSON

On the public Service For The Honourable Brigadier General Hand at Redstone

---

[39] Maj. Thomas Smallman and Simon Girty were both accused of being concerned in the Loyalist plot. Smallman's papers were searched but no evidence found. Girty was placed in the guardhouse, whence he escaped but on the succeeding day returned of his own accord. Girty thereafter served the patriot cause, but in March, 1778, escaped to the British.—ED.

RECRUITS FOR THE EXPEDITION

[Gen. Edward Hand to Col. William Fleming. IU92—A. L. S.]

FORT PITT 7th. Sept\r. 1777

SIR—on the 12th Ultimo I did myself the Honour of writing to you and requesting you to furnish 200 men properly Officered and equiped for an Expedition into the Indian Country. for Six months from the 1st. Inst. if so long wanted, and to order them to march to Fort Randolph on the Great Kanhawa as soon as possible, I can Assure you that what has Since happened encreases rather than lessens the necessity for Accellerating their March. I beg you may therefore Use every possible means to Accomplish my desire, and Inform me by express when your men March & the time you expect them to Arive at Fort Randolph. the Inclosed you will please to forward to the Officer Commanding at the Kanhawa by the Troops that march from your County Your Obie\t. Hble Serv\t.

EDW: HAND[40]

The County L\t. of Bottetourt

[Gov. Patrick Henry to Col. William Fleming. 15ZZ11—L. S.]

W\ms.BURGH Sep\r 7th. 1777.

SIR—Brigadier General Hand who is appointed by Congress to command the western Garrisons (the

---

[40] After dispatching this letter of Sept. 7 to Colonel Fleming, Hand received one from him dated Aug. 25, recounting the difficulties under which he labored in equipping and provisioning 200 men from his county. Hand therefore wrote Sept. 11 (Draper MSS., 2U2), saying that he would send flour by the first rise of the river, that cattle in abundance were already at Fort Randolph, and that the Botetourt mili-

DIFFICULTIES

Forts being under their Direction by Vote of our assembly) informed me that he should want the Assistance of Militia to chastize the offending Indians & desired permission from me to call out certain portions of them as the Safety of the Frontiers might require. In consequence, I did authorize him to call upon certain Countys & Botetourt among others, to furnish the necessary Number of men, & sent to each of the County Lieutenants Letters informing them respectively that they should comply with the Generals Requisition. These Letters I sent to him & expected he would forward them as he might have Occasion; for without such orders from me he well knew he had not Authority to call out the Militia. I find your Letter has miscarried. I wish you to comply with his Demand if possible. Indeed it is a delicate point as you observe, to march an Army ag^t. the western Tribes; but really their offences are so flagitious, that the Measure of their Iniquity seems to be full. Defensive operations cannot be productive of Safety to the Inhabitants, who have suffered abominable crueltys from the Savages. The Mingos are those whom the General wishes principally to scourge for the present. I am sorry for the Difficultys attending the Measure with y^r. Militia, but you will surmount them as well as you can. The continental commissary being not on the Spot, I fear Obstructions on that account. I send an order for some Lead. Congress wants a large Quantity & I must be frugal of it.

---

tia already sent to that garrison could be considered a part of the 200 requisitioned men.—ED.

I am glad to hear some Help is arrived at Kentucki.⁴¹ Gen¹. Hands operations will be effectual toward protecting that Quarter.

I beg Leave to congratulate you on the Success of our arms on the frontier of New York. Burgoine's Defeat if it is totally effected will deter the Indians. American affairs wear a promising aspect now. The Enemy who are landed at the Head of the Bay, are opposed by a well appointed Army ab^t. 12,000 strong & that will soon be reinforced by as many Militia who are very eager to turn out. I wish you Health & Happiness & prosperity to y^r. part of the country & am very respectfully Sir Y^r. mo ob^t. & very hble serv^t.

P. HENRY

P. S. The Evil of engrossing as practised with you, is a great one. It requires legislative authority to correct it. P. H.

DISTRESS AT WHEELING

[Maj. David McClure to Gen. Edward Hand. IU93—A. L. S.]

CATFISH CAMP 8th. September 1777

SIR—The Inhabitants of whelan are under Such Distress that the[y] are in hopes your Excellency will take them under your Consideration and Send them a party of Horses and men to Bring them into the Inhabitants as the have in Generall Lost all their Horses and Cannott Come in off themselves. Col^o. Shepherd sent orders to Alex^r. Douglass to bring down his Brigade of Horses to Assist the Inhabitants to Come in but s^d. Douglass having rec^d. orders from

---

⁴¹ This refers to Col. John Bowman's militia companies. See *ante*, p. 31, note 63.—ED.

Col⁰. Steel to Cross the mountain for Provision Could not obey Col⁰. Shepherds Orders. and Provisions is so Scarce at whelan that unless the Inhabitants are brought away the Provisions Cannott Last but a few days as the are obliged to Draw from the Publick Stores & Last friday there was but Seven Casks of Flower in the Store & Col⁰. Shepherd was affraid that unless your Excellency would order both men & Provisions down Immediatly he would be Obliged to evacuate the Garrison. I hope your Excellency will take those things under your Consideration & send them Immediate Assistance which will oblige your most humble Servᵗ

DAVID MᶜCLURE[42]

P. S I wrote the above by order of Col⁰. David Shepherd he gave me the orders when I Left the Garrison Last friday evening.

I believe Capᵗ. James Wright[43] Could Immediatly raise a party of men to Escort the Inhabitants if he Could get your Excellencys orders for it.

His Excellency Generall Eᵈ. Hand

---

[42] For this officer see *Rev. Upper Ohio*, p. 234, note 77.—ED.

[43] Probably this was James Wright, who with his brother Joshua removed about 1765 from the Cumberland Valley and settled on Peter's Creek, in the present Washington County. James afterwards removed to Kentucky, and was there killed by Indians.—ED.

RAIDING IN GREENBRIER

[Capt. John Van Bibber to Col. William Fleming. 3ZZ10—
A. L. S.]

CAPTAIN JOHN VAN BIBBERS[44] FORT GREEN BRIER
September 11th 1777

HON^d SIR:—Our present unhappy sittuation as well as the duty Incumbant upon me by the post the Country has thought proper to honour me with, Lays me under the greatest obligation of solliciting you for aid of men which I as well as the rest of my Neighbours are not in the least dubious of; When you hear the following Narrative of the Barbarity that was this day Commited by our most Inhumane & savage Enemys the Indians. The sequel runs as follows About Break of day this Morning they attacked the house of James Graham[45] which is sittuated within three hundred yards of the fort where they killed three and took one prisoner, and in about two hours afterwards a small Detachment of men which was going to the Assistance of some Adjacent Neighbours was again Attacked within two hundred yards of the Fort, when our Men gave them Battle & sustaind no damage only one man slightly wounded in the shoulder, what loss the Enemy sustaind is to us unknown, but we are in great hopes our men did some Execution as some

---

[44] For this fort and its builder see *Rev. Upper Ohio*, p. 177, note 7; also p. 192.—ED.

[45] Col. James Graham was born in Ireland in 1741, and died at his Greenbrier home Jan. 18, 1813. His daughter Elizabeth, who was captured, was adopted by a member of the Cornstalk family of Shawnee. Her father ransomed her with great difficulty in 1785, and she married Joel Stodgill. Settling in Monroe County, she died there in 1858. For a full account of the capture, see *West Virginia Magazine*, Jan., 1905.—ED.

of them had a tolerable good View of their Bodies, We got some few Implements belonging to them— Namely A Couple of Spears and Match Coats, Two Bows and a Case of Arrows & a scalping Knife. I hope you will be as assiduous as possible in sending us assistance of men. At the same time should be glad if you think proper to be Invested with such an Authority that I might have a small Body of men under my Command so that they may be under the Necessity of being Obedient to all Lawful Commands, and likewise that I may have the Liberty of sending out a Couple of Spies. Your Compliance with this request will greatly oblige all my Desolate Neighbours as well as Yr hble Servt

JOHN VAN BIBBER

Walter Kelwell [Caldwell], John Grimes [Graham], James Grimes Negro fellow, kild; Elizabth Grimes, Prisoner; Isaac Taylor, Wounded.

[James Henderson to Col. William Fleming. 3ZZ11—A. L. S.]

FORT HENREY[46]

Honour^d S^r.—this Morning I Rec^d the folowing Acct. from And^w. Kinkead[47] which is as folows—that he and Walter Caldwell was at James Greham on Green Brier River last wensday Night and a Thursday morning a litel before Day the Indians broke open the Dore upon them; and Shott Walter Caldwell &

---

[46] This was a local Greenbrier fort, named for Governor Henry. Its location is not certainly known.—ED.

[47] The Kinkeads were an Augusta County family, whence they removed in 1789 to Woodford County, Ky. Andrew was lieutenant of a ranging company under Capt. Andrew Lockridge.—ED.

kild one of Ja^{s}. Grehams Children and Negro Fellos; and one of his Children is taken prisenor; we are in great want of lead and I have sent up to the mines but Could not get Any. I have this Moment Rec^{d}. Acc^{t}. of Steel Loftus being murdred at the mouth of Indian Creek this Morning and what other Dammage is don is not yet known I, am Sr Your Humb^{l} & most Ob^{d} Servt

JA^{S} HENDERSON[48]

Sept. 12th 1777

On publick Service To Colo. William Fleming Botetourt County p^{r}. Express.

[Capt. John Stuart (Stewart) to Col. William Fleming. 3ZZ12—A. L. S.]

SIR—I Rec^{d} a letter from Capt Arbuckle last night which I have herewith sent you. I was also allarmed at the same time with an acc^{t} from James Graham about Sixteen miles down the river, who was yesterday attacked by a party of Indians at his house who killed Walter Caldwell as he was shuting the door to keep them out, several other persons were killed and taken at the same Time. I am told after the people got relief from Capt Jno Vanbibers who lives in sight of Grahams, & had taken in some of this Corps a smart firing was heard at Capt Vanbibers what the Issue has been there I have not yet larned also a number of guns was heard by sundry persons in our

---

[48] James Henderson was a brother of Col. John, noted in *Rev. Upper Ohio*, p. 183, note 16. The elder brother was with the Continental army, while the younger did militia duty at the frontier forts. By his father's will, James received large grants of land in Greenbrier County, where he became a prominent citizen and militia officer.—ED.

nighbourhood supposed to be at muddy creek fort about sundown last night I have sent of[f] some hands to see what they were but is not yet returned the people are in much confusion & flying to fort at Camp Union asoon as they got their women & Children someway secured shall endavour to take a party & pursue the enimy. They above acc\[t\] came so Imperfectly to me by sundry hands that I cannot presume giving the particulars but I make no doubt you'l receive them from Cap\[t\] Vanbiber before this reaches you. I have taken the first opportunity of writing you as I was last night some distance from home, the guard for escorting the cattle to the point was gathering yesterday for this purpose, but this allarm has scaterd them again & I am convinced untill we are relieved by men from the Interior parts of the settlement no escort can again be raised here for we appear to be exceeding scarce of men & I have sent by the bearer to Cap\[t\] Hendry Smith to send a Serg.['s] command at least to assist the people in muddy creek who is very few in numbers, & I am afraid will be much distress'd (this I hope you'l approve off) there is a report amongst us that Troops are to be here from augusta in a few weeks on their march against the Ohio Indians but of this I have [not] been rightly Informed how such an expedition has been proposed. I also find it very difficult to get good hands to go ascouting as the[y] complain of the wagges not being equal to half the Value they were formerly & those we had out has been som time returned & refused going back again I hope you'l do what you think will be Best Soon as our present circumstances is very alarming   Whilst I remain with due respect Your Ob{d}. Humb{e} Servt

JOHN STEWART[49]

Septr. 12th 1777
To the Colo William Fleming Comm{d}. of Botetourt.
Pr Express.

KITTANNING EVACUATED

[Gen. Edward Hand to Capt. Samuel Moorhead, dated Hanna's Town, Sept. 14, 1777. Draper's calendar in 3NN67, 68.]

Having found it impracticable to procure a reinforcement for your post, & being convinced that in your present situation you are not able to defend yourself, much less to render the Continent any service, orders withdrawal from Kittanning bringing every thing away portable, leaving the houses & barracks standing; & to take post at John M{c}Kibbin's house on White Pine Run, about six miles from the Allegheny river & four from the Kiskeminetas. There you will be joined by 50 or 60 who will assist you in erecting a small stockade fort for your & their own protection. Your duty will be to afford the neighboring settlements every possible assistance in securing themselves & their properties from the ravages of the enemy, & by small scouting parties to discover any, & to give notice of the enemies parties.[50]

---

[49] For a sketch of this officer see *Dunmore's War*, p. 104, note 51.—ED.

[50] This was Fort Hand, for which see *ante*, p. 41, note 83.—ED.

SITUATION AT FORT HENRY

[Col. David Shepherd to Gen. Edward Hand. 1U94—A. L. S.]

FORT HENRY Setembr. 15th. 1777

HONOURd. Sr—This if it Comes to hand will Inform you of the State of our Garrison, at this Juncture one Lieut. & twenty Rank & file fit for duty, Sick & wounded one Captain Rank & file four. the Reasons for this Seeming Evacuating of the post is to be attributed to Sundry Reasons some of which I shall here undertake to Enumerate & first Notwithstanding my Repeated orders to Captain Ogle to Martch to this place, agreable to your orders to me I am now Informed that your Honour has Incouraged him to support the Beetch Bottom Station & that a further Reinforcement will be sent to that place as soon as possible 2d. I have understood that you have Incouraged the Settlement about Catfishes Camp to fort strongly there, and your honour would aford them a Magazain for that purpose, thirdly as the Term of Supplying the posts By draughts from the different Militia Company's Ended the first of September, I have not Been able Since that time to keep up the Stations with a sufficient Guard of men partly for that I Expected this County's Quota of volantieres might Been made up to Go on the Expedition without being necessitated to draught for that purpose, which is still my opinion should an army martch into the Indian Country But notwithstanding our County men have been so Stiddy on service during the whole Summer that they in General protest against serving longer on the Station & what men I have now in garrison are only held upon my promise of being dismissed as soon as Relief Comes   Col°. Zackwell Morgan wrote me that he had order'd out Captn: Brenton[51] with fifty men for our Relief,   But he having not yet ariv^d. I have therefore for that Reason together with those above Recited thout it advisable to Retain Lieut James Spark & party untill such time as M^r: Brenton's Relieve or some other shall arive   I am of the opinion if your honour Could Consistantly spare for the use of this Garrison a Regular Lieu^t: or Captn: & twenty five Regular Soldiers to Join & intermingle with the Militia Business might much more advantageously be Transacted for the Interes of the Country in particular   with Respect to the Laying in of provision in store for should any pressing orders be given to the Militia at this time you may be assured that the Garrison would be abandoned in three hours for the Experiment has been try'd since the late action the Consequence of which was that the men woud fling their Budget & Gun over the Stockade & Slip out of the Gate unarm'd & Run off   I have sent you Inclosd the Bill of Costs for Repairing this fort & hope that your honour will Send the money p^r the Barer M^r. Zachariah Blackford[52] whose Rect: shall avail Death or Captivation only Excepted,   the particulars of the late action on the first of Septemb^r last is as follows: 1 Lieu^t: Killd & fourteen privates; Wounded one Captain & four privates; Escaped, five privates; on the 2^d:

---

[51] For Capt. James Brenton of Monongalia County, see *Rev. Upper Ohio*, p. 231, note 73.—ED.

[52] Capt. Zephaniah Blackford was commissary for Fort Henry. The Shepherd Papers (Draper MSS.) contain numbers of his receipts and other papers during this period of the war. His later history is not known.—ED.

of Septemb^r was kill^d. within five miles of this place Two, one scalp^d. yet alive; & one Missing; By the Best Judges here who have seen the plan Laid by the Indians & their Brestworks & blinds in the late action it is thought their Numbers must not have Been less than Between Two and three hundred the Destruction amongst Cattle Sheep horses hogs is not yet assertainable, the other day a number of the distressed families mov'd off yet a number Remain, for want of horses This from S^r: your very humb^l. Servt: to Command &c

DAVID SHEPHERD

To His Honour General Edward Hand   Pr Express

INDIANS MURDERED BY FRONTIERSMEN

[Gov. John Page to Gen. Edward Hand. 3NN 163, 164— Transcript.]

W^{ms}.BURGH, VA. IN COUNCIL, Sept. 17th 1777

SIR—Y^r. letter of 25th Augt. is just come to hand, in w^h. you apologize for y^r. large draughts of militia you have found it necessary to make. I can only observe, Sir, that the Board are perfectly satisfied with the steps you have taken, but are afraid that the late requisition from Congress for 1/3 of the militia of several of the Counties you had called on, may interfere with your plan, & the men you may receive may fall considerably short of your expectations. * * *

I cannot conclude without expressing our earnest desire that you will endeavor to discover & bring to justice the perpetrators of the horrid murders committed on the Indians at their late Treaty at Fort Pitt, which must otherwise expose us to the shameful reproach of being as treacherous & perfidious as the worst of savages.[53] We are the more shocked at this affair which would be disgraceful to the most barbarous nation, as it is a repetition of the same cruel & faithless behavior which the Cherokees experienced from us on a late similar occasion. I have the honor to be &c

JOHN PAGE

MESSAGES TO THE DELAWARES

[Gen. Edward Hand to the Delawares. IU96—L. S.]

FORT PITT Septr. 17th. 1777

BROTHERS THE DELAWARES—I lately told you it would be dangerous for any Indians to come near to this Place, owing to the foolish Conduct of the Mingo's & Wiandots, & therefore for fear of any Mistake I desired you not to send any Messengers this Way or to allow your young Men to scatter too much   I sent this word by our Brother Meymaconon & young Kilbuck. I now confirm them.

Brothers,   As I have Reason to rely on the good faith & friendship of our Brothers the Delawares, I

---

[53] This treaty did not take place, for there were in attendance only a few Delawares, who left hostages for their good conduct. On the attitude of the frontiersmen towards the friendly Indians, see Gibson's letter of Aug. 1, *ante.* Morgan wrote March 15, 1777: "Parties have even been assembled to massacre our known friends at their hunting camps as well as messengers on business to me; and I have esteemed it necessary to let those messengers sleep in my own chamber for security"—Craig, *History of Pittsburgh* (Pittsburgh, 1851), p. 141. Heckewelder relates that a party of Seneca coming to this treaty were fired upon by the white inhabitants. This is the incident to which Page refers; see John Heckewelder, *Narrative of the Mission of the United Brethren Among the Delaware and Mohegan Indians* (Phila., 1820), p. 159.—ED.

send the Bearer M^r. James Elliot[54] to inform you of the News of our grand armies, the cattle who you were told were pen'd up, have broke down the fences & trampled their Keepers to Death.

Brothers, The News Papers will give you a full Account of the great Battles our armies have gained. The Indians who were so foolish as to join our Enemies have found their Mistake & those who have not run away are quite sick of their Conduct. The Oneidas & Tuscororas have joined our army & are now in Pursuit of the Enemy.

Brothers, I expect very soon to send you an agreeable Account of another Battle as Genl. Howe who had run away from the Jerseys on board of his vessells has now landed with his army in Maryland whither Genl. Washington has gone with our army to drive the red Coats on board their Ships again. He will do little damage except stealing our sheep & Poultry

Brothers, I send M^r. Elliott not only to tell you this good News but to assure you that I am determined to preserve your friendship by a sincere & upright Conduct toward you agreeable to the repeated Orders of Congress. And notwithstanding foolish People occasioned a Cloud to overspread our Council fire & have filled the Road between you & me with Briars & Thorns I will soon clear the path & make it as broad & plain as ever, for this has been and is now the wish of all our wise Men, as a Testimony of my sincerity I sign & send you this.

---

[54] James Elliott was an Indian trader whose home was in the settlement known as Path Valley, in Franklin County, Pa.—ED.

Brothers, What I have told you is true but do not desire you to depend on Words alone. If you send to the Northward your Messengers may see with their own Eyes.

Brothers, If your Messengers get up to go for News I desire they may go the whole way & not take the reports of People they may meet on the Road.

Brothers, Your Uncles the Wiandots the foolish People on Scioto & every other Indian Tribe that has listened to the Advice of Governor Hamilton & Butler will see when it is too late that those Men do not regard the Interest of the Indians & will find them ready to tread them under their feet when they can't be of no further Use to them.

Brothers, You will be fully satisfied of my friendship when you see my Messenger M^r. James Elliott. I desire you to use him well & give him what he wants for which I will pay you as soon as I can see you. I desire you will also send by him all the News you have in Writing & convey him safe from all your Towns as far as may be necessary.

Brothers, Be strong & adhere to your Professions & depend on the friendship of your Brother

EDW^d. HAND

[Gov. John Page to the Delawares. 1U97.]

W^{ms}.BURGH Septr. 18. 1777

BROTHERS THE DELAW^s—I write now to you, by our Brother Col. Geo: Morgan to assure you that the State of Virginia is determined to hold fast the chain of friendship with and support you as she would her own children against all your Enemies as long as the

Sun or Moon shall shine & rivers flow. The same
assurance the Col. will give from all our 13 United
States for now B^{rs}. these states of america have broken
off the galling Yoke of the English & act for themselves they have been cruelly treated by the English
who have grown proud & insolent by the great riches
they had acquired in their Trade with our States &
by the Assistance we lent them in their Wars with the
french & other Nations as you can well remember,
began to treat us not like their Children, as we foolishly called ourselves but like their slaves & because
we complained of this Brothers & entreated their cruel
King to let us enjoy the same Liberty we enjoyed
under the old King his Grandfather he insulted us &
sent his fleets & armies to frighten us into a Tame submission to his will, we bore long with many cruelties
still hoping that we should not be forced to break off
from that Nation & shift for ourselves. but at last
when they had killed many of our People burned our
Houses & had endeavoured to make all the Indian
Nations on our frontier butcher our Women & Children, & the very Negroes born in our own Houses
cut our Throats, the 13 States laid hold on one strong
bright Chain of friendship, & resolved to be as one
People for ever and to take up the Hatchet & knock
off the hard Chains the English had bound them with
& with that Hatchet to clear their way to Liberty &
Peace. whoever strikes one of these States strikes
all & all will return the Blow the English know this
& have felt the weight of it & have therefore told you
lies & endeavoured to prevail on you to help them to
fight us, but consider well that God almighty has

seen their wickedness & heard their Lies & has therefore stretched out his hand to help us & has confounded almost all their cruel Schemes, we trust in God he is now our King & not a weak & foolish Man from him who is King of Kings & Govr. of all the World we expect support & we call on you yourselves to say whether we have not recd. it from him for how else did it happen B^{rs}. that the English who were so great a Nation with all the fleets & armies they Could raise have not been able in two Years to conquer one of our 13 States how otherwise can it be accounted for that we who had neither arms or Soldiers have now an abundance of both & that in several Battles with them we have Killed many of their Soldiers without loosing a Man we scorn to lie as they do we acknowledge that they have taken some of our Towns & that they still have a large army in one of our States, but we deny that they can ever conquer us or inclose us in a Pen like Bullocks as they falsely told you, our Way is open even on the Sea, where they are Most powerful for we trade with france & Spain Nations great & powerful now as England & as to being penned in by Indians the Cherokees know how unable they were to keep us in & that the English could not have hindered Us from destroying their whole Nation, if we had Chosen it & had not mercifully spared them, they have seen their folly we have forgiven them, & are now friends,[55] Brothers we are not like the English cruel & unrelenting we would forgive even them if they would leave off kill-

---

[55] For a good account of the Cherokee War of 1776 see Roosevelt, *Winning of the West,* i, chap. xi.—ED.

ing our People we have lately got the better of them in several Engagements & our army is now much larger than theirs so that we hope that they will soon carry them away to their own Country & leave us to ourselves, if they do we will forgive them, & not follow to fight them but trade peaceably with them when they send their People here to buy our Tobacco & Wheat & your skins & furs & many other Things which they will want & which we can let them have for their Goods. I hope I have now opened your Eyes Brothers that you may see your Way clearly & your Ears that you may hear the Truth let them not be stopped again. Hold fast the Chain of friendship with our States & remember that we look upon you as B^{rs}. born under the same Sky & living on the same Land & having the same Common Interests. We love you & sincerely Wish Peace & Happiness to all our Indian B^{rs}. We do not wish that they should ever fight for us none but the cruel English & their friends wish to see you engaged in a War. they indeed strong as they pretend to be, would prevail on you to help them to fight & I suspect have killed some of your people & then told you ours had killed them trust them not Brothers believe them no more but remember what I have told you & listen to our Brother Col. Morgan. I am Y^r. friend & Brother

JOHN PAGE
L^t. Govr.

[Col. George Morgan to the Delawares. IU97—A. L. S.]

FORT PITT 18 Septr. 1777

BROTHERS THE DELAWARES—You know that I never deceived you. It is my advice that you take

Care of your young Men, & I hope the Clouds which now interrupts our sight of each other will soon vanish. I intend to go immediately to Philad^a. to give an account of my Conduct to the great Council there. And I will not fail to assure them how strong you are in good Works. You may depend on their making the Sky clear again if you will assist them as you have done. Immediately after my Arrival there you shall hear from me if it is in my Power. You may expect a Messenger from me about the 1st. day of next Novr. when you shall know the Minds of Congress. 'Till then I desire you will wait with Patience & continue to be strong in good Works that we may tie down all those who study to do Mischief.

I committ M^r. Zeisberger &c. to your particular Care. He is sent to you from Heaven for your own Good, therefore be strong & do not let him suffer on any account.

Brothers, I desire you will give good Counsel to your Grand children the Shawanese & repeat this Message to them

I desire your Message to me may [be] directed for me at Philad^a. & that you will send it open under Cover to Genl. Hand who will read it & then forward it to me at the great Council by Express.

I therefore expect you will speak plain to me & tell me your whole Minds that Congress may see your Hearts.

I desire you will get M^r. Zeisberger to write for you.

TAIMENEND.[56]

---

[56] This was Colonel Morgan's Indian name, given to him by the Delawares. It was probably the same as the modern Tammany.—ED.

RAID ON MONONGAHELA

[Col. Zackwell Morgan to Gen. Edward Hand, Sept. 18. 1U98—A. L.]

May it please your Excellency—On the 13th. Instant at Coones Fort on the west fork the Indians killed and sculped a woman only 150 yards from the Fort, and Appeared to be Very impudent.[57] Whoever the Inhabitants seem to be Very Willing to Stand (if your Excellency Pleases to let them have Amunition, as what I Rec^d. I have Distributed to the Different Forts and have not any left I must Request your Excellency to give an order on Colo^l. Brown for what Quantity you shall think Edaquit for the Defence of the Inhabitants, of this Part of the Country I Expect to be Down in A few days, after I get my Drove of Cattle Delivered, I shall drive in a few days with what Colo^l. Evans[58] can Collect. I am Sir Your most Obedient and Most Hum^l. Sarv^t.

[Z. MORGAN]

P. S please send by the bearer 3 quir paper

To His Excellency Edward Hand Fort Pit Pr Express

REPLIES FROM THE DELAWARES

[David Zeisberger to Gen. Edward Hand. 1U99.]

CUCHACHUNK[59] Septr. 22^d. 1777.

May it please your Excellency:

SIR,—As Capt. White Eye will endeavour to try if he can get this Letter to the fort, I inclose here a Letter to the Honble. Congress because I suppose accord-

---

[57] For a detailed account of this incident see Thwaites, *Withers's Chronicles*, pp. 218, 219.—ED.

[58] For this officer see *Rev. Upper Ohio*, p. 234, note 78.—ED.

[59] For this town see *Ibid*, p. 46, note 73.—ED.

ing to the account we had that Mʳ. Morgan by this Time had left the Fort. Capt. White Eye & the Councellors Are very sorry that the Communication and Correspondence with you is stopped & they shall hear Nothing now from you not knowing in what Condition they are and what they have to expect, because we heard that the White People would come & attack Cuchachunk & the delaware Towns which has set all the Indians in Consternation & fear, expecting every day that they will be upon them. A late Report we had that the white People were already on their March hither caused our Indians at Gnadenhutten[60] to fly & left their Town and we are now altogether here nigh Cuchachunk. Therefore, pray Sir, let us know if we the Christian Indians, or the Delawares are in any Danger, & if we have any Thing to fear of the white People. I cannot leave my People the Christian Indians for I see it before hand that they all will be scattered if I leave them & the Brethren's Labour which they so many Years and with so much Difficulty have continued with success would be entirely lost. I venture my Life & am resolved to hold out with them relying next [to] our Lord & blessed Saviour on your Protection & Assistance. I hope you will remember us, & as much as lies in your Power to assist us that we may be able to keep our Ground & remain in Possession of our Towns. Capt. White Eyes and the Delaware Chiefs are yet determined to stand fast and not to meddle with the War, they want to live in friendship with the white People if they only knew that the white People has no bad

---

[60] For this town see *Ibid*, p. 45, note 71.—Ed.

design against them. As long as they remain quiet and peaceable I with my People shall keep with or nigh them, but should we see that they drop the friendship, then we should be obliged to seperate ourselves from them. But when they hear they have nothing to fear of the white People it will cheer up their spirits & be quiet. The Wiondots & Mingoes are all gone home again according to their Knowledge they killed 14 People at Weelunk, had one Wiondat killed & 6 or 7 Wounded one of the last died since. Wiondoughwalind's[61] son & another of his Company are badly wounded & it is said will hardly live. Both Capt^s. At present we know that 40 of the Wiondats are gone it is said to Weelunk[62] of any more that are out we know not. From Sandusky we hear that at Detroit they were gathering Men to meet the army which they expect to come up there. Pray let me know if possible with this opportunity if Messengers could come safe to the fort, & if it was dangerous for Indians perhaps we could send a white Man in Case of Necessity that we might hear from one another I am Sir Y^r. most Hble. Servt.

D. ZIESBERGER

[White Eyes to Congress. 1U100.]

CUCHACHUNK Septr. 22^d. 1777.

Capt. White Eyes Message to the Honble. Congress of the thirteen United States.

BROTHER,—When I was at Pittsburgh last I acquainted M^r. Morgan of all what passed in the Indian

---

[61] This is the chief noted *Ibid*, p. 46, note 75.—ED.
[62] Probably those who ambuscaded Foreman and his men. See *post.*—ED.

Country, that the Wiondats, Mingoes and others were coming to strike our Brethren the Virginians, & that it was no more in my Power to stop them, that they would march by Cuchachunk, as they also did, and we could not hinder it because they were too strong.

I informed M^r. Morgan that Wiondoughwalind with his Men had joined them. They marched from hence to the fort at Weelunk, from whence they returned again, where they told the White People that they came from Cuchachunk.

Brother, As I see the dark Clouds arising over my head, I still hold fast to the chain of friendship, and now more than ever, But since the Battle at Weelunk it seems by the account we had, as if you would drop the friendship, because you heard that these Warriors had said, they came from Cuchachunk, 'tho I told you before hand that their Chief Design was to bring the White People upon us to strike us.

Brother, We agreed with one another to hold fast & keep bright the Chain of friendship which our ancestors have made, and as a token that my heart was good and upright, I left two of my Men at the fort to keep the road open between us & you, that we might hear from one another.

Brother. I choose M^r. Morgan to transact Business & to assist us in the good Work of Peace & friendship & I always found him to be true upright & faithful. I also believe you know him likewise to be so, Let us therefore not drop our friendship for the sake of a bad Word of some foolish People. It is a Work of great Importance which the Honble. Congress of the thirteen United States has undertaken and continued until now. I should be very sorry that our Communication with one another should be stopped entirely.

Brother. We made out with one another, that if an Army should march in the Indian Country it should take its march above & below our Towns that our Women & Children might remain quiet & not be too much frightened, which I hope you will remember and order it to be done according to our agreement.

This is all Brother, I have to say at present, pray let us hear an answer from you as soon as possible. Your Sincere friend & Brother,

WHITE EYE.

FORT HAND BUILT

[Capt. Samuel Moorhead to Gen. Edward Hand. 1U101— A. L. S.]

JOHN McKIBBENS'S HOUSE Sep^t. 22^d. 1777

DEAR GENERAL—Arrived here last night with the Greatest Deficulties I ever had in my life, with Packhorses hevy loaded bad pack And untoward loading. Have Obeyd your Oarders as well As I Possably cou'd though it was not in my power to Accomplish the whole for the want of horses, likewise had an anvile And Some Other things that the people Coud not get Along And hid them in the woods. Hid another load by the way By reason of a horse Giveing Out in the Rear, thursday Night rec^d. your oarders, friday we spent in Packing, Saterday morning verry early Orderd the g[a]tes to be cut down and burnd As soon as them and part of the Stockades was set on fire The indeans Set to hupeing on a hill About 200

Yards from the fort we Cou'd just perceive them through the fog. I inquird By an interpreter who the[y] were or if they wanted to fight us they answerd they did. I told them to Come on they answerd they woud shortly, but we herd no more of them that day, yestard[ay] morning we march'd before day. One of My boys went back About half a mile for a shot bag and Powder horn, just as he got to the gate they rais'd a shoking huping and yaling in a Swamp just at the back of the fourt, he came off [being] descovrd suposed by their Sound there was a great maney. Came unmolested within about 2 miles of this place where our advansd Party was fird on by a party of indeans, our peopls arms was in bad Oarder by reason of the wet wether, which obleged them to retrate, they persud a little way nerly in Sight of the frunt of the party, two of my best men is a mising, but from what I Can learn, Am in hop[e]s one or both of them has made their escape. Thirty-five men has Assisted me in Coming here But there is verry few of them that I can prevale upon to Stay, Only the time that this express will be Coming back from your Honnour. Nor have I any Account of any more coming I expect to be treated in the Same manner here that I was at the Kittaning, by the Melitia. The indeans Apear to be verry Plenty in this Settlement by their tracks, the nomber my people Saw last evning was but Six though there apeard to be more by their Signes. Some of our people Say they heard indeans this day but am uncertain. Our Beef Cattle ran away ten days ago was not able to send a sofitient party to bring them back Untill M^r.

Jack came out, and hering of A removil thought it not prudent to send for them then, they have been tract through this Settlement expects they are near Fourt pit at this time, they are 19 in nomber. I would not chuse this situation for a fort by reason of a large thickety bottom about 100 yards distant, Though your Pleasure Shall be verry Agreeable to your Humble Servant providing we get Assistance which I can have but little dependance upon Am Dear General, with Respect Yr Mst. Obdt Huml Servt.

SAM^l. MOORHEAD

Returns you harty thanks for the newspaper it is all the medesin of the kind that has done me any good this long time.

Had to destroy two loads of flour. Put some medesion in part of it that may be of Some Service to the blks [blacks—Indians]. Have inclosed a Return of the Stores brought to this place. The Commisary had a wrong idea of the quantity of flour the last return. My men have done verry extrorny duty for some time past part of them has been three nights together upon guard and the greater part of them has not in the least Complaind knowing the necessity for it. they are now in wors Situation then before lying out in the open fields without blankets or Clothing fit for the Season of the year, the flux has been through a great many of them, are all recovrd except two

S. M.

On public Service Generl Hand Commanding the Westrin Departement. Fort pitt Per express

WORD FROM THE MUSKINGUM

[Capt. White Eyes's Message to Col. Morgan. 6ZZ7.]

CUCHACHUNK Septr. 23^d. 1777

BROTHER,—I was exceeding glad to see your Messengers coming to me & so much more I rejoiced to see them because I was already [at] a Loss what to do, to get some Intelligence from you, and I was just ready to send a Messenger to the fort when M^r. Elliott and his Company arrived to my great Joy & to the Joy of all my Men Women & Children. For 210 Warriors, Wiandots, Mingo's & other Nations who had joined & taken up the Tomhawk & struck our Brothers the Virginians had also agreed as we heard that when they should have struck the Virginians they would come here & leave the Tomhawk sticking in our heads, because they said we were Virginians. It is but a few Days ago since these Warriors went through our Town saying with great Joy, it would not be long that this Town would be no more. They went about, killed our Creatures & when the Women spoke anything about their Behaviour, they struck them & said we only kill your Creatures, but others will Come & knock you in the Head.

Brother, Therefore I am glad to hear you, that you encourage me to be strong and so I will do. That the other Nations have served me so ill shall not discourage nor make me faint, the faster I shall take hold to our Chain of friendship. You told me likewise that I should keep my young Men together & not let them scatter which I shall do they having already declared their Minds to me that they will do what I shall advise them. I have acquainted you that before this

Wiondoughwalend with his Men won't obey nor listen to me, but I am in hopes when they see that we are strong in keeping our Agreement that they will listen to me yet.

Brother, Let us be strong for our road is stopped & filled with Briars, Thorns & Logs, but I am very glad to hear from you, that there is hopes that it will be open again soon.

Brother, I shew you my heart that it is good & upright & you assure me before God Almighty that our Agreement of friendship will last as long as the Sun shineth, so I assure you likewise that I shall hold & keep to it so long as the Sun shall shine. Your Brother

CAPT. WHITE EYES

[David Zeisberger to Gen. Edward Hand. 6ZZ8.]

CUCHACHUNK Septr. 23^d. 1777

May it please your Excellency

DEAR SIR—I wrote to you yesterday & in the Evening your Messengers arrived at Cuchachunk to our great Joy & Comfort when I immediately in the Night was fetched where I read yours and M^r. Morgan's Speech to the Counsil when all rejoiced exceedingly as well over the good News you communicated to them as also especially when they heard that they had Nothing to fear, of the White People, & we can now thank God be quiet & without fear. I send the Letter I wrote Yesterday as it is, & inclosed here is a Message again to Col. Morgan. The Indians who shall conduct the Messengers to the river shall have the Packet in their Care in Case any Accident should happen by the Way, 'till they shall part from them & then deliver it to M^r. Elliott. Yesterday we had the following Intelligence which was sent by Wiondoughwalend to the Council here, to which so much more Credit we can give as he is no friend to the Virginians, Viz^t. that the Twightees [Miami] had rec'd the Tomhawk Belt from the Govr. at Detroit which they took home with them & called the Head Men & Capt^s. of their Nation & the Wawiaghtana [Ouiatanon] & Kickapoos &c^a together to consult about it when they all agreed not to take the Tomhawk but to follow the Example of their Grandfather the Delawares of whom they had heard by a Messenger that he would not receive the Tomhawk whereupon the Twightees sent it back again to the Govr. and said it would be the ruin of their Nation if they took it. Another Piece of News we had from the same Quarter,—That some Tawas & Chipways had been to war & were returned, who related, that they had attacked a fort at Kentucke where they fought awhile till on both Sides a Number was killed, when the white People hailed the Indians and desired them to come nigh and to speak with them which they refused to do & called the white People out; upon which one or two went out of the fort, & spoke with them, and told them that were sorry to see the dead bodies of both sides lying there, but neither they the Tawas & Chipways nor the white People were the Cause of it, but their father the Govr. over the Lake was the cause of it, they should blame him for it. That after this the white people invited them to the fort treated them handsomely & let them go home in Peace.⁶³ This News Capt. White Eyes desired me to inform you of. By information of a white Man from Detroit who came here two days ago but doth not choose to have his Name mentioned I can give you the following Account. That there are six Companies of Militia amounting to about 300 Men in the whole. The English are all for America. About 70 Men in Garrison only. An Entrenchment is round the fort on the Land Side & about 50 Pieces of Cannon in the fort & 7 Pieces of Cannon on the Wharff. If an Army should come against the fort every Man is to march out to meet it & they are to be reinforced from Niagara. Great Store of Provision is at Detroit & the Inhabitants full of Cattle. At the Sandusky there is 100 Head of Cattle & the People to whom they belong will have Nothing against it if they fall in the Hands of the Army. Six Vessels on the Lake the largest two of 16 Guns. If an Army should march there late then there will be a large Cargo of Goods at Sandusky. I beg the favour to forward the inclosed Packet to Lancaster by which you will oblige all the Brethren down the Country very much who will impatiently wait to hear from us. I am, Sir Y^r. most Hble. Servt.

D. ZIESBERGER.

---

⁶³ Boonesborough and the other Kentucky stations were repeatedly besieged during the summer and autumn of 1777; but no such affair as this reported to White Eyes is known to have occurred. The truth was, that a relieving force of 48 men entered Boonesborough Sept. 13, coming from the Yadkin under command of Capt. William Bailey Smith. Some lurking Indians withdrew and reported that 200 white warriors had come to relieve the fort, and it was now useless to attack it. See Draper MSS., 4B137, where Dr. Draper cites this letter of Zeisberger.—ED.

TROOPS FOR THE EXPEDITION

[Capt. John Bowyer to Col. William Fleming.   1U102
A. L. S.]

D^r S$_{IR}$—I received yours by the express but I am railey at a loss what to do, your orders was so long a Coming   I did expect that no men was to Go on the Indian expedition from this qarter and upon my hearing that the Enemy was a penetrateing some Considerable Distance into Pensylvania I determind to Raise 100 Vollenteers and go and Joine Genl Washingtons Army and expected to have march^d. on Tuesday next but did not attemp it before Last sunday when I made shure that the men would not be wanted for the Indian expedition as it was so late in the season the men seems to be Willing to go with the Greatest Cheerfullness   Each man was to have his horse and 7 or 8 days provision with a good Rifle   I want much to be their myself however I would be loath to have it said that I by any means had a hand in disapointing the Indian Expedition.   I shall without delay do as you have directed me and appoint the officers in this quarter Imediately to get the Number of men Either by Vollenteers or drafts from their Companys without delay and march with all expedition to the place of Rondevouse but I am afraid it will take some time before they will be got Ready as they will have everything to prepair for the Campain   I feel from my Very hart for our poor Country men to The Northward and should have march^d on Tuesday without fail had not these orders Come to hand   how it will be now I Cannot Tell   one of the other will fail but if I thought that the Indian expedition would be

Carried into execution this season I would decline my Going to General Washington but if I do I am afraid we will be disapointed in both if I was to go it will be an excellent Company of Rifel men and Cannot help thinking that we would be of as much service to our Country their as we Could be any where at this time Especially as it is so late in the year I could wish I had your advice upon the Ocasion I am loath to do any thing that I thought would be a prejudice to my Country but would do every thing in my Power that I thought would be for the Advantage of it had not these orders Come to hand at this time I should Certainly gon down and brought you up a true acc^t. of our Proceeding at Camp how it will be now I know not I am Certain the men Cannot be got to go to fort Randolph if I Proceed according as I was determined to do before these orders Come to hand the Augusta Troops are now at Cars Creek and are to march from that place in about two day

I am D^r. Sir with the Greatest Sincearity y^r. most Obed^t. & Very hble Servt.

JOHN BOWYER[64]

Sepr. 24th. 1777

To Col^o. William Fleming Botetourt p^r. Express

---

[64] John Bowyer, son of Capt. Michael Bowyer, settled in 1753 on Borden's Grant in Augusta County, Va., where he was for a time employed as schoolmaster. Later he married one of Borden's heirs, and became a substantial man in the community, being captain of militia (1763), justice of the peace (1770), and land commissioner (1776). In 1781 he enlisted a company of Rockbridge militia and joined Lafayette in the defense of Virginia, being wounded (July 6) at Jamestown Ford. He lived near Lexington and died on his estate in 1806, leaving no children.—ED.

FOREMAN'S DEFEAT

[Col. David Shepherd to Gen. Edward Hand. 6ZZ9.]

FORT HENRY Septr. 27. 1777.

To his Exc^y. General Hand.

Early yesterday a Party of 46 Men under the Comd. of Capt^s. foreman[65] & Ogle set out on a scouting Party. they Purpose reconnoitering as far as Capeteening[66] & making their ret^n. in 3 or 4 Days on their Arrival at Grave Creek they found the Place burned down[67] & all the Canoes or Crafts destroyed or carried off. this brought them to a resolution of returning as they could not conveniently cross the river. By 5 Men returned of whom Col. Linn is one,[68] we learn that about 11 oClock [this] forenoon they were fired on a little above McMahan's Narrows by a large body of Indians who lay concealed between them & the river & put our Men to flight such as did not fall

---

[65] Nothing is known of the previous life of Capt. William Foreman of Hampshire County. He came with a company of militia to take part in Hand's projected expedition and was sent to the relief of Wheeling. It is apparent from the accounts of contemporaries that Captain Foreman was unfamiliar with Indian warfare, and incautious as to an ambuscade. His son Hamilton was killed in the melée.—ED.

[66] Captina Creek, eighteen miles below Wheeling, on the Ohio side in the present Belmont County. It was a well-known haunt of the Indians. Washington mentioned a town thereon while on his visit of 1770. In 1780 several boats on their way to Kentucky were waylaid at this creek and their inmates killed or captured; among the captured was Catharine Malott, who became the wife of Simon Girty. In 1794 occurred the battle of Captina Creek, between a party led by Abraham Enochs from Baker's Fort, and a marauding Indian band.—ED.

[67] The fort at Grave Creek had been abandoned before the siege of Wheeling, and the building that had been left standing had been burned by Indian raiders.—ED.

[68] For Col. William Linn see *Rev. Upper Ohio*, p. 144, note 51.—ED.

before they had Time to discharge their Guns we have reason to believe by the reports that few are escaped the Number of the Enemy being So Vastly superior one of the men returned has recd two wounds with one Ball or shot, not Mortal. Our Situation calls for immediate assistance as we expect to have the Enemy in a few Hours at farthest we wholly depend on you for flour as we are not able to go to Mills as a Party would only fall into the Enemys Hand's 4 Men are come in but can give no further Account I am Sir with great respect

DAVID SHEPERD

There are wounded Men who lie in the Woods, particularly one with a broken Leg[69] & some others.

I am as before D. S.

[Recollections of Rachel Johnson.[70] 2S280, 281.]

Foreman's and Linn's companies came [to Wheeling], the next day went down to see if there were any signs of Indians at Grave Creek, where there was a deserted blockhouse. 46 turned out to go, camped [that night]; next morning [set out to return]. Linn,

---

[69] This was John Cullins, for whom see *post.*—ED.

[70] Rachel Johnson was a mulatto woman, born in Delaware (she said Oct. 20, 1736), who was brought to the Ohio by her master Yates Conwell, before Dunmore's War. She was in Wheeling at the time of the siege, and when the survivors of Foreman's party came in. Her memory was very good, and she had a reputation for truthfulness. Dr. Draper visited and interviewed old Rachel in 1845, and again in 1846; she died in 1847. She remembered to have seen Washington, George Rogers Clark, and a number of prominent Western heroes.—ED.

Daniel McLane[71] and a few others went up [over] the hill, the others marching in Indian file. The Indians had made blinds and were under the river bank &c.; when the whites were opposite [they rose and fired]. Foreman at the head was first shot down by a single fire; the others stopped suddenly and were fired on and shot down. McLane said he ran part way down the hill [when he heard the firing] and said he heard the tomahawks as if the Indians were cutting up beef. * * * In the afternoon a fugitive with his gun, but without his hat gave the first mournful intelligence [at Wheeling] of the defeat, not knowing of any beside himself who had escaped. Others between that and night kept dropping in. Next day a party turned out to bury the dead.[72]

---

[71] Daniel McLain was appointed justice of the peace of Ohio County early in January, 1777; he was likewise lieutenant of the county militia, and in service at Wheeling. He died some time before April, 1778, when his estate was administered.—ED.

[72] It was several days before a party ventured out to bury the dead; see letters *post*. A monument was erected on the spot to Captain Foreman and the other victims, all of whom were buried in one grave. It bears this inscription: "This humble stone is erected to the memory of Captain Foreman and twenty of his brave men, who were slain by a band of ruthless savages—the allies of a civilized nation of Europe— on the 28th [27th] of September, 1777.

"So sleep the brave who sink to rest,
By all their country's wishes blest."

Erosion by the river removed the soil on which this stone was placed; whereupon, by the order of Marshall County court, it was removed, in 1875, to Moundsville Cemetery. See *Southern Historical Magazine* (Charleston, W. Va.), March, 1899, p. 19.—ED.

[Petition of John Cullins[73] to Congress. 2E67.]

Your memorialist, John Cullins, of Muskingum County, Ohio, respectfully represents that in the month of August, 1777, your memorialist, then a resident of Hampshire County, Virginia, volunteered under Capt. William Foreman, at said Hampshire County, and marched to Pittsburg, and joined the

---

[73] John Cullins was at this time nineteen years of age and very vigorous. In his later life he visited a William Linn of Brownsville, Pa., thinking that he was the Col. William Linn who had rescued him at Grave Creek. He found himself mistaken, for his benefactor had removed to Kentucky and there been killed by Indians. William Johnson Linn, son of the Brownsville man, told Dr. Draper Cullins's story as he had related it (37J38, 39). The latter said that as Foreman's party emerged from the narrows, where they had been marching single file, they deployed to right and left, presenting a quite formidable front. They advanced in a wide bottom above the end of the narrows, to where a cone, breast high, jutted from the rock. Behind this the Indians were posted, and probably others on the left of the path, along the bushes by the river. No enemy was discovered until within a few paces of the ambuscade. The work of death was the result of an instant. Some of the survivors fled up the river, some down, and others up the hill. Among the latter was Cullins, who when two-thirds up was shot by an Indian below, and had his thigh broken. Just above lay a large log; over this he threw himself to escape a second shot. At this juncture appeared Capt. William Linn and a few other men, dashing down the hill, whooping and firing. The Indians fled to their canoes and put off over the river. Linn and his lieutenant came upon Cullins. Linn wished to carry him away, but his lieutenant thought that they should rather seek their own safety. After some dispute, Cullins was at Linn's insistence carried up the hill, over a second ridge, and secreted in a fallen tree-top. Linn left him some food, promised to return, and then retreated. Faithful to his promise, Linn came back after dark, and carried Cullins on his back for over eleven miles to Shepherd's Fort, fearing to attempt the shorter road to Fort Henry, lest Indians be lurking to waylay them. Another pioneer told Dr. Draper (17S62) that the doctor wished to amputate Cullins's leg, but the latter resisted and in time was able to walk.—ED.

troops then under the command of General Hand; thence, by order of General Hand, your memorialist with said Company, marched to Wheeling and was placed under the command of General Shepherd. After performing duty at Wheeling a few weeks, your memorialist was one of a party of forty-six men on a scouting party under command of Captain Foreman and some other officers, marched to the fort on Grave Creek, and on their return were attacked by a party of Indians, by whom the greater part of the party were cut off, and in this action your memorialist was wounded by a ball which broke his right leg in such a manner that he has never since that time recovered the full use of it.[74] * * *

[Capt. John Van Metre to Col. Edward Cook.[75] 6ZZ10—
A. L. S.]

BEECH BOTTOM OHIO Sept 28 1777

SIR—I am sorry that I have the following Account to give you that is on the 27th of this Instant Capt

---

[74] This petition was presented to Congress in 1834, and a pension was granted. For additional facts see 23d Cong., 1st sess., *Reports of Committees*, no. 268.—ED.

[75] Edward Cook was born in 1738 in the Cumberland Valley. In 1772 he removed to the forks of Youghiogheny River, where by 1776 he had built a large stone house, and was the prominent man of the region. As both Pennsylvania and Virginia claimed jurisdiction, Cook was an officer of both Westmoreland and Yohogania counties, alternately. His interest leaned, however, towards Pennsylvania, his native state, and in 1776 he was a member of her first state convention. At the time this letter was written he was colonel of the Westmoreland militia, of which from 1781-83 he was county lieutenant. As Van Metre commanded a Westmoreland company, he made his report to Colonel Cook. The latter died at his home between the forks of the Youghiogheny in 1808, leaving one son.—ED.

Linn with Nine Men Capt William Forman with 24
Cap Joseph Ogle from this Place with 10 Men Went
Down to Grave Creek to Make what Discovery they
could make   when Come there found grave Creek
Fort a[ll] Consumed to Ashes, the Corn Cut up and
Tottely Destro[yed] and on their Return to Weling
[Wheeling] About Eight Miles Below weling was
Actacted By A learg Number of Indeans   the kild
and wounded is unknown Aney ferder than Sixteen
that hath Came Inn and Fore of them wounded   sir
I Request the Favour of you to have another Company in Readiness and at this Place Against my Time
is up for I think there will be Great Nesesaty for them
here for the Times seemes to be now Dangerous and
More so hereafter   otherwise I Expect I shall have
to Guard the People of this Place away from here for
it is Imposable for them to stay for the Garrison will
be left Disolate   sir I am yours to serve

JOHN VANMATRE

N. B   SIR   In case Another Company should come
send with them Asufficent quantity of Flower to support them for it Appeairs that they Cannot be supported with Flower here   the times is so Difficult that
People that has wheat Cannot Thrush it Neither Can
Git it ground   As for Beef or Pork there is Plenty
to be had Convenient   also send asufficient Quantity
of salt and Amnition for it is not to be had here any
your Compliance will Amiably oblige the People In
General   sir I am

J. V.

To Mr Collonel Edward Cook   These

[Daniel McFarland to Gen. Edward Hand. 6ZZ11—A. L. S.]
MONONGAHALIA Sepr. 30th 1777

HON{rd} SIR—As I was returning home I heard Very Disagreeable News that Colo{l}. Lynn with a Party of About forty five Men was Defeated at the Narrows Above Grave Creek and the most part killed. Upon consideration thereof I Raised and Sent About forty Men this Day well Suplyed with Oficers they Being the most willing to go to their Assistance, I could not have raised them Unless I Promised them they Would Be Relieved In one week. I Shall Look to you for Directions By the Bearer. I am with Due Respects your Humble Servant

DANIEL M{c}FARLAND[76]

Genl. Hand   Pittsurgh

THE DELAWARES REASSURED

[Gen. Edward Hand to the Delawares. 1U103.]
FORT PITT Octr. 1st. 1777

Brothers, Capt. White Eyes, John Kilbuck &c. Delaware Chiefs at Coochocking &c.

BROTHERS—The Arrival of your People here Yesterday with my Messengers made my Heart glad. And our Women and Children rejoice. The Cloud will now soon disperse and the Day appear bright & Clear.

I thank you for the News you send me. I shall ere long be ready to speak to the Mingoes & Wiandots,

---

[76] Daniel McFarland was a Scotchman who before moving West lived for some time in Massachusetts. He made his home on Ten Mile Creek in Amwell township of Washington County. In 1777 he was chosen colonel of Monongalia County, to serve under Zackwell Morgan, because of previous experience in military affairs. After the Revolution he built a fulling mill on his property, and there died (1817) at an advanced age.—ED.

as I promised you I would & they will soon be ashamed of what they have done.

Brothers, You may depend that my Soldiers shall not hurt your Women or Children. They shall go the Road you have pointed out, & you shall have Notice when I move, agreeable to my Promise. I am determined to do every thing that is proper to convince you, that you have made a proper Choice of your Friends, and if any Nation strikes you on our account, I desire you will call on me & you shall be supported with as much Power as you wish for, & if you think it necessary I will build a fort & Garrison it either at your Town or at any other Place near to it that you think proper and when Peace shall be restored the fort shall be burned & our People shall all come out of your Country.

Brothers, I make this Offer to you to convince you of my Sincerity and that I am determined to promote an everlasting friendship between the Delawares & the United States. I say Brothers if any Nation strikes you on our Account, I will consider your Quarrel as our own.

Brothers, Two of your Messengers conclude to stay here some little Time longer for News. I now send the other two Back with this. They carry a Flag to make Use of when you send Messengers in future to this Place.

Brothers, Col. Morgan will continue to superintend Indian Affairs so long as he can render service & I rejoice that his Conduct has been so agreeable to you. He sets out for Philad[a]. to Morrow and carries all your good News to Congress. And you may expect to hear from him in thirty Days or perhaps thirty five Days. They will rejoice to see your good Words & the Sentiments of your Hearts. You may depend we do not listen to what bad People say but we are determined to hold fast to our agreements, and I desire you will not fail to speak to Colesqua[77] & the Shawanese whose Hearts continue to be good.

Brothers, If you can send Messengers to the Mingoes up the Allegany, whose Hearts are yet good, I desire you will do it & desire them to continue to sit still untill the Clouds disperse. I hope they will continue wise & not join the foolish People.

Brothers, The English landed lately in Maryland & endeavoured to march their whole Army to Philad^a. but our army went to meet them half way where a Battle ensued. We lost six hundred Men & killed eighteen hundred of the Enemy, this happened at Shadesford on Brandywine Creek. The two Armies now lye in sight of each other both preparing for another grand Battle which you shall have News of so soon as it arrives.

Brothers You may depend the English will soon be ashamed of their foolish Conduct. All the united States keep fast hold of the friendship of the Delawares & Yesterday Col. Morgan rece'd a Message for you from the Governor of Virginia which he now sends to you.[78]

Brothers Let us be strong in our Promises and keep true to our agreements as you may depend I will.

---

[77] This is possibly the English form of the Shawnee name of the chief Cornstalk.—ED.
[78] See letter of Sept. 18 from Gov. John Page.—ED.

[Col. George Morgan to the Delawares. 1U104.]

FORT PITT Oc^{tr}. 1 1777

Brother Capt. White Eyes & Capt. John Kilbuck—
Because James Elliott informs me you desire me to write something for you to speak when you go to Detroit, I now do it. You are wise Men and know what part to speak & what part to leave unsaid. I recommend to you when you speak to Govr. Hamilton to do it in writing as there are no good Interpreters at Detroit & desire him to give You his answer in Writing for the same reason. M^r. Zeisberger who has your good much at heart will assist you.

BROTHERS THE ENGLISH—I have often heard your Voice at a Distance & my Nation have thought proper to send me here that I might see your face again and hear you distinctly that they may not be deceived.

We have long lived in friendship with our Brothers the English, we have no desire to go to war with any Nation who will not strike us. The Big Knife are our Neighbours and we live in friendship with them. They & we have lately renewed our friendship & we wish it to last for ever. They constantly speak what is good & so long as their Actions correspond we desire to believe them. They have explained to us the Nature of their Quarrel one Way. You explain it another but we have Nothing to do with it. They have often told us so, & they tell us to sit still whilst you & they wrestle together. But Brother you have sent us a hatchet to strike them. We desire you will tell us why we should strike those who have done us no Injury & with whom we have long lived in friendship. If you can give us a Reason which is sufficient for wise men to listen to, We desire we may hear it. But if you have no other Reason to give than your own Quarrels, we desire you will say so, we are a free & independant Nation, we are in friendship with all Nations & we desire to remain so, & we particularly wish to live in friendship with you.

Brothers, If you have delivered the Hatchet to the Nations near you to strike the big Knife & to murder their Women and Children, tell us so, & give us a good reason why you desire it, that I may also consider it, but if you have not, we desire you will say so, & speak to them, to sit still for we fear the Big Knife will take a large Stride some of these days & hurt their Women & Children.

Brothers, Sir William Johnston [Johnson][79] took the Tomhawk out of our hands a long time ago, he buried it & told us we never should see it again, we desire you will not make him a Liar.

Brothers, We wish to see an End to your Quarrel with the Big Knife we are sorry to hear you speak to the Indian Nations to strike them & thereby involve their Women & Children in Trouble for I now tell them I hear the Big Knife is almost opened. It has been shut a long Time & when it is opened & ground it will cut sharp. We therefore wish to promote peace & to have Pity on our Women & Children.

Brothers, We have spoke our Minds freely, Now see our hearts & we desire you will speak freely to us that we may know what you wish. We tell you it is impossible for all the Indian Nations in the Woods to hurt the Big Knife, & it will be their ruin if they do not bury the Hatchet What will they say to you, or you to them when their Women & Children [are killed], Will they not tell you that you were the Cause.

Brothers, Be strong, & fight your own Battles like Men.

Brothers, You are wise Men. You will know what Part to choose. Be strong in all good Works.

TAIMENEND

---

[79] The former superintendent-general for North American Indians, who died at his New York home in 1774. Morgan here refers to the great Fort Stanwix Treaty (1768), when peace was made with all the Indian tribes of the West and North.—ED.

[Col. George Morgan to the Delawares. 1U105.]

FORT PITT Oct\. 1. 1777

BROTHERS THE DELAWARES—Yesterday I recd. your Message which pleases me very much. It shows that what I have told Congress is true & that I have not spoken lies. They know this & you may depend they will not suffer your friendship to slip out of their Hands, they are wise men chosen by all the united states to conduct the Business of the whole & they have ordered me to do every thing in my power to convince you of their friendship.

Brothers, I shall set out to Morrow for Ph^a. & will Carry your Message to Congress which will give them great Pleasure It was by their orders that I supplied you with Powder & Lead & if you want further assistance or want a fort to be built at or near your Towns & to be garrisoned by our Troops for the Protection of your Women & Children I desire you to speak. Consider well of the Matter first, You may depend Congress will never deceive you nor suffer you to be struck by any other Nation on their account, without supporting you

Brothers, Look again at my last Message, which I sent to you by James Elliott, & Robin George, When you see that my heart is good as a Man sees his face in a Looking Glass. I desire you to consider my Words & Advice the same as if I was your own flesh & Blood & if you do it will be good for both of us. I am sorry for Delaware George & Buckangehela's Son[80] but they should not have gone with foolish People.

---

[80] Delaware George was an important chief of that tribe who took part in the French and Indian War, and was a firm

You may expect to hear from you [me] in thirty five days.
TAIMENEND.

Yesterday I recd. the inclosed Message to you from the Govr. of Virginia which he desired me to forward to you. I expect the News Papers up every hour. If they come in Time I will send them to you. I send Capt. White Eyes some salt for the Money I have in my hands.

AFTERMATH OF FOREMAN'S DEFEAT

[Gen. Edward Hand to Jasper Yeates. MS. in New York Public Library; Hand Papers—A. L. S.]

FORT PITT 2d Octr. 1777

DEAR YEATES—From Intelligence rec^d. Yesterday from the Delawar[e] at Coochachunk, I find that the Tweetees, Wyachtanas, & Kickapoos,[81] have returned

---

friend of the English. See journal of Christian Frederick Post in Thwaites, *Early Western Travels*, i.

Buckingehelas was a noted war chief of the Delawares, called by John Johnston, Indian agent at Fort Wayne (11YY 35, 38) "the Delaware Washington". He was likewise an orator, and of great influence among his people. His village was in Logan County, Ohio, not far from the present Bellefontaine. He opposed St. Clair and Wayne and took part in the Treaty of Greenville (1795). In 1800 he visited Washington, and died subsequently on White River, Ind. According to Zeisberger's letter of Sept. 22, *ante*, it was the son of Wingenund, not of Buckingehelas, who was wounded at the siege of Wheeling. No doubt it is to this affair that Morgan refers.—ED.

[81] For a brief sketch of the Twigtwee (Miami) and Kickapoo Indians, see *Rev. Upper Ohio*, p. 3, note 8, p. 56, note 84.

The Ouiatanon (Wyactanas) were a branch of the Miami, who in the last decade of the seventeenth century had a village near the site of Chicago. After the founding of Detroit they removed to the Wabash, where they had a large village near Lafayette, Ind. The French built a fort at that village,

AFTER FOREMAN'S DEFEAT

the Tomahawk, and that the Tribe of Delawares headed by Wendaughaland are Wiavering. the Regular Troops at Detroit, am^t. to no more than 70, & the Militia to 300, so that we need not dread a Visit from that Quarter, tho the People here are well Disposed, savage like, to Murder a defenceless unsuspecting Indian. I do not find them much inclined to

---

which was destroyed during Pontiac's conspiracy (1763). The British never rebuilt this post; but the Indian village of Ouiatanon continued to exist until 1790, when two expeditions by American troops—the first in June under Gen. Charles Scott, the second in August under Gen. James Wilkinson—destroyed the Ouiatanon towns (called Wea by the English and French). In 1795 the Weas were present at the Treaty of Greenville, where their chief Little Beaver asked to be restored to their old home at Ouiatanon. They were at this time granted an annuity of $500. In various succeeding treaties of 1803, 1805, and 1809, they made to the United States government successive grants for additional annuities. During the War of 1812-15, the Wea were hostile; but in 1814 signed the second treaty of Greenville; and four years later ceded all of their Indiana lands, and agreed to remove to the West. They were at first located in Missouri, where they were closely allied with the Piankashaw. In 1832 this reservation was exchanged for one on the eastern border of Kansas. There they pursued agriculture and gradually adopted a civilized life. A Baptist mission school was maintained among them from 1847 to 1856. In 1854 the Wea amalgamated permanently with the Peoria, Kaskaskia, and Piankashaw, and ceded most of their lands, agreeing to take allotments in return. During the Kansas border troubles and the War of Secession they were much harassed: by 1859 the confederated tribes numbered only 217. In 1867 they made a new treaty, ceding all their Kansas lands and agreeing to remove to a reservation in northeastern Indian Territory. There they rapidly advanced in the arts of civilization, and in 1889 they agreed to have all lands allotted to them in severalty. They still live in the northeastern portion of Oklahoma, and while largely mixed with white blood, their condition compares favorably with the average white farmer of the region. According to the last few census reports, the population of the federated tribes is slightly increasing.—ED.

enter the Indian Country, and believe that no great matter will be atchieved in the West this Season. 46 men from the Garrison of Wheeling, fell into An Ambuscade the 27th Ult: about 8 miles below the Fort, they were entirely Routed, & but few had come in when the Acc[ts]. came away

Our Eyes & Ears are Open to the East, much will depend on the Operations there. Jessy is well & joins in love to every Creature About your house Farewill D[r]. yeates your Very Affectionate Kinsman

Edw[d]: Hand

To Jasper Yeates Esq[r]. Lancaster p[r] Col: Morgan.

[Col. David Shepherd to Gen. Edward Hand. 4ZZ11—A. L. S.]

Fort Henry, October 3[d]. 1777

Dear General—Your timely Releif by Maj[r]. Chew, was very Exceptable as we Could not Bury the Dead before he Came. The party, that went on the late Unfortunate Excursion, went not at my Request or Order, but from Motives of their Own, as they were tird of being Cooped up in the Fort Idle, & Purposed the Same Several Times before I would at any rate Consent. Indeed, I myself thought their party was Sufficient for any Scouting party of Indians they might fall in with as it was hardly to be Supposed, that Forty Six of our best Riffle Men well Equipt Should be Over power[ed] by Numbers of Indians from the Known Manner of their Sending Small parties to Annoy the Settlements

I Hope Maj[r]. Chew has made a Sattisfactory Report to you of Action as well as of the Strength of the Garrison, I am Sure Notwithstanding our Repeated

AFTER FOREMAN'S DEFEAT 121

loss's that we Shall nearly Make Up our Quotoe for the Expedition, tho the Situation & Danger of Leaving their famileys Prevent their going to the Stations, Yet Upon the Officers Receiving Marching Orders for Joining the Main Bodyes their Quotoes will be immidiately Compleat.

The Friends of those Unfortunate Men that have been Kill'd in these Two Attacks, have Request me to Apply to you to Know Whither they will be paid for the Gunns & Blanketts lost, in those Engagements, as they Were mostly taken from Others by Consent and appraised[82] I refer you to Maj^r. Chews letter for what has happen^d Since his Arrival and am Sir with the Greatest Respect Your Most Ob^t. Hble Ser^t.

DAVID SHEPHERD

Brig. Gen. Hand Fort Pitt

[Maj. James Chew to Gen. Edward Hand. 1U106—A. L. S.]

FORT HENRY, October 3^d. 1777

DEAR GENERAL—It was out of my Power to Send you the Inclosed Account sooner as it was Difficult to find out who was Kill'd, in that Unfortunate Affair near the Narrows Agreeable to your Instructions, I Have made out the most Authentick Reports of that affair, as well as the Strength of the Garrison of Fort Henry, and tho they are imperfectly done, as to the Manner Yet I Hope they will Answer the End design'd. Youll find by the Report of the Garrison, that I Have made a note, to the Several Cap^{ts} from Monnongalia, as those Gentlemen on Hearing of the Late Disaster near this place, March^d Immediately

---

[82] See the Appendix for list of appraisals of effects.—ED.

with what Men they Could Collect for fear others Might not Come Since my arrival Col° Shepard & myself March^d & Buried those Unfortunate Men, in the late Action a Moving Sight. Twenty One Brave fellows, Cruelly Butcher'd, Even after Death.

this day, there was some fresh Tracks Di[s]coverd about Two Miles from this Fort, every Method of Discovering of the Enemy shall be made use of tho the Monongalia Militia Will Return in about Ten or Twelve Day, As they were Raised only for the Intent of Burying the Dead, & not more than One Capt. One Lieut. & One Ensign of the said officers, Expects pay as Officers. If any News from the Eastward Please Let me Know by the Return of the Express, also when I am to Sett out With the Boats &c I am Sir With the Greatest Respect Your most Obt. Hble Ser^t

JAMES CHEW

On Public Service To Brigadier General Hand at Fort Pitt
Pr Express

REINFORCEMENTS FOR FORT RANDOLPH

[Capt. John Bowyer to Col. William Fleming. 1U107— A. L. S.]

SIR—Imedeatily upon receiving your orders I appointed the officers as you Directed and with all expedition the Several Companies on the forks were Drafted I attended all the musters my Self except Capt. Gilmers where ten of the Number you ordered was to be raised and as a Lieutinent is to go from that Company I make no doubt but they will be ready Capt. Paxton and Capt. Hall are the two Captains with the proper Number of other officers According to the Number of Men required the two Companies will be ready to march from Collins Town Next Tuesday morning with out fail and I belive will amount to Near 100 men they have got the Number of Pack horses ready also Beef & flower sufficent to Serve them down to the point also Tents and Kettles you mentioned in yours to me that Donely Mathews would furnish the men but I was informd by Mr Sampson Mathews[83] that they had no flower at Greenbrier which made me Give the Captains orders to Take a Nuff of Provisions with themselves least that they should be disapointed I got also 25^{lb} of Powder & 44^{lb} of lead for the men they will march Next Tuesday I sepose you have heard before this time That General Washington has give How a Compleat Drubing near Schoolkill it is Taken for fact this way pray God it may be true If Col^o Skilleron[84] goes on the expedition these men will be at greenbrier before him I shall do every thing in my Power to get them away my Comp^{ts} to Madam Fleming and

---

[83] For a sketch see *Dunmore's War*, p. 223, note 54.—ED.

[84] Col. George Skillern was an Augusta County pioneer, who as early as 1758 was paid for express services in the army. In 1764 he was commissioned justice; and when Botetourt County was set off in 1770 this commission was renewed. In 1776 he received appointment as lieutenant-colonel of the county militia. This expedition of 1777 seems to have been the extent of Skillern's active service. In 1780 he became county lieutenant for Botetourt, in place of Col. William Fleming, and the following year was active in the defense of the state during the invasions. He was in the same office as late as 1793. His home was about two miles from Pattonsburg, of which town he was an incorporator in 1788. He was wealthy and hospitable, and one of the prominent men of his day west of the mountains. He seems to have left no descendants in the male line.—ED.

am with the greatest Sincarity Y^r most obed^t. and Very Hble Servt.

JOHN BOWYER

Octr. 4^t. 1777
On the publick service   To Col^o. William Fleming
Botetourt   P^r express

[Col. George Skillern to Col. William Fleming. 1U108—
A. L. S.]

SIR—By the Inclos^d: it appears that there is Near 100 men Rais^d: in the Forks   Maj^r Poege[85] was hear this Day and is preparing with all Expedition to March as allso I will be Ready Shortly and Should you think that the Number of men Rais^d. on green brier and the Forks will Admit of me to go on the Expedition you will please to Send me particular Instructions How I am to act as I am a Stranger in Sum respects to the Buisness as allso where you think on Greenbrier the Troops had Besst Randivouse, we will want a pack horse to Carry our Tent Cloath & Bagage whether you think it ought Not be a public Expense   Should there Not appear to Bee 150 Men when we Come to the place of Randivouse Maj^r. Poege offers to Re[sign] his Command to me if Aprovd of   But if I goe with my Quoto he is ready allso to March   as to a Commisary if M^r. Lewis Dus not Chuse to Act I would think Mr David May[86] a

---

[85] Probably this was Maj. John Poage, son of the pioneer Robert. The former was assistant surveyor in 1760; three years later he was appointed vestryman; in 1778 he qualified both as county surveyor and high sheriff, and died at his Augusta County home early in 1789.—ED.

[86] David May was clerk of Botetourt County court for many years before 1776 and as late as 1791. Probably the

proper person   However what Ever Instructions you send me I will Indeaver to Comply with to the utmost of my power   I am with Esteem your obed^t Humble Servt

GEO SKILLERN

ye 5th Octr. 1777
On the publick Service   To Col^o William Fleming Pr Express. Botetourt

---

[Capt. Matthew Arbuckle to Gen. Edward Hand. 3NN74-78— Transcript]

FORT RANDOLPH, 6th. Octr. 1777.

SIR—I rec^d. yours of the 17th ult^o. by sergt^t Flinn,[87] who arrived at this garrison the 25th. do. I detained said Flinn & his party until the arrival of Captn. McKee[88] from the settlement whom I daily expected: said McKee & 8 or 10 of a party were detained in order to assist in escorting a drove of beeves from the settlement to Kelly's on the Kenhawa, which escort was to have been militia. I likewise was ordered to send an escort from this garrison to that place in order to relieve the militia in case any circumstances would admit of it, which order I complied with: said McKee is not yet arrived here; but by 4 of the escort who are returned, I learn he is with the cattle about 3 days march from this place.

In respect to the troops who are to assist in the expedition, I am verbally informed those from Au-

---

Lewis mentioned was Col. Andrew, for whom see *Dunmore's War, passim.*—ED.

[87] Probably the John Flinn mentioned in *Ibid,* p. 325, note 47, who in 1786 was killed by Indians.—ED.

[88] For William McKee, see *Ibid,* p. 348, note 69; also *Rev. Upper Ohio, passim.*—ED.

gusta are on their march, but for more particular information I refer you to Col. Fleming's [letter] which I send enclosed. In respect to the junction of the troops I would for various reasons advise to be at this garrison. In the first place should it be at any other place on the Ohio, there must be a number of men left as a guard to the boats; besides I think this garrison as nigh to the heads of the Scioto as the mouth of the Hockhocking.

Likewise expect to have in my custody six or eight of the Shawanese Chiefs before you arrive. The case stands thus: On the 19th. ult°. two Shawanese arrived here with a string of white wampum, & likewise delivered a speech with strong protestations of friendship—in the meantime producing a black string which they say they had sent them by the Delawares, which was sent them by Col. George Morgan. Their principal errand was to know the reason of it. They had likewise information of an army that was to march into their country, & they beg strenuously for Cornstalk & his tribe. They likewise informed me that the Indians had embodied themselves immediately upon receiving the black string, with the information of a campaign. I thought proper to detain these two. In about 8 days afterwards, Cornstalk's son came to know the reason why they were detained, & gave me the strongest assurances that his father, the Hardman,[89] & some more of their chiefs should come immediately to this place. I have the two still detained, and intend detaining & confining as many as fall into

---

[89] For this chief see *Ibid*, p. 57.—ED.

AFTER FOREMAN'S DEFEAT

my hands (unless it should be to carry intelligence for me to & from this place) until I have further instructions from you.

I had two scouting parties sent out—one of 20, the other of 17 men, two of whom in endeavoring to drive some beeves towards the garrison, & by disobeying my positive instructions, got killed & scalped on the 31st. of Augt. And since, they have killed two men, one child, & one negro, & taken a little girl prisoner from Greenbriar.[90]

The number of men in this garrison—in my company, 1 Lieut, 4 sergt^s, 1 drummer, & 34 privates: In Capt. McKee's company, 2 Lieuts, 4 sergt^s, 1 fifer & 51 privates: In Capt. Henderson's Company of militia, 1 Lieut, 1 ensign, 2 sergt^s, & 25 privates—total 130.

The provision on hand this day I began to issue of the boat load I rec^d. of Sergt. Flinn, which is all the flour at this garrison. No beeves until Capt. McKee arrives with the drove, which amounted to 112 head in number at Kelly's, which is 80 miles distant from this garrison. Only one keg of salt, scarcely 1 cw^t.; of amunition, between 16 & 17 w^t. of powder, & 6 w^t. & 50^{lbs}. lead. No country arms. Every man a good rifle his own property in good order; scarcely 200 flints in the garrison. I have sent with M^r. McNutt[91] two boats, which are all fit for use at this place. Your boats, I suppose, would carry 50 men each down

---

[90] This refers to the affair at the house of James Graham; see *ante,* pp. 78, 79.—ED.

[91] Lieut. James McNutt of McKee's company was probably a son of John McNutt, an early settler of Augusta County, in that portion afterwards set off as Rockbridge. See Draper MSS., 8ZZ35.—ED.

stream, but 35 w^d. be load sufficient up stream, as the men would require room to work. For particulars relative to this garrison, I refer you to M^r. McNutt. I am Sir, with Esteem Y^r. very humble serv^t.

MATHEW ARBUCKLE

Genl. Hand

NEWS FROM FORT PITT

[Gen. Edward Hand to Jasper Yeates. MS. in New York Public Library; Hand Papers—A. L. S.]

FORT PITT 9th. Octr. 1777

DEAR YEATES—I rec^d. your favours of the 13th. & 17th. Ultim. wish I could hear from you at this time, to clear up our perplexitys respecting the many & various reports of the progress of the Enemy in your Quarter. I believe I told you in my last that we here had nothing to Apprehend from Detroit. I some weeks ago sent a Small party towards Niagara for Intelligence but they have not yet returned. the Clamor against Messrs. Morgan & M^c.Kee was wrong-founded nothing appeared agains[t] either of them.

* * *

Since my last about 200 men Arived here from Frederick & Dunmore Counties.

* * * * * * * *

Your Affectionate Kinsman
EDW^d HAND

Jasper Yeats Esq, Lancaster   Pr fav^r of Mr. J^{no}. Anderson
* * * * * * * *

THE BLOCKHOUSE OF FORT PITT

Built by Bouquet in 1764, and now possessed by Daughters of the American Revolution of Allegheny County, Pa.

CONDITIONS AT FORT HENRY

[Maj. James Chew to Gen. Edward Hand. 4ZZ12—A. L. S.]

FORT HENRY, October 10th 1777

MY DEAR GENERAL—by the Return of the Express I had the pleasure of Receiving your very Kind Letter and Instructions and can really Assure you nothing gives me more Sattisfaction than to Obey every Order, but the Task you have injoind on me is almost, beyond my abilities. the Militia I Have with me was only Raised for One Month, and that Time is past, about Ten or Twelve days, nothing is more inconsistant than Militia, when their Time Or Engagements are at an End. However, I have by Letting four or Five return with the last detachment from the Monnongehala Prevailed on the rest, to Stay, for the Ten days you have Mentioned, in which Time, Perhaps Col°. [Zackwell] Morgan may Send the Company you Order'd Here, as I Have Wrote to him on that Subject, and Let it be as it will I am fully determined to pay the Attention due to your Orders, in endeavouring to fulfill every part of them. I very readily agree with you that our M[MS. torn] Cheifs, Vallorous for Killing their Allies, when at Treaties, may now Rest Sattisfied on the direfull Consequence of Such, Vain Exploits should they not think of it, every Sensible Person must, & the Cruel Strokes the People Here, have felt, from the Occasion [of] those Ignominious, Heroes, will ever be Rememberd. what will not Men do for want of Thought, or Rather to be Thought brave [by] the giddy Multitudes. this last was the Occasion of the loss in the Narrows. Beleive me I never Saw, on this River, a Likelier platt of Ground, for a Battle, for Such a Party, and their [MS. torn] Conduct in the March, was the Occasion of the fatal Event [that] Followed. all the Particulars of which when I have the Pleasure [of] Seeing you shall relate; I have Sent the Necessary Instructions to the Beach Bottom Commanders, Dividing the Gatering With them by the Return of the Men from that place am informed that Capt. Vanmeters Company are daily leaving him, so that that place will be straitned much if no Releif is Sent them. Captain Williamson[92] of the Ohio Vollenteers is to bring the Cattle M^r. Robinson wrote you about the Said Captain Choosing this duty himself.

---

[92] David Williamson was born in Carlisle about 1752. In 1846 Dr. Draper interviewed his eldest daughter, who gave the following facts (2S34) concerning her father's life: When a young boy he was ambitious to go West, and at the age of thirteen accompanied a party hunting and trapping toward Pittsburgh. Soon after, he made a settlement on the waters of Buffalo Creek, and going home brought out the families of his father John and his uncle Joseph. They all settled, and built a stockade, or station, near the present Taylorstown, Washington County. David Williamson was very active in frontier defense, and popular with his neighbors. In the spring of 1782 he was chosen commander of a force embodied to raid the Moravian towns, whose inmates were accused of encouraging attacks on settlers. This disgraceful affair ended in the massacre of a number of peaceful, unoffending Indians. Williamson's share in the affair has received just obloquy, although he is said to have desired to spare the prisoners. The same year he was second in command of Crawford's disastrous Sandusky expedition, wherein his courage was of value in securing the retreat. His popularity did not suffer by these expeditions, and in 1787 he was elected sheriff of the county. But he is said to have been too lenient with offenders, and lost his property through giving security therefor. He died in 1809 in poverty, having lost his large landed estate. His descendants are numerous. Several are still living in Washington County, where as late as 1882 remains of his farm buildings were yet standing.—ED.

AT FORT HENRY 131

Upon my Arrival Here I found everything in the utmost Confusion, Without any Kind of Order & the Very Garrison, Enough to Poison Men. I Have now Erected Some faint Emblem [semblance] of Order and Got the Garrison neat & Clean so that How [who] ever Comes after me, Will be Enabled to Live Comfortable & Keep up the Disipline. the Armourer that was Employed by Col^o. Shepard for the use of this and the Neighbering Garrisons has, as I am inform'd by all the People Here, as well as from the acc^t. of his Work, done his duty in Every Respect, and is an Exceeding Good Workman. Yet I am at a loss to Know whether he is to be Employed any Longer, or upon What Terms. this I am Sure that he is as Good for that Purpose as any that is to be had, besides for the Work done Heretofore he has found all the Matereals, and has worn out a Number of Files as well as Tools of Other Kinds and if he should not be paid it will Ruin him to all Intents. I would be much Obliged to you for Instructions on this Head. the Doctor Likewise Informs me that he has no Convenience for to Keep the Wounded Men as they should be Kept. Neither have they or Can they be supplyed, with Proper Cloathes having Lost their Blankitts, and if it is agreeable to you When I Return with Boats Purposes to Move Two of them to Pitt as he informs me the Rest Can do without a Surgeon but this Cannot be done without a Supply of Blankitts for them.[93] I am afraid I have tired your Patience

---

[93] In reply to this appeal, General Hand wrote Major Chew, Oct. 12, 1777 (3NN58): "Your wounded men are as well where they now are as they could be here. I have not blank-

with this Long Letter. Shall only Add that I will do
every[thing] in my Power to Discover the Enemies
Motions, & beg you well send me by the first Convey-
ance Two Quire of Paper, as I owe the Greatest part
[of] one Borrowed Already in my next Shall Send
you a Return of the Strength of this Garrison in Men
Provisions & Ammunition &c I am Sir with the
Greatest Respect Your most Ob^t. Hble Ser^t.

JAMES CHEW

I have Directed the Commissary to Supply Several
Distressed Families with the allowance of Soldiers.
Untill I Receive your Orders. myself and all that
Came with me from Pitt Left our Clothes So that if
we Continue Longer the Garrison will. be numerous
Enough, tho of no Great addition to our Strength.

TROOPS FOR THE CONTINENTAL ARMY

[Capt. William Linn to Gen. Edward Hand. 1U110—A. L. S.]

CATFISH CAMP Octr. ye 11th 1777

SIR—M^r. MClure[94] Has Arrived. He Brought A
Letter from M^r. Lightfoot Lee[95] In which He Informs

---

ets to give them when here, much less to send down for them."—ED.

[94] Probably David McClure, for whom see *Rev. Upper Ohio*, p. 234. The following additional facts are noted: April 6, 1778, David McClure was chosen justice of the peace; Aug. 3 of the same year, he took oath as lieutenant-colonel of the Ohio County militia; and at the September court he was appointed clerk of the county, to succeed James Mc-Mechen, who had removed from the state.—ED.

[95] Francis Lightfoot Lee (1734-97) was a member of the Continental Congress from its first session until 1779, when he resigned and the same year entered the senate of Virginia. He was a signer of the Declaration of Independence, and only less famous than his elder brother, Richard Henry Lee.—ED.

me that He thought it proper for M^r. MClure to Return Home Again As the Congress at that time Had Left Philadelphia And Had Not Met Before He Left that M^r. Lee told M^r. MClure that they Could not Determine it Under two Weeks But as Soon as they Concluded Upon it that they would Send an Express Out which I Suppose will Come to You You will be Kind Enough to Send me Express As Soon as the Express Comes from Congress to You And Inform me What they Have Agreed Upon As I Intend to Rais Men as fast As possible if they Congress Grants what We Concluded Upon Pleas When You write me Direct it to Colo. Brown[96] Redstone Fortt From Your Obleg^d. Humble Servt.

W<small>ILL</small>^m. L<small>INN</small>

To His Excellency Gen. Hand Fort Pitt P^r. favour Col. Shepperd

---

TROOPS FOR EXPEDITION

[Calendar of letters, 3NN57, 65, 180; 1U111; and Darlington's *Fort Pitt*, p. 227. Oct. 13-16.]

Oct. 13. General Hand writes to Col. John Piper[97]

---

[96] For Col. Thomas Brown see *Rev. Upper Ohio*, p. 233, note 76.—E<small>D</small>.

[97] Col. John Piper was born in Ireland in 1730. When ten years of age his family emigrated to America, but soon after landing at Wilmington, Del., the father died. The widow and her sons removed to Shippensburg, in Cumberland County. John Piper was out with Bouquet in 1764; and in 1772 removed to Yellow Creek, in Bedford County, where he had a large place on Piper's Run. About 1776 he built a large stone house, which in 1860 was still standing, and in possession of his descendants. In 1776 he raised a company and served one year in the Continental army; after that he was charged with the defense of the frontier, as colonel of Bedford County militia. Piper later served in the state legislature, and as associate justice of his county (1790). He died at his home on Piper's Run in 1816. See Draper MSS., 7E48.—E<small>D</small>.

that he has ordered 150 men from Bedford and 250 from Westmoreland for an expedition into the Indian country. Of the former, Captain Shearer with seventeen men have arrived.[98] Urges that the remainder be sent, as Virginia militia are partly arrived and partly on their march. The same day he sent word to the county-lieutenant of Westmoreland to hasten on his men and the provisions.

Oct. 14. General Hand writes to Col. William Russell[99] or officer commanding the 13th Virginia: "We have had two severe blows at Wheeling on the 1st and 27th ult°—14 killed the first, and 21 the last. Capt. Wm. Foreman of Hampshire and his son fell the 27th. Forty six of them suffered themselves to be led out by Mr. Wm. Linn, fell into an ambuscade of 50 Indians and were totally routed. The Kittanning I was obliged to evacuate for want of men. I have many difficulties to encounter, yet hope to drink your health in pure element at Sandusky[1] before Christmas."

---

[98] A William Shearer accompanied the Sandusky expedition of 1782. Probably, however, the present allusion was to Robert Shearer, a prominent citizen of Robinson township, in the later-formed Washington County. He may have acted with the Bedford militia at this time. It would seem from Major Chew's letter of Oct. 16, that Hand stationed Shearer and his men at Beech Bottom Fort. Robert Shearer was killed by Indians in 1780, while cultivating corn at his homestead.—ED.

[99] For sketch of Col. William Russell see *Dunmore's War*, p. 6, note 9.—ED.

[1] This is an interesting evidence of General Hand's purpose in his proposed expedition—that it was to strike the Sandusky towns, where were collected the bands most hostile to the Americans. For a sketch of Sandusky see *Rev. Upper Ohio*, p. 218, note 61.—ED.

RAISING TROOPS 135

Oct. 14. Maj. James Chew writes from Fort Henry, enclosing lists of the garrison and Captain Shearer's report from Beech Bottom. Sent Captain Williamson with thirty men to escort in the beeves. On their return it is learned that on Friday last one man was killed near Van Meter's mill on Short Creek. Scouts report fresh tracks; but he flatters himself that few scalps will be taken while he is with the garrison. Purposes setting out with the boats next Thursday. Garrison will be weak unless reinforced. Militia will not remain after time expires.

Oct. 16. Thomas Baldwin, James Ratchkin, James Parsons, Edward Lucas, John Baldwin, and Michael Rader,[2] captains of militia from Frederick, Loudoun, Berkeley, Hampshire, and Dunmore[3] Counties assem-

---

[2] A family of Baldwins was forted at the present site of Blacksville, Monongalia County.

Edward Lucas was one of the earliest settlers of Frederick County, arriving there from Pennsylvania in 1725. This is probably Edward Lucas Jr., since the elder Lucas died Oct. 3, 1777. The son served in the Continental army as well as in the militia.

A German family of Rœders (Rader) was located in the Shenandoah Valley, in what was later Rockingham County.—ED.

[3] Frederick was the pioneer county of the lower Shenandoah Valley, and was erected in 1738; but owing to insufficient population it was not organized until 1743.

Loudoun, east of the Blue Ridge Mountains, was formed from Fairfax in 1757, and named for the British General Earl of Loudoun.

Berkeley was formed from Frederick in 1772. It then comprised all of what is known as the Eastern Panhandle of West Virginia. Berkeley's quota for this campaign was to be a hundred men. See letter from Hand, dated Aug. 12, 1777, to Col. Van Swearingen, militia officer in Berkeley, published in Danske Dandridge, *Historic Shepherdstown* (Charlottesville, Va., 1910), pp. 179, 180.

Hampshire County was erected in 1754 from both Augusta

bled at Fort Pitt, address General Hand to the effect that in their opinion a campaign down the Ohio is impracticable, the season being far spent and there being only 360 men in their combined companies. Allude to Captain Foreman's loss.

GOOD NEWS FROM THE EAST
[Col. George Morgan to the Delawares. 1U113.]

YORK [PA.] Octr. 16. 1777

Taimend, To the wise Council of the Delawares at Coochocking

CHIEFS AND BROTHERS.—When I wrote to you last I told you you should hear from me again in thirty Days: I then expected to have been back at Fort Pitt in that Time but as I have much Business to do with the great Council [Congress] I shall not return quite so soon as I expected, they have desired me to write to you to tell you some of the good News we have from our Armies. They thank you for your last Message, what you desire shall be done. They place great Confidence in your wise Councils & are determined that you shall never have reason to be sorry for being strong in good works.

Brothers, I lately wrote a Letter to Genl. Hand informing him of the Success our Northern Army then had. He will send a Copy of it to you, I now confirm the Contents.

---

and Frederick. It comprised the upper waters of the Potomac, and lay between Alleghany and Shenandoah mountain ranges.

Dunmore County was formed from Frederick in 1772. The name was (in October, 1777) changed to Shenandoah, on account of Lord Dunmore's unpopularity in the state.—ED.

NEWS FROM THE EAST 137

Brothers, Since I wrote that Letter Viz^t. on the 4th. Inst. our Army surrounded a part of the British Troops at Germantown when 1500 of them were killed, wounded & taken Prisoners. Their Courage begins to fail for they did not fight strong that Day. However their whole Army out & a part of ours only being engaged we brought our prisoners off to our main army all of them are now taking Possession of such Grounds as will effectually surround our Enemies. We are making good strong fences to Pen them up so that they shall not get off unless they steal out of some hole in the Night Time for now they are out of reach of their Shipping.

Brothers, On the 7th. Ins^t our Army to the Northward routed the british Army commanded by their greatest Genl's, who sent orders to Detroit last Spring to employ the Wiandots & other western Nations & to hire them to do Mischief that he might Succeed the Better. They were so foolish as to be deceived & he is now defeated. I send you a particular Account of this because I know it will make your Hearts glad. Listen to the annexed Letter.[4]

---

[4] Annexed is the copy of a letter from Commissary-General Trumbull to the President of Congress, dated Albany, Oct. 9, 1777. After describing the battles of Oct. 7 and 8, he says: "The Canada Indians have deserted the British Army and the Six Nations have joined ours. In the late action the Oneidas & Tuscaroras were of great Service. In this they had little share, but they have determined to send a War Belt through all their own & other Nations to take up the hatchet in favour of the Americans agst the British Troops on account of ill Treatment they have rec^d. The Southern Indians have also sent us the Eagles Tail & Rattle. So that the Western Nation[s] will soon repent their folly."—ED.

Brothers, So soon as we take Genl. Howe & his Army Prisoners (which I hope to inform you of before many Moons) our Army will have nothing else to do, but to divert themselves with the Mingoes, Wiandots &c[a]. but as they & we are all born of one Mother, and live on one Land, I wish they would now come to their Senses and ask for Peace before their women & children get hurt or are carried into Slavery. If they lose this opportunity, I tell you they will repent it.

Brothers, you shall hear from me three Weeks after you receive this. Continue Strong & let Capt. Pipe, Colisqua &c[a] know this News.

TAIMENEND

HAND VISITS WHEELING: MILITIA ATTACKED
[Archibald Steel to Gen. Edward Hand. 1U125—A. L. S.]
PITTSBURGH Octr. 21th 1777

DEAR GENERAL HAND—I Need Not inform you how the Militia Behavd after you Set out for wheeling. But Refers you to there Conduct whilst you were Present. they Left this at 10 of the Clock on Sunday Evening. yesterday they Stoptd at Logs toun[5] in the morning where the met with two or three indians, which By all acounts Defeated the whole Party killd one and wounded one. Magor Chue hapned to Com to them Just after the indians fired and fled. he found the whole Party So alarmd that he Could Not get one Man to assist him to Surround a Cornfield where the thought the indians were. But I Beleve they Proceeded on their Jorney.

---

[5] For this place see *Rev. Upper Ohio*, p. 26, note 52.—ED.

INDIAN DEPREDATIONS 139

Just Now one hundred and forty horses Came Loaded with flower. I Expect in a Day or two one hundred More horses. I will Detain them to [till] the Express Returns. I have Just Convers^d with Capt. wm. Loughry[6] about the Militia of westmorland. he Cannot Give any acount whether one man from that Place will Com to your assistance or Not. I am Dear Sir your humble Servant

ARCHIBALD STEEL.[7]

To The Honorable Edward Hand Brigad^r General on his way to or at wheelen By Express.

---

[6] William Lochry was a brother of Archibald, county lieutenant, and was in 1774 a justice of the county court of Westmoreland. It would appear that he was at this time captain of militia.—ED.

[7] Col. Archibald Steele was born in Lancaster County about 1741; at the outbreak of the Revolution he assisted in raising a company of riflemen, of which he was commissioned lieutenant. They proceeded to Boston, and were enrolled in the regiment of which Hand was lieutenant-colonel. In September, 1775, Steele was one of a company detached to accompany Arnold on his perilous march to Quebec. He attracted the attention of the commander by his enterprise and endurance, and undertook several difficult reconnoissances. At the siege of Quebec, Steele was wounded and taken prisoner. Being exchanged in 1776, he returned home, and was appointed deputy quartermaster-general. In that capacity he was with General Hand at Pittsburgh. Later he served as military storekeeper to the United States army, making his home in Philadelphia. He was honorably discharged from the army in 1816, and died at his Philadelphia home in 1832. Three of his sons served in the War of 1812-15.—ED.

[Maj. James Chew to Gen. Edward Hand.   1U122—A. L. S.]
Fort Pitt, October 21st 1777

Dear General—this Morning I arrived at this Garrison. a few minutes after I Passed by. Loggs Town, I was informed by one of the Officers of my detachment that Call'd at that place, that the Indians Killd a Man of Capt Lucas's Company & Wounded one Other, which I Brought with me to Pitt. I am very sorry I had not Staid untill you Came to Wheeling, as I am at loss to know, What I am to do As the Monnongalia Militia, have left this Fort, indeed, my Leaving Fort Henry was Owing to the Impatiance of the Men to get other Cloaths, and fit themselves out Should Occasion Call them again this Fall, which I Heartily Hope it will be the Case and that it will also be in your Power to Cross the River, that the Indians may be Paid for Some of their Misdeeds. I beg you will Let me Know by Express if I am to Continue Here, or where, Untill the Campain goes Forward. Believe me any Post is Agreeable to me that you may think Proper, As I will make my Inclination & duty always Coincide with your Orders, and am Sir With the Greatest Respect Your most Obd^t Hu'ble Ser^t.

James Chew

On Public Service to Brigadier General Hand at Fort Henry p^r Express.

[Col. John Gibson to Gen. Edward Hand.   1U123—A. L. S.]

Dear General—By the Inclosed letters you will be informed of the state of the Garrison at Konhawa not knowing what Quantity of Amunition and provision you wou'd Choose to send by them, has enduced me to

INDIAN DEPREDATIONS 141

Send this Express for your further orders. After all the Care that has Been taken to prevent the Infection of the Small pox from Spreading, I am sorry to Inform you that a man at McClellans house in town has Been lying there sick of that Distemper these sixteen days past, the pox is quite turned on him and I am afraid the Distemper is Spread. Major Chew and his party arrived here last night he will Remain here until further orders from you. Capt. [William] Lochry is just come in with 150 Packhorses loaded with flour, he informs me that the Indians have Burnt a number of houses near Kiskemonetto. Nothing new from Below. If you should think it proper that any more flour or Stores should be sent to Weling please to acquaint me. Capt Lochry seems to think it will Be very hard to Get the Militia of Westmoreland to turn out, and I wish it may not Be the Case with the people of this County. I shall Be happy in hearing of your safe Arrival at Weling. I am Dear General your most obedient humble Servt.

JNO. GIBSON

FORT PITT Octr 21st 1777.
To Genl Hand.

TORY DROWNED; ZACKWELL MORGAN ARRESTED
[Col. John Gibson to Gen. Edward Hand. 3NN182—
Transcript.]

FORT PITT Oct. 22ᵈ. 1777.

DEAR GENERAL—Just after the express left this on the 21ˢᵗ [Oct.], James Shirley came in here with an account of his being attacked by Indians, between Capt. Cisney's place & Samˡ. Newells on the road to Logstown. They killed one Smith & his daughter, & tomahawked his son, a boy about 6 years old, & after scalping him, left him; the boy is still alive, but I am afraid will not recover.

I am sorry to inform you that the militia of Monongahala county are in the utmost confusion, occasioned by the drowning of Higgison, the noted Tory. The report is that he in company with Col. Zach: Morgan and four others were crossing a flat at the mouth of Cheat River—Higgison was handcuffed & had bolts on his legs & whether he tumbled out, or was thrown out, is uncertain. Some say he was thrown by Col. Morgan: However, the coroner's inquest have found it wilful murder, & a called court has been held, & Col. Morgan is ordered to Williamsburg for further trial. Capt. Pigman & most of the Captains have resigned, & have publicly declared they will not go on an expedition without Col. Morgan. As I thought the communicating this to you was of the utmost importance, I have therefore sent this express[8] &c.

JOHN GIBSON

Gen. Hand, Fort Henry.

---

[8] The Virginia assembly passed a law in the autumn of 1777, appointing three commissioners to proceed to Fort Pitt

A TORY DROWNED

[Maj. James Chew to Gen. Edward Hand. 1U124—A. L. S.]

FORT PITT October 23ᵈ. 1777.

DEAR GENERAL—by two men from the County of Monongalia Yesterday evening I was inform'd that Hickison, the Cursed Tory was drown'd in Crossing Cheat River, in Company with Colº. Morgan and Several others, the Magestrates of that County have Accused Colº. Morgan, as the Person who threw the said Hickson into the River and Proceed to find him Guilty & have Past Sentence for his further Tryal at Williamsburgh by the Accounts my informant Gives me no Positive Proof Could be made Appear, against the Colº. Please Receive the Accᵗ. in their Own Words. Colº. Morgan after Ironing Hickson was

---

and examine the extent of the dissatisfaction in that neighborhood; Hening, *Statutes*, ix, p. 374. The Loyalist disaffection in this region seems to have been a direct result of Hamilton's letters and proclamations, already cited. In the autumn of 1777 the affairs of the colonists appeared desperate, and many thought to save their lives and property by giving adherence to the king. British agents sent a test oath, which was secretly taken by a number of poor and ignorant people in that part of Pennsylvania and Virginia that borders the Monongahela and Youghiogheny rivers. Col. Thomas Gaddis and Col. Zackwell Morgan were especially active in arresting and quelling this uprising. A skirmish was held, and the Loyalists dispersed. Higginson (or Hickson) seems to have been the only one who was killed, and his drowning was claimed to be accidental. His grave was marked for many years at the forks of Cheat River. Col. Zackwell Morgan was arrested and tried for the murder of this prisoner, but was acquitted at the trial. For a detailed account of the episode, see the reminiscences of John Crawford in Draper MSS., 6NN86-101. The excitement in the West was intense. Many prominent men were suspected. Col. George Morgan was placed under arrest for a brief time; and even Hand's fidelity was in question. The disaffection finally culminated in the flight to the British (March, 1778) of Col. Alexander McKee and his party. See *post.*—ED.

seen to turn away from him, and was not seen by any Person, tho, there were six others in the Boat or flatt, besides some others on the shore, to lay hands on the said Hickeson but on Getting a Cross went off without making any Schearch for him, tho his Hat was seen on the River. the Court notwithstanding, have Done the fatal stroke & Ordered him to Williamsburgh. This will stop the Militia from that County, which will Ruin the Expédition. Good Heaven that the Death of a Vile Tory should Effect us so nearly & Ruin what you have with so much Labour, pains & Dificulty almost Accomplished. Yet, Sir, Without Some Method Can Timely be thought of that will set aside the ill timed Judgm^t. of Court, The Militia from that County are not to be Expected. I know the People there well and am sensible that it is not in the Power of any other Man but Col^o. Morgan to march them. You Good Sir, saw the Intrepid behaviour of those People at the Apprehending of the Torys, also heard how the Popular Voice, was to Hang them on the Spot, it is easy for you to Judge, how much Louder, that Cry is now Extended against the Court for Condemning the Col^o. Provided the fact had been Proved, which it seems was not done, impolitic when no other Man, Can do any thing with the Militia to still Irritate them by Condemning, the only Man that could, much more at this Juncture when you had Honored him with your Instructions; Might it not be to Presuming in me I would intreat you to go to that County Your Presence Could do every thing that is Required for the People there look up to you as their Protector.

A MEETING OF OFFICERS

Any Commands you in the Mean time shall be Please to give me shall be most Cheerfully Obeyed. I will Repair any where, do any thing, so that the Expedition goes On, and Let me add that my Dear freind the Col⁰. may be extricated from the Heavy Charge Laid against him. Will you be so Kind as to forgive the faults of this Letter as I am much imbarrassed & Confused for the best of Freinds & the Disapointments you have Experience[d] on this side the Mountains I am Dear General With the Greatest Respect Your obliged & most Hble Serᵗ.

JAMES CHEW

Col. Gibson writes all the News in this part of the Country and gives a much better Accᵗ. of Col. Morgans affairs than I can Posible do at this Time.

On Public Service To. Brigadier General Hand at Fort Henry

COUNTY LIEUTENANTS MEET; EXPEDITION ABANDONED

[Calendar of letters. 3NN49, 58-62, 187, 188; 1U127. Oct. 26-Nov. 5.]

Oct. 26. General Hand writes to Col. Daniel McFarland of Monongalia County asking him to come to a meeting of the officers at Fort Pitt, Nov. 1.

Nov. 1. General Hand writes from Fort Pitt to Col. Archibald Lochry that he has just returned from Fort Henry to meet the commanding officers of the counties of Yohogania, Monongalia, Ohio, and Westmoreland, and get their positive answer as to the practicability of an expedition. Mentions Burgoyne's defeat, and General Potter's attack on Hessians.[9] Orders an officer and a few men to White Pine Run, as the commander-in-chief has sent orders to withdraw Capt. Samuel Miller.

Nov. 2. General Hand writes to Mrs. Hand: "I am just returned from a visit to Fort Henry on the Ohio, and am sorry to inform you that I despair of being able to do anything effectual this season. If I can assist the inhabitants to stand their ground, and wait the event of our success to the Northward, shall now deem myself doing a great deal."

Nov. 2. Col. Archibald Lochry writes to General

---

[9] The report was, that "General Potter with the Cumberland militia attacked 1000 Hessians on their march from Philadelphia to Chester with baggage, killed some, took 300 prisoners, and seized all the baggage and 13 pieces of brass artillery." This seems to have been incorrect, although in December General Potter attacked a foraging party from Philadelphia, with great bravery and effect, and was commended by Washington.

Gen. James Potter was born (1729) in Ireland, coming to America while young. His father John was sheriff for Cumberland County, and the son began his career during the French and Indian War, when he served on Armstrong's campaign against Kittanning. At the outbreak of the Revolution he joined the patriot forces, and was commissioned brigadier-general in the spring of 1777, after serving through the Trenton-Princeton campaign. In the autumn of this year he commanded the Pennsylvania militia, and was assigned the task of watching the west side of the Schuylkill and cutting the enemy's communication with Chester and Wilmington. The latter part of the year he retired, because of illness in his family. Rejoining the army, he was in 1782 commissioned major-general, after serving on the executive committee of his state. He was in 1784 a member of the council of censors, and died at his home in Penn's Valley, near Bellefonte, Centre County, in 1789. A portion of his papers was secured by Dr. Draper from his descendants. It was unfortunate that the entire collection was not entrusted to Draper's care, for it has since been scattered and destroyed.—ED.

Hand that they can furnish but 100 men for the expedition, as their frontier is much distressed, the savages daily committing hostilities, burning and plundering.[10]

Nov. 2. General Hand writes to Col. George Morgan that he expects little aid from the neighboring counties. He has returned to Fort Pitt to meet the county-lieutenants, who have not all arrived, owing to excessive high waters. Narrates the Indian attacks at Logstown and in the vicinity. "Tom Nichols and party are returned; they were out 6 weeks and a day; he has been at Muncy and Musquaghty towns,[11] Le Bœuf and to the head of French Creek, but could not discover any appearance of a regular enemy."

Nov. 3. General Hand sends to the Delaware chiefs additional good news from the Eastward.

Nov. 3. General Hand requests of the county officers their sentiments in writing about the expedition. Only seventeen men have come from Bedford, three from Westmoreland, a few are assembled at Fort

---

[10] See Lochry's letter in *Penna. Archives,* v, p. 741.—ED.

[11] Probably Thomas Nicholson, who had lived with the Indians, and on several occasions was guide and interpreter; see *Dunmore's War,* p. 13, note 26.

The Munsee were a division or clan of the Delawares, who had several villages upon the upper Allegheny. Thence issued the parties that struck the Westmoreland frontier. These villages were established some time previous to 1748, when Céloron in his voyage mentions several "Loup" towns—the Munsee were the wolf—loup—clan of the Delawares. Céloron likewise mentions one town containing a number of Renard (or Fox) Indians—see *Wis. Hist. Colls.,* xviii, p. 40. This would seem to be the town to which Hand here refers under the name of "Musquaghty". The Foxes called themselves Musquake, and the remnant of the tribe in Iowa is still known by this name. These were the villages raided by Brodhead in his expedition up the Allegheny in 1779.—ED.

Henry. There are at Fort Randolph 130, from which he could not draw more than 100.

Nov. 3. John Campbell, county lieutenant of Yohogania, Daniel McFarland, colonel of Monongalia, John Gibson, lieutenant-colonel of 13th Virginia, Alexander Barr, colonel of Westmoreland,[12] and James Chew, major of Monongalia, submitted their opinion to General Hand. The number now collected will not exceed 800; not more than 150 more available. "And as the cold season is now setting in, and the militia destitute of the necessary clothing—give us leave, Sir, to offer it as our opinion, that under these difficulties, the stationing a number of men, not less than four hundred, on the frontiers of Monongalia, Yohogania, & Westmoreland, this winter, is all that can be done; and from the distressed situation of Ohio county, a number not less than one hundred and fifty men."

Nov. 5. General Hand countermands orders for militia, expressing his great mortification at finding he could not collect a sufficient body of men to march into the Indian country.

---

[12] Alexander Barr was one of a group of Scotch-Irishmen who as early as 1769 removed from Cumberland Valley to Derry township, Westmoreland. The Barr settlement was about a mile from the village of New Derry and contained a blockhouse known as Fort Barr. During an attack in 1778 on Wallace's Fort, one of the Barrs while hastening to the relief of his friends, was shot and killed before attaining the safety of the fort. Alexander Barr went down the Ohio about 1785, locating lands in company with Richard Wallace; he was at that time killed by the Indians for trespassing on their lands. See Hand's letter to Colonel Lochry, dated Nov. 5, 1777, with regard to the disposal of Colonel Barr's troops, in Darlington, *Fort Pitt*, pp. 228, 229.—ED.

CORNSTALK 149

FORT RANDOLPH REINFORCED; CORNSTALK DETAINED

[Capt. Matthew Arbuckle to Gen. Edward Hand. 3NN 78, 79—Transcript.]

FORT RANDOLPH, 7th Novr. 1777

SIR—I have the pleasure to inform you of the arrival of the troops from Augusta and Bottetourt here the 5th. inst, under the command of Col°. Dickinson & Col. Skilron [Skillern].

I am very uneasy concerning the batteaux which I have daily expected for some time past—by which I expected to hear more particularly from you relative to the ensuing campaign. I am somewhat suspicious that some misfortune has befallen them, being convinced you would have despatched one down with flour with the greatest expedition, knowing the condition of this garrison both with respect to flour & salt. We were totally out of salt three days ago, & our beeves are daily losing.

I have here detained Cornstalk and two other Shawanese[13] whom I'm determined to keep confined until I have further instructions from you.

I much doubt you have been disappointed in the troops you demanded from the several counties, which might probably have defeated your design. Should you be so circumstanced, I desire you would despatch as many boats with flour as would be sufficient during the winter, as I make no doubt but the river may be frozen up.

---

[13] The other Indians were Redhawk and a chief who having lost one eye was familiarly known as "Old Yie." His Indian name appears to have been Petalla. See *West Virginia Magazine*, April, 1902, p. 57.—ED,

Should you be prevented from proceeding, would desire you would give particular directions relative to Cornstalk as I am well satisfied the Shawanese are all our enemies. The last arrived troops had scarcely flour sufficient to carry them to this garrison. Inclosed I send you the n°. of troops last arrived. I am, with respect, Sir, Y^r very hble serv^t.,

MATHEW ARBUCKLE
Genl. Hand

[Col. John Dickinson to Gen. Edward Hand. 1U128—A. L. S.]
POINT PLESENT NEAR FORT RANDOLPH 7th Novr 1777

DEAR S^r.—Col°. Skilron from Bottetourt and myself from augusta arived here with our Troops from Each County the 5th Instant whare we flattered our selves of the hapyness of meeting y^r. Excelency but being Disapointed Do greatly fear that som accident or Disapointment has fell in y^r. Way Which I should be hearttely sorry for our N° of Troops are Not mentined here as the strength of the Whol is Inclosed in Capt. Arbuckels Letter agreeable to y^r. Excelencys Instructions to your County Lieu^{ts}. We brought Flour and salt seficiant only to bring us to this place as We ware greatly Detained on our march by Rain and high Waters.[14] We Expected to have met with a seficient

---

[14] In an application (1832) for a pension in Tyler County, Virginia, Peter Berting thus describes the outward march of the Augusta troops (6ZZ44) : He volunteered in a company commanded by Capt. John Hopkins, which was part of a regiment headed by Col. John Dickinson, and Major McClanahan. They rendezvoused at Staunton and marched to Warm Springs, Bath County, thence to Jackson's River and across Alleghany Mountain to Camp Union (Lewisburg), in Greenbriar. There they formed a junction with Skillern's forces

supply of provisions here but to our great mortification found the garison out of salt and very scarce of Flour tho Wile we have Beef am Willing to surmount Every Deficalty and hardship untill We Either see or hear from y^r. Excelency. our Troops are Exstreemly good In general and in high sperits Keen for the Expedision under a Commander of so great a Carecter as y^r.self

I am Dear general tho unacquainted Y^r. Excelencys most obediant and very Hble Servt.

JOHN DICKINSON

WALLACE'S FORT ATTACKED

[Col. John Proctor to Gen. Edward Hand. 1U129—A. L. S.]

TWELVUE MILE RUN Nov. ye 8th 1777

HONORED SIR—I am Just Returned from Bedford with My famaly and find this Quarter of the Contry Mutch Destresst, and in the greatest confusion there was a party of the Bedford Millita at my House on theire Martch to Joyne you and receved youre orders to return the necessity of this Distresst frunt^r [frontier] Calls for Asistiance Coll^n. [James] Smith being one his martch with a bodey of about Eighty men thought it nessery to order them With him I hope his conduct will Meet youre aprobation. Wallases fort was Attacted one tuesday last[15] with a body

---

from Botetourt, and crossed Sewell Mountain to the Great Kanawha. They halted for several weeks four miles below the falls, and then descended the river to Point Pleasant.—ED.

[15] According to a note on the manuscript, written by Dr. Draper, this attack occurred Nov. 4, 1777. The following details are given in a contemporary journal written at Ligonier during the autumn of 1777. See George A. Albert, *Frontier Forts of Pennsylvania* (Harrisburg, 1896), ii, pp.

of about forty or fifty White Men and indeans the peple in the fort kild one of the white men and oblidged the rest to retrate but the[y are] Seen Evory Day in the Neibohud we havue though[t] it would answer [every] avaluble End To Send out a Strong party in order to fall in with them if Posable.

I Congratlate you on the Good Nuse from the Norward and am Sir youre Most Obed Humble Servt

JOHN PROCTOR

N. B. I just now recaved intiligance that our batrys has blue up by hot bals at Bilingsport a Ninty gon Ship & 2 others and kild three hundred Hesions and a number of Helandors who had landed and made an atempt to storem the Garason but failed in their Desires.[16] I am your Hu^e [servant]

J. P

244, 245: "[Novr.] 5th. The Light Horse Men return'd with the news that yesterday about 11 o'clock Wallace's Fort was attacked by a number of Indians on one Side while a White Man on the Other Side came wading up the Tail Race of his Mill with a Red Flag which seem'd to be intended as a deception for the attack. When the Man appear'd open to the Fort in the instant of the Attack 7 Balls were fir'd thro' him. * * * 2 of the Balls went thro' 2 Letters he had ty'd in a Bag which was hung round his Neck down his Breast. * * * From what cou'd be discover'd by the Letters they were proclamations from Detroit to the same amount of those found with Col. Campbell. The same day the People about Palmers Fort were fir'd on."—ED.

[16] This is an inaccurate account of the attack, Oct. 22, on Fort Mercer in New Jersey, by a body of Hessians under Count von Donop. Col. Christopher Greene, in command of the fort, repulsed the enemy with great loss. He was assisted by Commodore Hazelwood, whose batteries fired into the British ship "Augusta", 64 guns, causing a great explosion that destroyed the vessel. The "Merlin" was likewise burned. These events occurred the day after the attack on Fort Mercer. Billingsport, where the stockade was unfinished, had

ATTACK ON WALLACE'S

[Col. James Smith to Gen. Edward Hand. 1U130—A. L. S.]
FROM COL^l. PROCTOR'S November the 8th. 1777

Dr GENERAL—Whereas I am persuaded that you had not heard of Wallaces fort being invaded and other Damages Done by the Indiens near this place when you gave orders to the Bedford Melitia to Return and Whereas there is a loud Call for men here at present to Defend and protect this Distressed frunteer; I have orderd the Bedford Melitia to march in Connection with a party of my men over Conemah[17] to Reconoitor and Scour the woods and if posable to anoy the Enemy or Drive them over the alegany; and I hope Sir I will be Justified by you in So Doing. I am Sir your most obedient Humble Servt.

JAMES SMITH
To His Excelancy General Edward Hand   Fort Pitt

N B my intention is to Detain those men but about ten Days; and by that time your pleasure may be known

---

been abandoned by the Americans several days previous to this attack.—ED.

[17] The word Conemaugh is said to signify an otter. The stream rises in the Alleghany range and flows westward through Laurel and Chestnut ranges, until, uniting with the Loyalhanna, it forms the Kiskiminitas. The valley of the Conemaugh was early settled by Scotch-Irish from the Cumberland. John Pomroy and James Wilson formed the nucleus of this colony, which was known as the Derry settlement. These two men came out as early as 1772. A few settlers may, however, have preceded them, on the north side of the Conemaugh near Black Lick Creek. The region was unusually exposed to Indian raids, most of which originated with the British authorities at Niagara. Wallace's Fort suffered at least three attacks within the year 1777-78.—ED.

HAND REPORTS ABANDONMENT OF EXPEDITION

[Extract from a letter of Gen. Edward Hand to Gen. George Washington. 15S113—Transcript.]

FORT PITT 9th Novr. 1777.

"When I last did myself the honor to write to your Excellency, I fully expected to be able to penetrate the Indian country. But, alas! I was disappointed; the whole force I was able to collect, including drafts from Hampshire, Berkley, Dunmore, Loudon, Frederick & Augusta, did not exceed 800 men. I am therefore obliged to content myself with stationing small detachments on the frontiers to prevent as much as possible the inroads of the Savages, and rely on the success of our arms to the Northward, & your Excellency's operations, for the rest." The writer expects to start next day for Forts Henry and Randolph to establish order and make winter arrangements.

[Gen. Edward Hand to Gov. Patrick Henry. 3NN 62, 63—Transcript.]

FORT PITT, 9th Nov. 1777.

SIR—When I addressed your Excellency the 8th. ult^o. I fully expected to be able to give the Wyandotts a specimen of what their perfidy so greatly deserves, but to my very great mortification I am obliged to relinquish that design. The militia from Hampshire, Berkley, Dunmore, Loudon & Frederick arrived here, tho' not the number I expected, Hampshire excepted— that county exceeded; the number I called for from Augusta I suppose are now at Fort Randolph. My last letter from Col. Fleming, Cot^y: Lieut. of Bottetourt County, gave me little reason to hope that I could expect any men from that county in time. The Counties of Yohogania & Ohio are not able to assist. From Bedford & Westmoreland in Penn^a. I did not get 50 men for the expedition—so that on summing up my force I found it did not exceed 800 men, including the few regulars here & at Kanhawa—these badly clothed, & the cold season advancing. For these reasons I was obliged to content myself with ordering 150 men to be stationed in each of the frontier counties to prevent, as much as possible, the inroads of the savages and assist the inhabitants in securing their grain and other property. I hope Yohogania & Monongalia will furnish for themselves; for Ohio I intend detaining 100 of the militia from some of the other Counties, if they are to be preváiled on to stay.

Since my last the savages have chiefly aimed at Westmoreland County. They killed a soldier at Logstown & wounded another; a man & two children have been murdered about five miles from this place; in Monongalia two Indians were seen and I apprehend both killed. In Ohio nothing has happened.

[Extracts from a letter of Gen. Edward Hand to Richard Peters, secretary to Board of War. 3NN64—Transcript.]

Nov. 9, 1777.

[Says that he] expected making a move with about 300 men assembled here from over the mountains, to draw out those I expected from the frontiers—but to no purpose. But I conjecture it has had a tendency to alarm the savages as they have not appeared in this quarter in any considerable number, since they now aim at Westmoreland—I believe they are yet ignorant of our movements this way. * * *

About the end of August I found it necessary both to appease the popular clamor and for his own security to bring M^r. Alex^r. McKee[18] from his farm & confine him to his own house here; he had given a parole to the Committee of this place obliging himself not to correspond with or give any intelligence to the enemies of the United States, or to leave the neighborhood of Fort Pitt without their leave—which on inquiry found he had not violated. During the violence of the outcry he was desirous to move down the country to Lancaster County; and he now wishes to continue here, having a considerable interest in the neighborhood, which I did not think necessary to refuse him until I learn the sense of Congress on that head. He has taken up the old parole, & given a new one which I enclose.

[Gen. Edward Hand to Mrs. Hand. 3NN50—Transcript.]
FORT PITT, 9th Nov. 1777.

I believe I informed you in my last that I could not accomplish an expedition into the Indian country. I was much deceived in the real strength & spirit of this part of the country; but hope that the prosperity of our affairs to the Northward will have a happy influence on the Western Indians.

Jesse [Ewing] & myself intend a voyage to the Kenhawa & are to set out to-morrow; on our return, which will be by Staunton, in Virginia, I will apply for leave to go down the country.

---
[18] For a brief biographical sketch of Alexander McKee, see *Rev. Upper Ohio*, p. 74, note 3.—ED.

CORNSTALK'S ATTITUDE

THE MURDER OF CORNSTALK

[Portion of the narrative of Capt. John Stuart.[19]
6NN105-112.]

The preceeding year 1777 the Indians again began under the influence of british agents to manifest signs of commencing hostilities, and the Corn Stak warrior with the young Redhawk paid a visit to Capt Arbuckle's garrison he made no secret of the disposition of the Indians declaring that he was opposed to joining the war on the side of the British, but that all the rest of the nation but himself and his wife were determined to engage in it; and of course he should have to run with the stream (as he expressed it) on which Capt Arbuckle thout proper to detain him, the

---

[19] Stuart's *Narrative* was first published in 1833 in the first volume of *Collections* of the Virginia Historical and Philosophical Society from a copy furnished to the editor by the son of the author. The latter says, in his accompanying letter, that he does not know the date at which the narrative was written; and that in presenting the copy he has made some minor changes in spelling and punctuation. In 1877 the *American Magazine of History* printed this narrative (vol. i, commencing pp. 668, 740) from a manuscript said to be the original by John Stuart, and then owned by a subscriber in Salem, Va., who signed himself "Wm. McC.". This is dated December, 1820. Among the Draper MSS. is what appears to be a portion of the original manuscript, from which we print the extract relating to Cornstalk's murder, of which Stuart was an eye-witness. Dr. Draper was long in correspondence with Charles A. Stuart, son of the writer, from whom he may readily have obtained this document. Both this and that at Salem may have been originals prepared by the author. The circumstance of the date would go to show that the latter was a second edition, since the son testified that the original in his possession showed no date. This narrative of Stuart has been made the basis of all detailed accounts of Cornstalk's death, by Doddridge, Withers, and later writers. The accompanying documents and letters throw additional light on this tragic episode.—ED.

young Redhawk and another fellow as hostages to prevent the nation from joining the British. In the course of that summer our new Government [ordered] an army to be raised of volenteers and General Hand was appointed to the command, who as soon as sufficient forc could be collected at fort Pit was to begin his march down the river to point pleasant, and there to meet a reinforcement expected to be raised in Augusta and Botetourt counties.

* * * * * * * *

We collected in all 30 or 40 men and joined the rest of the men on their march under Colo. Skillern to point pleasant when we arrived there, there was no account of General Hand or his army and but little provision made to supply our troops save what we had taken with us down the Kanawha; and we found the garison unable to give us any relief, being [having] nearly exhausted what had been previously furnished before our arrival. we concluded to remain at the garison until General Hand should arrive, or some accounts from him; during our stay two young men of the name of Hamilton, and Gilmore, crossed the Kanawha one day to hunt deer; on their return to camp some Indians had approached to view our encampment and had concealed themselves in the weeds of the top of the bank at the mouth of the Kanawha; and as Gilmore came along they killed him on [the] bank Capt. Arbuckle and myself were standing on the point of the opposite bank when the gun fired and wondered what any one was doing there firing contrary to orders; when we Saw Hamilton run down the bank and call out that Gilmore was killed. Gilmore was one of the company of Capt. John Hall from that part of the country now called Rockbridge county [The captain was] a relation of Gilmores and whose familey wer chiefly cut off by the Indians in 1763[20] when Greenbriar was cut off. Halls men instantly jumped in to a canoe and went to the relief of Hamilton brought the corpse of Gilmore down the bank scalped and covered with blood, he was put into canoe and as the[y] passed the River I observed to Capt. Arbuckle the[y] would be for killing the hostages as soon as the canoe would land but he supposed the[y] would not commit so great an out rage on the innocent who were not accessary to Gilmore's murder.

but the canoe was scarsely landed in the creek when the cry was raised let us kill the Indians in the fort and every man with his gun in his hand came up the bank pale as death with rage. Capt. Hall was at their head. Captain Arbuckle and myself met them endeavoring to disuade them from so unjustifyable an action but they cocked their guns threatened us with instant death if we did not desist and rushed into the fort.

On the preceeding day Corn Stalk's son had come from the nation to see his father and to know if he

---

[20] The Gilmore family lived on Carr's Creek in Augusta (later Rockbridge) County. On Oct. 10, 1759, this settlement was attacked by a band of Shawnee, headed by Cornstalk, who massacred John Gilmore and his wife and son Thomas, and the wife of William Gilmore; after killing Thomas they captured his wife and three children. The marauders were pursued and the prisoners retaken. The same settlement was again raided in 1763, in which some of the Gilmore connection suffered, as well as their neighbors the Hamiltons.—ED.

was alive; when he came to the River his father was that instant delineating a map of the country and waters between the Shawanee town and the Mississippi at our request with Chalk upon the floor. he instantly knew the voice of his son, went out and answered him, when the young fellow crossed over and they embraced each other in the most tender and affectionate manner. The next day the Interpreter's wife who had been a prisoner with the Indians and had recently left them, hearing the uproar and seeing the men coming to kill the Indians for whom she seemed to have an affection, run to their cabin informed them the people were cumming to kill them and that the[y] said the Indians that killed Gilmore came with Elinipsico the day before. he utterly denied it declared he knew nothing of them, and trembled exceedingly; his father incouraged him told him not to be afraid, for the great Spirit above had sent him there to be killed. the men advanced to the door, the Corn Stalk arose and met them, seven or eight bullets were fired into him, and his son was shot dead as he sat upon a stool. Redhawk made an attempt to go up the chimney but was shot down, the other Indian was shamefully mangled. I grieved to see him so long a dying. Thus died the great Cornstalk warrior who from personal appearance and many brave acts was undoubtedly a Hero. I have no doubt if he had been spared but he would have been friendly to the Americans for nothing could have induced him to make the visit to the garison at that critical time, but to communicate the temper and disposition of the Indians, and their design of taking part with the British. on the day

Monument to Cornstalk

At Point Pleasant, W. Va. From a recent photograph

MURDER OF CORNSTALK 161

he was killed we held a council in which he was present; his countenance was dejected and he made a Speech all of which seemed to indicate an honest and manly disposition. he acknowledged that he expected himself and his party would have to run with the stream, for all the Indians or those Indians on the lakes and to the north were joinin the British.[21]

* * * * * * * *

When he made his speech in council with us he seemed impressed with an awful presentment of his aproaching fate for he repeatedly said, when I was a young man and went to war I thought that might be the last time, and I would return no more but now I am here among you and you may kill me if you please, I can die but once and its all one to me now or at another time. this sentiment concluded every period

---

[21] The British reports of the murder of Cornstalk are as follows:

Jan. 15, 1778, Hamilton, then at Detroit, wrote to General Carleton: "Different parties of Indians have related that a Sergeant from that place [Fort Pitt] having been killed by some Shawanese, his officer required of the Commandant to deliver up The Cornstalk (a Shawanese Chief at that time at Fort Pitt being in the Virginia Interest) and some of his followers, this was refused, on which the Cornstalk and his people were seized on by force, taken out of the Fort and put to Death, that the Commandant dissatisfied with this act of violence had gone off to Philadelphia."—*Mich. Pion. & Hist. Colls.*, ix, p. 481.

Jan. 31, 1778, Joseph Galloway wrote from Philadelphia: "I have received an Account from Fort Pitt that Col. Hand had called to a Treaty the Great Corn Stalk an Indian Chief with other Sachems of the Delaware and Shawanese Tribes, and while in Treaty a Number of the Frontier People, as is supposed under the Direction of Hand, rush'd in upon them and put them to Death."—Dartmouth MSS., reproduced in B. J. Stevens, *Facsimiles of Manuscripts in European Archives relating to America*, no. 2078, p. 11.—ED.

of his Speech he was killed one hour after. A few days afterwards General Hand arrived but had no troops and we were dismissed and returned home Shortly before Christmass.[22]

Not long after we left the garison a small party apeared in sight of the fort, Lieutenant More[23] was ordered with a party to pursue them, they had come to retaliate the murder of Cornstalk. Moore had not advanced ¼ of a mile when he fell into an ambuscade and was killed with 1 or 2 of his men.

[Deposition on the murder. 3NN80—Transcript.]

FORT RANDOLPH, BOTTETOURT COTY., 10 Novr. 1777

The deposition of Capt. John Anderson, W^m. Ward, & Richard Thomas,[24] being first sworn on the Holy

---

[22] Nov. 19, 1777, General Hand issued orders to Col. George Skillern, commanding the Botetourt militia, and Colonel Dickinson, commanding the Augusta militia, with their respective troops assembled there, to return home as the expedition is relinquished; Draper MSS., 3NN68.—ED.

[23] There were at this time several families of Moores in southwestern Virginia; Andrew and William Moore of Rockbridge County; James Moore, founder of Abb's Valley settlement; William Moore on Clinch, who was a lieutenant in the Island Flats battle of 1776. All of these men were known to have been living after 1777. The Moore here mentioned was probably related to one of these families.—ED.

[24] John Anderson was one of the first settlers of Augusta County, being a magistrate there as early as 1745. His home was on Middle River, not far from Staunton. Probably this deponent was a son or nephew of the first settler.

William Ward was the eldest son of Capt. James Ward, noted in *Dunmore's War*, p. 276, note 93, and a nephew of Capt. Matthew Arbuckle. He afterwards emigrated to Kentucky and thence to Ohio, becoming in 1806 founder of the town of Urbana, and grandfather of John Quincy Adams Ward, the American sculptor.

A Revolutionary pensioner named Richard Thomas was living in Kentucky as late as 1840.—ED.

MURDER OF CORNSTALK   163

Evangelists, deposeth & saith: That they were present when Rob{{t}}. Gilmore was brought over the Kanhawa River killed & scalped; on which a n°. of armed men appeared to be coming into the garrison in a riotous manner, on which said deponents suspected that they were determined to kill the Indians in custody in said garrison; & further say, that Capt. Mathew Arbuckle told them, that they should not be killed, as they were his prisoners, & it appeared to them that it was not in his power to stop their supposed intentions. And further say, that they proceeded into the garrison, & a number of guns was shortly fired, on which the Indians were all killed, being four in number, as they afterwards understood—& further saith not.

J{{n}}°. ANDERSON,
W{{m}}. WARD
RICH{{d}}. THOMAS.

Sworn before me, the date above said.

GEO. SKILRON

I do certify that I know the above deposition to be just & true.

SAM{{l}}. SMYTH, Surg{{n}}.

[Stanza of a popular ballad related to Dr. Draper by Capt. James Ward of Kentucky.[25]   9BB54.]

King Cornstalk, the Shawnee's boast
Old Yie, by whom much blood we've lost,
The Red Hawk and Elinipsico
Lie dead beside the Ohio.

---

[25] Capt. James Ward, second son of the one of that name killed at the Battle of Point Pleasant, was born in Staunton, Sept. 19, 1763. When a boy of six years his parents removed to the Greenbriar country, where he continued to reside after his father's death in 1774. In 1780 he and his brothers made

NEWS FROM THE DELAWARES

[Rev. David Zeisberger to General Hand. 3NN81-84—Transcript.]

COOKING,[26] Nov[r]. 16, 1777.

D[r]. SIR—As Capt. White Eyes is going to the fort, I will not omit to acquaint you how matters are here now with us. Since my last we have been quiet, & not any warriors have passed by here except a small party of Mohickons & now 8 days ago, 14 Wyandotts & two white men with them who came from Detroit; & as much as we know went to Weelunk [Wheeling], John Montour being in their company.

Some time ago, as we heard, 50 Frenchmen came over the Lake to Cuyahoga, & gave the Delawares and Muncys[27] who live there the tomahawk, & desired

---

an exploring tour to Kentucky, whither they removed in 1785 and settled near Washington in Mason County. Captain Ward went out in Logan's expedition against the Indians in 1786; again with Edwards in 1791; and on Kenton's Paint Creek expedition of 1793, when the only person killed was John Ward, brother of the original Captain Ward, who had been captured when three years of age and reared among the Indians. In 1794 James Ward was in Wayne's campaign. He later became a Presbyterian elder in the Washington church, under Rev. Robert Wilson. In 1845 Dr. Draper visited Captain Ward at his Kentucky home, and had a prolonged interview with him. Ward died Feb. 27th of the next year.—ED.

[26] A mistranscription of the Indian term for Coshocton, which the German Moravians spelled in several different forms. It was the chief town of the Delawares during the Revolutionary period. See *Rev. Upper Ohio*, p. 46, note 73.—ED.

[27] The early Indian history of Cuyahoga River is obscure. Some of the Six Nations seem to have removed thither at an early date, and probably occupied the village denominated on Evans's and Hutchins's maps as "Cuyahoga Town." It would seem likewise to have been the site of an Ottawa village and a French trading house; and may have been the "Rivière Blanche," so frequently mentioned in the reports of the

NEWS FROM DELAWARES 165

them to go with them to Ligonier.[28] Capt. Pipe not being at home, they consented, & 40 men went with the French, but Pipe met them on the road, reproved the French for deceiving his people in his absence, & told them that they were only servants, & had no power to hand the tomahawk to them: Nobody could force him neither to take it—whereupon the greater part of the Indians turned back.

French officials, 1742-53. See Charles A. Hanna, *Wilderness Trail* (New York, 1911), i, pp. 315-339. George Croghan had a trading house in the vicinity in 1747, which seems to have been abandoned by 1750 for one on the Muskingum. During the French and Indian War there was an entire readjustment of Indian villages, but the Cuyahoga town is still shown on later maps. It would seem, however, to have been the abode of Delawares rather than of Mingo, and the inference from this letter is that it was the headquarters of Captain Pipe before his removal in 1778 to the Sandusky region. The Indians reported in the autumn of 1777 that the British were building a storehouse at Cuyahoga to supply the neighboring Indians with goods; but during the later years of the Revolution the region seems to have virtually been deserted. In the late autumn of 1782, Maj. Isaac Craig was ordered out from Fort Pitt on a reconnoissance to the mouth of the Cuyahoga, to discover if the British were there building a post. He reported on his return that there was no sign of occupancy—*Washington Irving Correspondence*, pp. 137-139; Draper MSS., 1NN111, 4S10. In 1786 the Moravian Indians lived for a short time at the old Ottawa village, on the east side of the stream, just north of Tinker's Creek, in Independence township; but the following spring they removed to Sandusky Bay. The preceding year, by the Treaty of Fort McIntosh, the Cuyahoga had been made the dividing line between white and Indian territory. With the exception of an occasional wandering trader, this locality appears to have been unvisited thereafter until the settlement (in 1796) of the Western Reserve.—ED.

[28] Fort Ligonier was built during Forbes's campaign in 1758, on the site of a well-known Indian town, probably of Shawnee origin, on Loyalhanna Creek, just west of Laurel Hill. While the advance of the army was encamped there, the enemy attacked them, after having inflicted (Sept. 14, 1758) a severe

Capt. John Killbuck & Pipe are gone to Detroit—upon what business Capt. White Eyes can tell you better. They did not desire me to write for them, so I suppose they did not approve of what you proposed to them. The Shawanese—Cornstalk's people, perhaps, will move from their place & come to Cuchachunk this winter. They lately sent messengers who consulted with the chiefs here about that matter; & as no messengers from hence are on their way thither, we shall soon hear what they are resolved to do.

Of the Mingoes we have heard nothing since the

---

defeat upon Grant's skirmish line that had penetrated to the neighborhood of Fort Duquesne. The attack upon Ligonier was repulsed, and was the last battle between French and British in this section. A garrison was maintained at this point until after Pontiac's War, when Fort Ligonier was besieged, and relieved with much difficulty. About 1765 the permanent garrison was withdrawn, and in 1766 Capt. Harry Gordon reported that the fort was much shattered and rotting away. He also mentions some inhabitants clustered about the fort. More would come, he says, if right of possession was secured—Hanna, *Wilderness Trail,* ii, p. 40. In 1769 a land-office was opened at Ligonier and settlers flocked in rapidly. The land on which the fort stood was patented to Gen. Arthur St. Clair. The ravages of the Revolution did not reach the Ligonier Valley until the summer of 1777, when Col. Archibald Lochry set about establishing a stockade fort at Ligonier, probably on the site of the former British fort. This was officially known as Fort Preservation, but ordinarily received the well-known appellation of Fort Ligonier. From this date until the close of the Revolution, Ligonier Valley was constantly exposed to the Indian ravages. Nov. 7, 1777, it was reported that all of the settlers had fled to a distance forty-two miles from Ligonier—*Frontier Forts,* ii, p. 245. The party to whom allusion is made in this letter is doubtless the one that attacked Fort Wallace; see *ante.* Palmer's Fort, in Ligonier Valley, was likewise attacked and eleven persons killed and scalped, among whom was Ensign Woods; *Penna. Archives,* v, p. 741.—ED.

Half King[29] was here; & it seems as if they were tired of going to war, or rather frightened. We heard that after their last ret^n. they went over the Lake & asked the Wyandott Chief's counsel & advice what they should do, because the Virginians would soon be upon them. The Wyandot Chief answered them, that they had begun the war, & had always encouraged others to go to war; they had now brought it to pass what they always had wished for; he therefore could give them no other advice than to be strong & fight as men.

Capt. White Eyes intends to stay at the fort two or three days, & wish you would let him return again as soon as possible, for none of the Counsellors are at home to do business, if any thing should happen; but if occasion should require to detain him longer, please to let the people here know of it that they may not be uneasy about him, for some apprehend because the Cornstalk is taken fast at the Kanhawa, White Eyes may be served so too: If he therefore stays out above the time he has appointed them, they will surely think so. The letter Genl. Hand had sent to me last, the messenger lost. I suppose you will by this time have some news from before—if you can favor me with any you will much oblige Sir, Your Hbl^e. Servt.

D. ZEISBERGER

---

[29] In his *Narrative*, pp. 160, 161, Heckewelder describes a visit of Half King (for whom see *Rev. Upper Ohio*, p. 91, note 14) to the Delaware towns in August, 1777. The Wyandot having sent to the Delawares the war-belt, which the latter had refused, next dispatched thither their head-chief and a deputation of 200 warriors. The Delawares, especially the Christian Moravian Indians, were much alarmed at their approach; but all ended well, for the Half King made a covenant with the Christian Indians and acknowledged their

NEWS OF CORNSTALK'S MURDER
REACHES VIRGINIA

[Col. William Preston to Col. William Fleming. 2ZZ43—
A. L. S.]

SMITHFIELD Decr 2^d 1777

DEAR SIR—Last Night I rec'd your most obliging Favour of the 10th of November, for which I thank you. The News it confirms is glorious, and Interesting to every Friend to the American Cause; and I have the greatest hopes that it will have a happy Effect in our Favour, by striking a Damp to our Enemies and encouraging our Friends both in America and Europe. God Grant that a proper and prudent use may be made of this signal success; & that the Americans may not relax in their Duty by "crying Peace when there is no Peace;" and thereby loosing sight of the great Object they have in View, in hopes that no further Efforts will be made by our Enemies. I wish the dividing Counties here, the rating whiskey &c. in Pennsylvania, may not too much engross the Attention of the Legislatures of the States, while proper Provision to cloathe and recruit the Army & lessen the Quantity of Currency in Circulation are neglected. I only mention these Doubts to my Friend, as I am not certain they have any real Foundation.

Parson Smith[30] came here last night, and Informs that the Augusta Troops &c. are on their way from the

---

chiefs as "Fathers". He likewise agreed to leave the Delawares in peace, and permit them to retain their much-prized neutrality.—ED.

[30] Rev. Adam Smyth (so he wrote the name) was a native of Ireland, and in 1772 served for five months as curate of the Augusta parish at Staunton. Resigning from his cure, he was the following year appointed rector of Botetourt par-

Point, after killing the Cornstalk and some other Shawnesse Chiefs in cold Blood. This Account he had by a Letter from his Friend at that Place. I am apprehensive this Conduct will be followed by very bad consequences to the Frontiers, by engaging us in a war with that Revengful & Warlike Nation and their Allies.

This County affords no News worth your Notice, only that Capt. Burke[31] & his whole Company except four or five & near forty of my Neighbours have Positively refused the Oath of Allegiance to the States. I have laboured with them untill I am wearied out and to no Purpose; and next week I intend to order them to be disarmed, having given them this week to come in and take the Oath, and I have the greatest reason to believe that it will be attended with much Trouble and perhaps Resistance. The Ringleaders, such as Price, Bane, Shull & the Heavins, dont realize the Punishment as the Law now Stands; and I am convinced that they, and all such will stand out untill their Property or Persons can be more Affected than what the Law subjects them to. The present Punishment

---

ish. But little is known of his history. He appears to have been an American sympathizer during the Revolution, and in 1781 applied for leave for a visit to Ireland. In 1782 he was again in his parish, where the Virginia assembly ordered an accounting of the tithes due him before the disestablishment of the church in that state. He was living as late as 1792. His youngest son was Gen. Alexander Smyth, prominent in early nineteenth-century Virginia.—ED.

[31] Capt. Thomas Burk had for some years been a militia officer; see his letter in *Dunmore's War*, p. 398. In 1775 he accepted a commission from the Virginia committee of safety, and served until Feb. 18, 1778, when he tendered his resignation; see letter, *post*.—ED.

is really a matter of Divirsion to them. They bring no Suits, they never Elect, they dont attend Court; they can dispose of their arms and they dont want to purchase Land; by these means they entirely evade the force of a Law, to which I sincerely wish some amendments could be made to stop this growing Evil.[32] They speak with Caution therefore do not come within the Law for punishing certain Offences. In short they do as they Please.[33]

I would beg the Favour of you to lay the Enclosed stat[ement] before Mr Jefferson and any other of the first Lawyers & take their Opinion in writing for which pray pay their Charge & I will repay you with Thankfullness. You will readily Judge that it relates to Col Pattons Will.[34] I am my D^r S^r your Sincere Wellwisher & most Obed^t Servt.

W^m. PRESTON

---

[32] Colonel Preston is here referring to the law passed in May, 1777, entitled, "An act to oblige the free male inhabitants of this state above a certain age [sixteen] to give assurance of Allegiance to the same, and for other purposes." This provided for the taking of an oath renouncing all allegiance to the king of Great Britain, and that the county lieutenant shall disarm recusants. It further provided that all refusing the oath shall "be incapable of holding any office in this state, serving on juries, suing for any debts, electing or being elected, or buying lands, tenements or hereditaments"; Hening, *Statutes*, ix, pp. 281-283.—ED.

[33] The act referred to was passed at the October session of 1776, and provided a fine of £20,000 and an imprisonment of five years for openly maintaining and defending the authority of the king or parliament of Great Britain. *Ibid*, pp. 170, 171.—ED.

[34] Col. James Patton was one of the earliest settlers of the Valley of Virginia. He was a Scotch-Irishman who had served in the royal navy, and later owned a passenger vessel trading to America. In connection with Benjamin Borden, his father-in-law, he obtained a large grant for land west of

DIFFICULTIES 171

Perhaps it would be Possible to get two or three Lawyers together & get their Opinion, all Expense shall be paid as I am very anxious in this matter.
Col. Wm. Fleming p`r` Fav`r` of Cap`t` Cloyd.

HAND AT FORT RANDOLPH

[Gen. Edward Hand to Col. William Fleming. 17J2—
Transcript.]

BOTTETOURT COUNTY[35] Dec`r`. 3`d` 1777.

SIR: I take this opportunity of thanking you for your readiness in granting me the assistance I requested of you, & am extremely sorry that the mutual exertions of your county & Augusta were so badly seconded as to put it out of my power to carry my designs into execution for the benefit of the distressed frontiers; but hope that the rapid successes of the American arms to the Northward will do more for us than we can do for ourselves. Should that unhappily not be the case, I have every reason to expect that you

---

the Blue Ridge, and after 1738 was busily employed bringing out families for its settlement. He was a Presbyterian, and largely instrumental in founding Tinkling Spring Church, of which Rev. John Craig was pastor. In 1742 he qualified as colonel of the county militia, and in 1745 as member of the county court. Later he was county lieutenant, and in the early years of the French and Indian War was entrusted with the defense of the vast frontiers of Augusta County. In 1755, while Patton was on a tour of the Western country, he stopped at Draper's Meadows and was killed during the massacre at that place. He is said to have cut down two Indians with a broadsword, before he was himself shot and killed from without the house. His will was admitted to probate at Staunton in November, 1755. His nephew, Col. William Preston, was its chief executor.—ED.

[35] The fort at the mouth of the Great Kanawha was at this time within the limits of Botetourt County.—ED.

will on a future occasion, show the same readiness to assist your neighbours.

I ordered your troops under Col. Skilron to march back from Fort Randolph, and to be discharged on their return. Their number fell short of your orders, but beg that this circumstance may not exclude Major Poag from his appointment; his readiness to serve in any capacity merits that mark of respect. I am, Sir, with respect, Your obed^t. hble serv^t.

EDW^d. HAND.

Col. W^m. Fleming, Co. Lieut. of Bottetourt.

INDIANS OF THE ALLEGHENY

[Col. John Gibson to Gen. George Washington. 15S114— Transcript.]

FORT PITT. DEC^r. 5th, 1777:

Gen. Hand has gone down the Ohio to regulate the garrisons in that quarter; Since he left this place (Nov. 10th) Nothing Material has happened. Simon Girty,[36] a Messenger dispatched by General Hand to

---

[36] In view of his later history, the employment of Simon Girty by the military authorities at Pittsburgh at this period, is interesting. No doubt he was a good spy and ranger. As such he was employed by Dunmore—see *Dunmore's War*, p. 152, note 4; and again by Wood in 1775—*Rev. Upper Ohio*, pp. 28, 43. He was interpreter in 1775 at Fort Pitt (*Ibid*, p. 67), and in May, 1776, was made official interpreter for the Seneca, among whom he had been a captive in boyhood. This position he retained only for three months; but afterwards was employed in enlisting volunteers, and received a commission as second-lieutenant in the Continental army. His conduct in the summer of 1777 caused General Hand to suspect his loyalty, and for a short time he was under arrest. But after examination before a magistrate, he was acquitted and was sent by Hand on this important mission to the Seneca towns. For Girty's official report of this expedition, made to Col. George Morgan, commissioner for Indian affairs at

ALLEGHENY INDIANS 173

the Seneca towns on the heads of the Alleghany, returned here a few days ago. he informs us Gu-a-sho-ta,[37] a chief of them, had returned from war; that he had killed four people near Ligonier; that another party returned and brought in a white man and three scalps whilest he was in the towns; that they told him all the Nations, excepting White Eyes & a few Delawares, would strike us in the Spring; that they told him he Must go with them to Niagara;[38] that he made

---

Pittsburgh, see William M. Darlington, *Christopher Gist's Journals* (Pittsburgh, 1893), pp. 214-216.—ED.

[37] For a brief sketch of this chief see *Rev. Upper Ohio*, p. 38, note 65. This note is, we find, erroneous in regard to Guyashusta's attitude during the Revolution. In the first years, the chief, like the other Seneca, was in favor of neutrality. But after the council at Oswego (1777), he was pledged to the British and went on the Oriskany expedition. His relative, Governor Blacksnake, told Dr. Draper (4S64) that Guyashusta (Giasodo) was not on any other Revolutionary campaigns. This referred to the war on the New York frontier; whereas Guyashustá seems to have been instigated by the officers at Niagara to attack the Pennsylvania frontier. The raid which Girty reported was doubtless that against Wallace's Fort. Guyashusta also led the Hannastown raid in 1782, and throughout the Revolution terrorized the border.—ED.

[38] There is still much obscurity concerning conditions at Niagara during the Revolution. Frank H. Severance, secretary of the Buffalo Historical Society, has, however, made two important contributions to the subject in *Old Trails on the Niagara Frontier* (Buffalo, 1899), pp. 63-103; and Buffalo Historical Society *Publications*, ix, pp. 221-308. During the period covered by our volume, Col. Mason Bolton of the 34th Royal Artillery was commandant-in-chief. Niagara was the headquarters of the New York Loyalists, and thence parties issued to harry the New York frontier. The Pennsylvania frontier was likewise exposed to the Indian allies of the British. The Seneca made headquarters at Niagara, and in February, 1778, Col. John Butler of the Queen's Rangers wrote from that place: "The Indians of the Six Nations & those from the westward have exerted themselves in laying

his escape by going to hunt for his horse; he says the news of Burgoyne's Surrender had not reached there.[39] [Gibson then speaks of having sent Capt. Sullivan[40] down the Country for clothing for the 13th Virginia regiment, & hopes Gen[l] Washington will so direct as to enable him to return with a supply as soon as possible.]

[JOHN GIBSON]

---

waste the Country most exposed to them from the east branch of the Susquehanna to the Kiskismenitas Creek upon the Ohio & from thence down to Kanhawa River an extent of many hundred miles is now nothing but an heap of ashes such of those miserable people as have escaped have taken refuge in small forts." Commandant Bolton wrote Dec. 14, 1777, that he had 2300 savages at Niagara, who had all received presents—*Mich. Pion. & Hist. Colls.*, xix, pp. 335, 342. Under these circumstances it seems remarkable that any settlements were maintained west of the Alleghany Mountains during the years of the Revolution.—ED.

[39] Girty declared (in report cited in *ante*, note 36) that the Seneca had not heard of Burgoyne's surrender, and would not believe his report of this event. When they reached Niagara they learned these tidings, for Colonel Bolton wrote (*Mich. Pion. & Hist. Colls.*, xix, p. 335): "The accounts of the unfortunate affair that happened to General Burgoyne's Army reached this place a considerable time before the Chiefs assembled here, which put it out of Colonel Butler's power to execute what was intended."—ED.

[40] As early as 1769, Capt. James Sullivan had settled on the west side of the Monongahela; and upon the enlistment of the West Augusta or 13th Virginia regiment (see *Rev. Upper Ohio*, p. 250, note 94) was chosen one of its captains. In 1779 he served at Fort McIntosh, and the next year emigrated to Kentucky, settling a station not far from Louisville. In Clark's campaign of 1780 he acted as master of horse, and was captain in the expedition of 1782 (Draper MSS., 36J4). He was one of the early trustees of the town of Louisville, and owned many lots therein; in 1783 the trustees met at his house. He was a large, powerful, and active man, and prominent in the new community. He died early in the nineteenth century near St. Louis, at the home of his son, John C. Sulli-

HAND REPORTS CORNSTALK'S MURDER

[Gen. Edward Hand to Maj. Samuel McDowell. 3NN67—
Transcript.]

CAMP NEAR KELLY'S[41] ON KANHAWA, Nov. [Dec.] 5, 1777

SIR—As I understand that a mare belonging to one of the Shawanese Indians lately murdered at Fort Randolph has been sold at vendue by the desire of the soldiers, & that the money she sold for is to be paid into your hands—I hereby request that you may remit it to Capt. Mathew Arbuckle for the benefit of the representative of the dece^d.

[EDWARD HAND]

[Gen. Edward Hand to Gov. Patrick Henry. 3NN69-71—
Transcript.]

STAUNTON, 9th Decr. 1777

SIR—When I wrote your Excellency from Fort Pitt in Nov^r., I promised myself the honor of addressing you from Fort Randolph before now, but as I found

---

van. Another of his sons was George Rogers Clark Sullivan.—ED.

[41] For the location of Kelly's, on the Kanawha, see *Dunmore's War*, p. 112, note 82. Walter Kelly emigrated from the Carolinas to the Greenbriar settlement in 1773, and against the protests of his friends made an advance settlement on the Kanawha in the autumn of that year. He was there killed by a marauding Indian party, early in 1774. The place was thereafter known as Kelly's. Soon after the Battle of Point Pleasant, Kelly's improvement was purchased by William Morris, likewise of Greenbriar, who soon removed his family thither. Morris was one of the notable men of Kanawha Valley history. He was at the Battle of Point Pleasant, where he was wounded. After settling at Kelly's he built a fort and had many a skirmish with the savages. In later life he was a member of the Virginia assembly for Kanawha County. The Morris family had many descendants and connections of note, among whom was Bishop Thomas A. Morris of the Methodist Episcopal church.—ED.

this the only rout by which I could return with propriety I deferred it until my arrival here.[42] Before I left Fort Pitt I received a letter from Capt. Arbuckle informing me that he had confined two Shawanese Indians, suspecting them to be spies, & that he expected a number of their chiefs in a short time & was determined to confine them also, until he had more particular instructions from me. On my way down, I rec^d. another letter from him, a copy of which is inclosed together with a return of the militia from Augusta & Botetourt, & the deposition of some people respecting the murder of four Shawanese Indians. On my arrival at Fort Randolph the 18th. ult^o., I was much concerned to hear that the Cornstalk, his son, the Red Hawk's son, & another Indian had been murdered by the militia, tho' in close confinement in the garrison, more especially as the Cornstalk appeared to be the most active of his nation to promote peace. I understand that Ensign Gilmore of the Botetourt militia & two others straggled over the Kanhawa to hunt; soon after they crossed the river they took different routs, & Gilmore was killed & scalped within a trifling distance of the fort. This so enraged the men, that a party immediately proceeded to the fort & mur-

---

[42] It is an interesting commentary on means of communication at this period, that the only practicable route from Fort Randolph to Fort Pitt was by way of Staunton. Probably General Hand followed the same route as the Augusta troops had taken going out; see *ante*, p. 150, note 14. Staunton was the county town for Augusta, and was settled by the Lewis family in 1732 at the Beverly mill-site. It was surveyed and platted in 1748, and incorporated in 1761. The origin of its name is uncertain; possibly it was intended to honor Dr. Edmond Staunton, an eminent English Presbyterian preacher of the seventeenth century.—ED.

MURDER OF CORNSTALK 177

dered the Indian prisoners, notwithstanding Captn. Arbuckle's endeavors to prevent it. Both Capt. Arbuckle & the field officers of the militia—indeed every officer at the Point, expressed great abhorrance of the deed, but unhappily none of the militia officers were at hand, & Capt. Arbuckle had not influence enough to prevent it. It would be vain for me to bring the perpetrators of this horrid act to justice at that time, therefore must comfort myself with giving your Exc^y. this detail, & informing you that the most active of the party are known to Col. Dickinson, Col^o. Skilron & many other officers.[43]

* * * The number of men now at the Point, including Capt. Arbuckle's & Capt. McKee's companies does not exceed 100, the strength of one company. I think they had best be consolidated, & supernumerary officers sent to recruit. Captn. Arbuckle will wait on you about the beginning of next month to settle some public accounts, & know your pleasure on this head.

I ordered 150 men from Yohogana County, & same number from Monongalia, to be stationed on the frontiers for their defence. I detained 100 men from the militia of Frederick, Berkley, Dunmore and Loudon Counties, to remain in Ohio, and to be joined by 50 men from that county.

[EDWARD HAND]

---

[43] April 13, 1778, Capt. James Hall was brought to trial in the Rockbridge County court for the "murder of the Cornstalk Indian, his son and two other chiefs of the Indians on the 10th of November last." Hall appeared and denied the charge. The trial adjourned until April 28, when no witness appearing against him, he was acquitted. Three other militia-

TEMPER OF WESTERN INDIANS

[Col. John Gibson to Gen. Edward Hand.   1U132—A. L. S.]

FORT PITT Dec[r] 10th 1777

DEAR SIR—A few days after you set of from this place for Kanhawa, James Kelly[44] and Tho[s]. Nicholson the Messengers, who were sent by you with Despatches to the Delawares returned they informed me that they went to a Small town of the Delawares on Beaver Creek,[45] where they were kindly received by the Indians, that on their Acquainting them with their Business, and desiring some of them to Accompany them, the Chief told them it would not be Safe for

---

men—Hugh Galbraith, Malcolm McCown, and William Rowan—were tried in like manner and acquitted for lack of witnesses. See "Rockbridge County Records," in *Virginia Historical Magazine*, xvii, pp. 324, 325.—ED.

[44] A family of Scotch-Irish Protestant Kellys lived in Lancaster County. Their founder was John, who emigrated to America before 1730, and became a well-known Indian trader. One son was Maj. John Kelly, who served in the Pennsylvania line of the Revolutionary army. There was likewise a son James, who may have been this messenger to the Delaware towns. He was born in 1749, married Elizabeth Forster, and was buried in the Derry churchyard in the present Dauphin County, Pa.—ED.

[45] There were several Indian towns on Beaver Creek and its branches. The most famous was Kuskuskies—probably a group of three or four contiguous towns, built originally by the Six Nations, but later occupied by the Delawares. These towns were near the forks of the Beaver and along the Mahoning, its western branch. Salt Lick town, near the present Niles, Ohio, was a well-known locality; but the town here noticed was probably the one known as Mahoning. Most of the Delawares had before this period removed to the Tuscarawas and Muskingum, but a small town seems to have been maintained at Mahoning, probably about the site of the present Newton Falls in Trumbull County, Ohio; this was on an important trail to the West. See A. B. Hulbert, "Indian Thoroughfares of Ohio," in Ohio Archæological and Historical Society *Publications*, viii, p. 270.—ED.

ENEMY INDIANS 179

them to proceed any further, as they might fall in with the Enemy Indians, he told them he would take the Messages himself and goe with them to Gyahoga, and from thence to Cooshachkung.[46] he Gave them a String of Wampum as a Token of their holding fast the Chain of friendship.

Simon Girty another Messenger who was also sent by you with Messages to the Seneca towns on the Heads of the Allegheney, Returned and Informed me, that he went to the towns without meeting any Indians, tho by the Marks of the Warriors on the Roads he could Discover they had Been at War, that on his arrival there he acquainted them with the Success of our Army to Northward and Asked them if they had not heard of it. they Replied they had not. he then told them they might depend on it for truth, and desired them to sit still as they would hear it in a few days from their own people. they then told him they looked upon him as a Spy, and that they would take him to Niagara they informed him that all the Western Nations had taken up the Tomhawk against the Americans Excepting White Eyes and a few Delawares and that they would be Ready to Strike in the Spring. he Learned that Seven parties were then actually out against our frontiers, that Guashota had Been twice at war against our Settlements, that he had killed four people near Ligonier, that the White

---

[46] This would be the natural order of the route from Mahoning, which was nearer Cuyahoga than Coshocton, and on the direct trail toward the former—probably to the town of Captain Pipe, mentioned *ante*, p. 165.—ED.

Mingoe[47] had also Been at War, that the flying Crow[48] Brought in a White Woman Daughter of Dudley Dougherty who was taken near Ligonier, whilst he was there and some scalps,[49] that All face the head Warrior[50] was out with a party of 25 five [sic] Men. that the Evening Before they were to set of[f] for Niagara he pretended to hunt his horse, and after going out he Returned in a Great hurry saying he saw a flock of Turkeys and snatched up his Gun and Came

---

[47] This chief is noted in *Rev. Upper Ohio*, p. 27, note 53. It is apparent from this document that he did not die before 1777. Governor Blacksnake stated to Dr. Draper (4S67) that he had no knowledge of the White Mingo having had part in the Revolution, and therefore supposed he must have died before this date. Blacksnake appears to have been well informed regarding operations against the New York frontier, but not of those ravages in Pennsylvania for which the Allegheny Seneca were responsible. The date of the death of White Mingo is uncertain. The map republished as frontispiece in *Rev. Upper Ohio*, seems to have been made from information secured on a trip down the Ohio in 1794. The "Mungo blanc" who gave that information was doubtless the White Mingo. One of that name is said to have died on the site of Fort Wayne in 1790; see Louise W. Murray, *Old Tioga Point* (Athens, Pa., 1908), p. 109.—ED.

[48] For this chief see *Rev. Upper Ohio*, passim. He was in attendance at the treaty of 1775.—ED.

[49] A contemporary journal written at Ligonier (see *ante*, p. 147, note 10) has this entry for Nov. 2: "About 3 miles from Richardsons [which was three from Ligonier] 2 men were killd & Scalp'd & a Woman missing. 24 of our Men turn'd out and bury'd Richardson." There was a Dougherty family captive at Niagara, apparently in 1780; but probably was not connected with the person here mentioned. See Severance's list of captives in *Buffalo Hist. Colls.*, ix, p. 250.—ED.

[50] This chief has not been identified. He may be the same as Hodowndaoga, head chief of the Conowango village. At the time of Brodhead's expedition (1779), this chief and his people abandoned their village on the site of Warren, Pa. Later he settled on the Catteraugus, where he lived to be an old man, dying early in the nineteenth century.—ED.

away. that in the night he came to another town on the River where he got a Canoe and Came by Water, that near the Kittanning Early in the Morning an Indian from the Shore haled him and asked him who he was, that he told him his name was a Chiefs name who he left in the towns, that the Indian told him he Lyed that he knew him to be Girty and desired him to come ashore, that on his Refusal he fired several shot at him.

He Girty says that he thinks, they will wait to hear from the Northward as they are guided by a Chief of the Senecas there, and that the Surrender of Burgoynes Army will have a Good Effect on them I am Dear Sir with Respect your most Obedient humble Servt.

J^{No}. GIBSON

To Brigadier Genl Hand

THE KENTUCKY SETTLEMENTS

[Col. John Bowman to Gen. Edward Hand. 3NN192-196—Transcript.]

HARRODSBURG, December 12th 1777

SIR—We received yours by M^r. John Haggin,[51] dated Fort Randolph, 19th. November, 1777. Which

---

[51] Capt. John Haggin was born in 1753 near Winchester, Va. In early life he removed to western Pennsylvania, where he married and served on Dunmore's campaign of 1774. He was one of the earliest settlers of Kentucky, coming out in the spring of 1775 with his wife's uncle, Col. John Hinkston. The next year he brought out his family and built a cabin on Hinkston's fork of Licking; but because of Indian hostilities he removed that summer to McClelland's Station, on the site of the modern Georgetown. Haggin was at McClelland's when George Rogers Clark arrived at Limestone (Maysville) with gunpowder for the Kentucky settlements, and was one

news gives great satisfaction to the poor Kentucky people, who have these twelve months past been confined to three forts, on which the Indians made several fruitless attempts.[52] They have left us almost without horses sufficient to supply the stations, as we are obliged to get all our provisions out of the woods.[53]

---

of the party who helped to carry it in to Harrodsburg. About that time (Jan., 1777), McClelland's Station was broken up, and the Haggins removed to Harrodsburg. There he had numerous adventures with Indians, was closely pursued, and at one time he was supposed for over two weeks to have been killed or captured. But later he walked into his cabin quite unconcerned, greeting his wife with, "How are you by this time, Nancy?" In May, 1777, Haggin was sent express to Fort Pitt, where it was understood that an Indian treaty was to be held. The Kentuckians had wished to have a representative at this affair to recover their stolen horses and obtain what reparation was possible. The treaty, as we have seen, did not take place, but Haggin would appear to have spent the summer in the neighborhood, and to have been, at the time of this letter, on his return to Harrodsburg. In 1778 he joined Clark's expedition for Kaskaskia, and the following year was in Bowman's campaign. In 1780 he settled Haggin's Station, not far from Harrodsburg, and there became a planter and landholder. His wife died June 15, 1821, and he March 1, 1825. For these dates our thanks are due to James B. Haggin of New York, a grandson of the Kentucky pioneer.—ED.

[52] On the situation in Kentucky see *ante*, p. 103, note 63; also *Rev. Upper Ohio*, p. 205, note 47, and p. 242, note 85. The three forts were Boonesborough, Harrodsburg, and St. Asaph (or Logan's) Station. All these were founded in 1775. Logan abandoned his station during 1776 and retreated to Harrodsburg. During March, 1777, he returned to his old location, near the present Standford, Ky., and rebuilt his fort, which he occupied with his own and a few other families. Twice during the summer of 1777 Logan had sought relief from the Holston settlements, for his beleaguered garrison. After September the raids of the savages appear to have been diverted to the Fort Pitt neighborhood, and the Kentuckians enjoyed a comparative immunity.—ED.

[53] James Ray, one of the Harrodsburg defenders, had one old horse left out of a drove of forty that he and his step-

KENTUCKY GARRISONS 183

Our corn the Indians have burned all they could find the past summer, as it was in cribs at different plantations some distance from the garrisons, & no horses to bring it in on. At this time we have not more than two months bread,—near 200 women & children;[54] not able to send them to the inhabitants; many of those families are left desolate, widows with small children destitute of necessary clothing.

Necessity has obliged many of our young men to go to the Monongohale for clothing (their former place of abode), intended to join their respective companies as soon as possible, as there will be a sufficient guard, I think proper to order some corn to this place for our support: we intend to keep possession and plant crops the ensuing spring, as we have no other place to expect relief from. If we are denied this request we must do without bread, till we can get it from what we intend to plant.

I find it difficult to keep the garrisons plenty in meat, & if we have no bread we must at any rate suffer. I am, Sir, with due respect, Your humb. Servt,

JOHN BOWMAN[55]

Genl. Hand, F^t. Pitt   Favored by Lieut. Linn.[56]

---

father Hugh McGary brought to Kentucky. In later life, Ray related that he would steal out from the Harrodsburg fort before daylight and hasten to the woods as hunter for the garrison, returning after dark with a horseload of game for food; Draper MSS., 4B118.—ED.

[54] A census taken May 1, 1777, reported the presence of 201 persons at Harrodsburg, about fifty at Boonesborough, and thirty at Logan's Station; *Ibid*, p. 125.—ED.

[55] For a sketch of this pioneer see *Rev. Upper Ohio*, p. 170, note 94.—ED.

[56] Lieut. Benjamin Linn was a younger brother of Col. William Linn. Being born in New Jersey in 1738, Benjamin

LOYALISTS AT FORT PITT

[Gen. Edward Hand to a committee of Congress. 3NN85-88—Transcript.]

FORT PITT, 21st. Decr. 1777.

GENTn.—Before the arrival of your favor of the 24th. Octr. I had gone from this place to Fort Randolph, from whence I did not return till yesterday, which prevented my complying with your order sooner.

The report of Col. George Morgan's being arrested here was well founded. The express (a militia officer) who brought the enclosed letter from Col. Zach: Morgan informed some of his acquaintance in town that the principal people here concerned in the conspiracy, were Col. George Morgan, Col. John

---

lived during early life in western Maryland. In 1769 he removed with his brother to the Monongahela and devoted most of his time to hunting. Before hostilities broke out he had lived much with the Indians. Early in 1776 he went out to Kentucky and formed part of the Harrodsburg garrison, aiding in removing the powder thither (Jan., 1777), and distinguishing himself for bravery in the attack of March 7, 1777. When the militia was organized for Kentucky County, in the spring of the same year, he was chosen lieutenant. In April he was, with one other companion, sent by George Rogers Clark to discover the situation at Kaskaskia, in the Illinois. Here he narrowly escaped detection as a spy, and at the instigation of an American friend, retired in haste. A contemporary letter indicates that this was not Linn's first visit to Illinois—"Kaskaskia Papers," in *Illinois Hist. Colls.*, v. p. 8. After Linn's return to Harrodsburg he married (July 9, 1777) Hannah Sovereigns. Linn did not go out with Clark on his Kaskaskia or Vincennes expeditions, but with several men joined him at the latter place in July, 1779. In 1782 he founded the first church in the Green River country, and the second Baptist church in Kentucky. Three years later he settled in Larue County, and became a Baptist minister of note. His death occurred at the residence of his daughter, Mrs. John Chisholm, at Huntsville, Ala., Dec. 23, 1814.—ED.

LOYALISTS 185

Campbell, Capt. Alex^r. McKee, & Simon Girty—& that the reason they were not pointed out in the letter was, that I was myself suspected. From this information I judged it prudent to secure these persons to prevent their escaping the punishment they deserved, if guilty, & to repair myself to where Col. Zack: Morgan was, to sift the affair to the bottom. Col°. Campbell before he had learned my intention of arresting him, waited on me & desired permission to accompany me, which I assented to; & told Col. Geo: Morgan he might have the same liberty, which he declined, being then, he said, very busy—& remained a prisoner in his own house. Capt. McKee was sent for to his farm house & confined in the same place; & Simon Girty to the common guard-house. I was present at the examination of the greatest number of the prisoners, & heard from the Magistrates who examined the whole, that no more than one man mentioned Col. Morgan's name; his expression was, that he allowed him to be of their party; & some few of them mentioned Girty's name—but none of them either Col. Campbell's or Capt. McKee's. For this reason on my return I took off Col. Morgan's arrest. Simon Girty was examined before a civil magistrate & acquitted; & Capt. McKee I put on a new parole, after obtaining the old one from the Cot^y. Co't.:[57] His parole I have en-

---

[57] "Minute Book of the Virginia Court held for Yohogania County," published in Carnegie Museum *Annals*, ii, p. 106, contains the following entry under date of Sept. 23, 1777: "A letter from General Hand addressed to Col. Campbell [re]questing that Capt. Alexander McKee's Parole given to the Committee of West Augusta be given up to him, the said General Hand, in order to enable him to put Capt. McKee

closed to the Board of War & wait the direction of Congress as to his future residence.

The remarks made in the enclosed letter by Capt. Arbuckle on McKee's conduct, tho' coming (in my opinion) from a bad author, knowing her to have an implacable hatred to the woman who lived with McKee, may yet have some weight with Congress. The same person[58] was at Fort Randolph when I left it the 21st. ultimo—she assured me that McKee had written letters to Detroit. I mention these circumstances to your Honb^{le}. Committee, as I think them applicable to the present subject, & by that you may also communicate them to Congress.

Col. George Morgan left this place in a few days after my first arrival here, & did not return until about the 25th. of July—he staid until the beginning of October, since when he has been absent. I recollect that the day after he arrived here in July, he told me he would cross the river to talk with the Indians then waiting to see him, & probably not return that night. As I had confined the day or two before two Indians, I judged it unsafe, and advised him against it; but he still persisted—early next morning I understood he lay at Capt. McKee's; on his return, told him what I had heard—he said it was so, & that he had a conference with the Shawanese Indians; who was his inter-

---

on a New Parole, as he finds it necessary to remove said Alexander McKee. Ordered that the said Parole be given up to General Hand and that he deposit a Copy of the New Parole to be taken from the said Capt. McKee in lieu thereof, Certified by the said General Hand."—ED.

[58] Without doubt a reference to the **Grenadier Squaw**, see *ante,* p. 26, note 57.—ED.

preter I don't know, certain it is, he can't discourse in that or any other Indian language. Except this part of his conduct may be found exceptionable, I must declare in justice to him that every proceeding of his that came to my knowledge, either as Indian Agent or Com^y. appeared to me to be that of a zealous & faithful servant to the United States. I should have made early mention of his arrest, but as it was on a groundless assertion, I wished to have it buried in oblivion. I am, gent^n., with much respect Y^r. most obed^t. hb^{le}. serv^t.

EDW^d. HAND

To The Honb^{le} Rich^d. Henry Lee, Rich^d. Law, and Danl. Roberdeau, Esq^{rs}.[59]

---

[59] Oct. 22, 1777, Congress having heard that Col. George Morgan was unfriendly to the American cause, appointed a committee composed of the three men here mentioned to investigate the report—*Journals of Congress* (new ed.), ix, p. 831. In November following, the case was placed in the hands of the commissioners for the Western frontier, who on April 7, 1778, fully acquitted Morgan and restored to him all his honors, offices, etc. The letter here published was Hand's reply to the inquiry of the first committee.

Richard Henry Lee (1732-94) was one of the most prominent of the Virginia patriots, a member of the Continental Congress from its inception, president thereof in 1784, and the first senator from his state.

Richard Law (1733-1806) was a Connecticut patriot, son of a colonial governor, a graduate of Yale, and long a member of the Continental Congress. He was a lawyer of repute, chief justice of his state, and after 1789 the federal judge for his district.

Daniel Roberdeau (1727-95) was a Philadelphia merchant, and was of great service to the Revolutionary cause.—ED.

ALLEGHENY INDIANS AT WAR

[Gen. Edward Hand to Col. George Morgan. 3NN89— Transcript.]

FORT PITT, 24th. Decr. 1777

D^r. SIR—As I communicated your first relation of Genl. Burgoyne's defeat to the Delawares, & as the last is no more than a repetition, I don't think it necessary to repeat the expense. Indeed I don't think it advisable to send any person among them at present, not knowing what effect the death of Cornstalk, who, with his son, the Red Hawk's son, & another Indian, being prisoners, were [killed] at Kanhawa the 10th. ult^o. Kayashuta, the White Mingo, All-Face, the Flying Crow, &c have been lately at war.

EDW^d. HAND

Col. Geo: Morgan

HAND RETURNS TO FORT PITT

[Gen. Edward Hand to Jasper Yeates. MS. in New York Public Library; Hand Papers—A. L. S.]

FORT PITT 24th. Decr. 1777

D^r. YEATES—Your fav^{rs}. of the 23^d. & 31st. Octr. 1777 I have rec^d. and thank you heartily for the good news you Communicate, & am More happy that the domestic Acc^{ts}. you are likely to give me next will be still better.

hope the Political [situation] will also mend—Jessy can give you the Particulars of Our late Ramble, & of the Murder of Cornstalk, his son, & two other Shawanese Indians at Fort Randolph. if we had anything to expect from that Nation it is now Vanished. the Senecas have been often at war this fall. Bedford & Westmoreland have been the Scenes of Action.

I am so heartily tired of this place that I have petitioned Congress to be recal'd. hope it may be Granted me.

* * * * * * * *

Farewell D^r. Yeates y^r. Affectionate Kinsm[a]n
E_{DW}^d: H_{AND}
Jasper Yeates Esqr.
Kayashutas the White Mingo, Allface, & all the Seneca Chiefs have been repeatedly at War

---

[Gen. Edward Hand to the Secretary of War. 3NN89-94—
Transcript.]

F_{ORT} P_{ITT}, 24th. Decr. 1777

S_{IR}—When I wrote you last, I acquainted you of my intention of visiting Fort Randolph. You will find by the enclosed letters from Capt. Arbuckle that before my arrival there he had confined some Shawanese Indians, & his reasons for so doing. On the 10th. ult°., the day I left this post to go to Kanawha, three men, one of them an ensign of the Bottetourt Militia, straggled over the Kanawha to hunt. The Ensign was killed & scalped within a small distance of the fort, which exasperated the militia to such a degree that a party of them rushed into the fort, & put the Cornstalk, his son, the Red Hawk's son, & another Indian to death, notwithstanding Capt. Arbuckle's endeavors to prevent it. From this event we have little reason to expect a reconciliation with the Shawanese, except fear operates on them; for if we had any friends among them, those unfortunate wretches were so. Though from information brought me from the Seneca country, which Lt. Col. Gibson has already

communicated to you, we have little reason to expect that will be the case. * * *
Col. W^m. Crawford has arrived.[60] I hope his activity and influence will have a very good effect. If Major John Stephenson[61] could have any appointment worth his acceptance, I think he also would be a valu-

---

[60] For a biographical sketch of Col. William Crawford see *Dunmore's War*, p. 103, note 48; his early Revolutionary service is sketched in *Rev. Upper Ohio*, p. 250, note 94. After joining the Continental army in August, 1777, Crawford served with efficiency, commanding a detachment of scouts and skirmishing with the British under Howe. November 20, Congress resolved "that General Washington be requested to send Col. William Crawford to Pittsburg to take command under Brigadier General Hand of the Continental troops and militia of the Western department." In this way Crawford lost his place and rank in the Continental line, and it was never restored to him. He seems to have spent part of the winter of 1777-78 at his own home on the Youghiogheny. In March and April he was present at Yohogania County court, acting as magistrate and commissioner to lay out prison bounds. His subsequent career will be outlined in later documents in this volume.—ED.

[61] Maj. John Stephenson was a half-brother of Col. William Crawford, and was born in Virginia about 1737. He was out in the French and Indian War, and about 1768 removed to the West, settling on Jacob's Creek, in Fayette County. There in 1770 he was visited by Washington, who was then returning from viewing Western lands. In 1774 Stephenson commanded a company under Dunmore, and was active on the Virginia side during the troubles between that state and Pennsylvania. In 1775 Stephenson enlisted a company for the colonial cause, and joined Col. Peter Muhlenberg as captain in the 8th Virginia; this regiment saw service at Charleston and Savannah. In the summer of 1777 Stephenson contracted disease, and returned home that autumn. He did not again enter the Continental army, but served as a volunteer on Hand's campaign (1778), and that of McIntosh (1778-79). About 1790 he removed to Kentucky, where he lived and died on the South fork of the Licking, leaving no children. He was a large, active man, brave, kind, and popular. For Samuel Murphy's reminiscences of Stephenson, with whom he lived, see Draper MSS., 3S1-10, 5S1-9.—ED.

able acquisition. I wish much to be permitted to lay my proceedings here before Congress. I assure you that I have fully exerted my poor abilities to accomplish the end for whch I was ordered here, yet am sorry to say that little advantage has arisen from it; & unless some other measures can be fallen on, I have little reason to promise myself better success for the time to come.

I think that as it is now winter, & Col. Crawford present, my absence for some time would not be attended with inconvenience. If Congress have no particular objection, would esteem it as a most singular indulgence to be recalled & suffered to join the grand army, with them to share the honors & fatigues of the field. Indeed, unless our affairs will admit of the assistance of a regular force, I had rather resign my office than continue here in command of militia.

Capt. Willing[62] had arrived here a few days before my return from Fort Randolph. I have in the best

---

[62] Capt. James Willing, youngest son of Charles and his wife Anne Shippen Willing, was born in Philadelphia Feb. 9, 1751. The Willing family were prominent in colonial affairs, and James's oldest brother, Thomas, was a partner of Robert Morris, and aided in financing the new nation. James removed in 1774 to Natchez, where he dissipated his patrimony. In 1777 he returned to Philadelphia, and received from Congress a commission as captain in the navy, with permission to proceed to the Mississippi River to secure the neutrality of the inhabitants along its banks and to bring back provisions to the states. He enlisted a company for this purpose (see roll in *Penna. Archives*, 2nd series, xv, p. 658), and in an armed boat christened "Rattletrap" left Pittsburgh Jan. 10, 1778. Arrived at Natchez he succeeded in securing a pledge of neutrality from the chief inhabitants (see Almon's *Remembrancer*, vi, p. 343), but was accused of having in a wanton manner pillaged and inflicted damages on their property. Having proceeded to New Orleans, Willing captured a small

manner I could supplied him with such things as he wanted, but am afraid the river will be shut up before he gets away. * * *

Ed^w. Hand

To Rh^d. Peters, Sec. of B^d. of War

[Gen. Edward Hand to Jasper Yeates. MS. in New York Public Library; Hand Papers—A. L. S.]

Fort Pitt 27th. Decr. 1777

Dear Yeates—Just as the Major [Jasper Ewing] was about to set out for Lancaster I rec^d. your favours of 24 & 26 Nov^r. & 8th. Instant, and need not mention my joy at the agreable tidings you give me, my absence from this Place for some time prevented my Answering your Many Favours Sooner, I refer you to my last & the Major for every thing worthy Relating from this Place. I wish much for an Enquiry into the Causes of the Indian Expedition failing & hope judicious men will be Appointed

Adieu D^r. Yeates remember me to every Body & Believe me to be most Affectionately y^{rs}

Ed^{wd} Hand

Jasper Yeates, Esqr. pr. Major Ewing

British vessel at Manchac, and used this for further depredations on the property of British sympathizers. In the following year he sent his troops back up the river under charge of Lieut. Robert George, who placed them under the orders of Gen. George Rogers Clark. Willing himself proceeded to Mobile, where he was captured and narrowly escaped being hung. He was finally shipped as prisoner to New York, and kept on Long Island, under parole, with other American officers. Having resented an insult offered by a British officer, Willing was incarcerated in New York City and loaded with irons, where he remained for three months. One of his sisters, wife of a British officer, interceded for him with Sir Henry Clinton, who finally permitted him to return to Phila-

AN ATTACK SUGGESTED 193

NEW EXPEDITIONS PLANNED

[Gen. Edward Hand to Westmoreland officers. 3NN94—Transcript.]

FORT PITT, 27th. Decr. 1777.

D^r. SIR—I am informed that the gent^n. in Westmoreland have it in agitation to make a descent on one of the Indian Villages on the Alleghany. I think that it might be put in execution without much hazard—would therefore gladly consult with you on the occasion, as I can make you acquainted with many circumstances you are now a stranger to   I am, dear Sir, very sincerely y^{rs}.

EDW^d. HAND

Col. Jno. Proctor or Col. Jas. Smith

[Gen. Edward Hand to Col. William Crawford. 3NN95—Transcript.]

FORT PITT, Dec. 28th. 1777.

D^r. CRAWFORD—As I expect the pleasure of seeing you in a few days, shall defer communicating a matter I much wish to set on foot, until that time.[63]

There are at Kayahoga about 100 miles from here, a magazine of arms and provisions sent from Detroit, & 15 batteaux lie there. You may guess the rest. Y^{rs}. &c.

EDW^d. HAND

Col. W^m. Crawford

---

delphia on parole until exchanged. He is said to have been exchanged for Henry Hamilton, governor of Detroit. Willing was never married. He made his home in Philadelphia, where he died Oct. 13, 1801.—ED.

[63] See Crawford's reply of Jan. 4, 1778, published in C. W. Butterfield, *Washington-Crawford Letters* (Cincinnati, 1877), p. 66.—ED.

NEWS FROM FORT RANDOLPH

[Capt. William McKee to Gen. Edward Hand. 1U133— A. L. S.]

SIR—Messrs Bailey[64] & Lynn Express from Kentucky to you Call^d here on their way with whom I transmit your Excellency some acc^t of the state of this Garrison and what has happened since your Departure on the 29th Nov. last Lt Moor with a Reconoitring party fell into an ambuscade of about 20 Indians within about 100 y^{ds} of the turnip field M^r. Moor & one private belonging to my Comp^y were kill^d. we

---

[64] John Bailey was born in Northumberland County, Va., May 4, 1748. He came to Kentucky as early as 1776, and appears to have lived at Harrodsburg. In 1778 he was commissioned lieutenant, and joined Clark's Kaskaskia expedition. In August of that year Clark sent him to the aid of Capt. Leonard Helm at Vincennes. Having returned to Kaskaskia, Bailey became a member of the expedition to recapture Vincennes, and was sent in advance with a detachment of fourteen men to make the first attack on Fort Sackville. When Clark left Vincennes, Bailey was placed in command of part of the garrison. November, 1779, found him at a council of war at Louisville, when he is first designated as captain. In 1780, Bailey accompanied Montgomery on his expedition to Rock River, and early in the following year was in command at Fort Jefferson on the Mississippi. Thence he was detached in January, 1781, to take command at Vincennes, where he remained until November under great difficulties, due to lack of provisions, hostility of the Indians, etc. In 1782 and 1783 he was still in service at Fort Nelson, and in 1784 was one of the commissioners for the Clark grant of land in Indiana, wherein he received his captain's allotment. At the close of the Revolution, Captain Bailey became a Baptist preacher, and was influential in laying the foundations of that church in Kentucky. In 1792 and 1799 he was a member of the constitutional conventions for the state, and voted in favor of an emancipation clause. He died at his home in Lincoln County, July 3, 1816, leaving the reputation of an honored minister of the gospel, and a loyal, efficient soldier and public servant.—ED.

CAMP DISEASES 195

sally^d from the Garrison with all Possible speed but on our approach the Enemy fled in diffrent parties so that we Got none of them nor any thing belonging to them only one Blanquet & a Tomhawk. about 8 Days Afterwards one came to the other side the Ohio Just as it got Dark Fired his Gun and Call^d. over that He was Morgan[65] and was perishing with cold & Hunger wanted to be brought over I wou^d not let any of the men go over But sent Katty & Fawney[66] as they wer[e] setting off he ask^d. how many were coming with her was told none but the two; he told her not to come till morning But we have [heard] nothing of the Gentleman since I suppose he wanted some hair [a scalp] but was Disappointed nothing of Importance has happened since The small Pox & Meazles both spread through the Garrison there is now 17 men lying in them. Capt Arbuckle left the Garrison the 5th Inst^t. 11 men went with him four had gone before make 15 on Furloe the state of the Garrison at present as follows—Capt Arbuckles Compy 1 L^t. & serg't 19 Rank & file fit for Duty 5 serg^t. 8 Rank & file sick 1 sergt 7 Rank & file on Furloe.

My Compy 1 Capt 1 L^t. 2 Serg^ts. 39 Rank and file fit for Duty 8 Rank & file sick 1 Serg'^t 6 Rank and file in Furloe 1 L^t absent You will Sir see by this our

---

[65] No doubt this was an Indian who had taken the name of Col. George Morgan, long a trader in the Western country.—ED.

[66] Katty [Katy] was the Grenadier Squaw, for whom see *ante*, p. 26, note 57. Fawny [Fanny] was probably her daughter, who is known to have been at Fort Randolph with her.—ED.

Garrison is verry weak and in all probability will be weaker as many of the men have those Disorders to take.

The Commissary has wrote you and (I suppose) has given an acc^t. of the Provisions.

Please Present my Comp^{ts}. Maj^r Ewing & other officers at your post tho' unacquan[t]ed. I am your Excellencys Most obed^t. Hble Servt

W^m. M^{c}KEE.

FORT RANDOLPH 31st. Decem 1777

P. S. We have Nominated M^r. David Wallace[67] my Eldest Sergt to act as second L^t in my Comp^y I hope you'll approve of & signify your approbation in your next.

On Continental service   To His Excellency Edward Hand
B. Genl.

PLANS FOR CLARK'S EXPEDITION

[Gov. Patrick Henry to General Hand. 3NN196—Transcript.]

WILLIAMSBURGH, Jan. 2^d 1778.

SIR—I was favored with your two last letters which shall have my attention.

I have to request that you will please to furnish Major G. R. Clark with boats sufficient for conveying seven companys of militia on an expedition of great consequence.[68] Besides the immediate advantages

---

[67] Probably belonging to the Wallace family of Augusta County, early settlers near Staunton.—ED.

[68] George Rogers Clark (1752-1818) was born in Albemarle County, Va., and as early as 1774 was surveying on Ohio River. For his commission as captain in Lord Dunmore's War see volume thereon in the present series, p. 156. In 1775 he visited Kentucky, and was occupied with its defense until the autumn of 1777, when he returned to Virginia to obtain authority for his plan to capture the Illinois settlements.

arising from the success of it, the consequential benefits will be many. A good understanding with [New] Orleans is a desirable object. And I must entreat you, Sir, to give Major Clark every assistance which he may want. The boats I hope will not long be wanted; & the use of them, & every other thing furnished by you will be amply compensated by the Major's success, which I beg leave to assure you I am most anxiously concerned for. I refer you to that gentleman for an explanation of the errand on which he goes. It is needless to inform you how necessary it is that the whole affair should be kept impenetrably secret. I have the honor to be, Sir, Y^r obedient hble. Servt

P. HENRY.

P. S. I should have consulted you on the expedition, but time would not permit. I direct the Major to get his powder & lead from your quarter. Please to let him have what is necessary. P. H.
Genl Hand, Pittsburgh   Fav^d by Maj^r Clark.

EXPEDITIONS FOR NEW ORLEANS
[General Hand to Jasper Yeates. MS. in New York Public Library: Hand Papers—A. L. S.]

FORT PITT 6th. Jany. 1778

DEAR YEATES—Since I wrote you by Major Ewing have nothing to mention but the Arival of Mr George

---

This proposal was approved by Gov. Patrick Henry, and the accompanying letter was one of several issued on this date, destined to promote the expedition. Clark had at this time been commissioned lieutenant-colonel of Virginia militia; but Henry uses familiarly his former title of major, given while in command of Kentucky forts. The object of the expedition had necessarily to be kept secret, to insure its success.—ED.

198 FRONTIER DEFENSE ON UPPER OHIO

Clymer[69] (one of the Commissioners) Yesterday.[70] I have not yet heard of the Other Gent^n. hope they may soon Arive and that I may be Able to return with M^r. Clymer as our Army has gone into Winter Quarters, suppose nothing material will take place before Spring My love to every Body Adieu! D^r. Yeates Affectionately y^{rs}.

Jasper Yeates Esqr.

EDW^d HAND

[Capt. James Willing to General Hand. 3NN198—Transcript.]

F^t PITT, Jan. 7, 1778.

As I expect to bring at least five boats from New Orleans laden with dry goods, & navigated by 20 or 25 men each, I request the favor of you to give the necessary orders for a sufficient quantity of flour & pork to

---

[69] George Clymer was a prominent Philadelphia patriot. Born in that city in 1739, he was educated by his uncle, William Coleman, and early entered into the colonial disputes. He opposed the landing of tea, served on the first committee of safety, and was a signer of the Declaration of Independence. For several years he was a delegate to the Continental Congress and to the Constitutional Convention. He was first collector of excise for Philadelphia, one of the directors of the Bank of North America, and a commissioner (1796) to treat with Cherokee Indians. He died in 1813 at his home in Bucks County, Pa.—ED.

[70] Nov. 20, 1777, Congress took into consideration the state of the Western frontiers of Pennsylvania and Virginia and the disaffection existing there as the result of Hamilton's proclamations. It determined to appoint a commission of three to investigate the rise, progress, and extent of the disaffection and to provide means both for checking it and the Indian ravages. Col. Samuel Washington, Mr. Gabriel Jones, and Col. Joseph Reed were appointed. The last named having withdrawn, George Clymer was (Dec. 11) elected to take his place. See *Jour. of Cong.* (new ed.), ix, pp. 942-944, 1018.—ED.

ROGERS'S EXPEDITION 199

be lodged for me by the beginning of April next at the Arkansas.[71] Not less than 60 or 70 barrels of flour, of 250 to 300 lbs each, & 20 or 30 bbls of pork. I will supply my crews with the remaining quantity of meat necessary below.

[Gov. Patrick Henry to General Hand. 3NN199—Transcript.]

W^{ms}BURG, Jan. 15th 1778.

SIR—Col. David Rogers has my instructions to proceed to New Orleans on business of the greatest concern to the State.[72] He must have boats, provisions, Men, &c. without which his journey will be stopped. I trouble you, Sir, on this occasion, so important to the interests of America, hoping for your warmest Exertions to fit out the Colonel in the Most Speedy manner. His principal difficulties will probably be in procuring boats & men. But I've hopes that in a Matter of such high moment to your part of the country, everything necessary for the trip will be got with alacrity. Ammunition & arms will be delivered him by you, Sir, I hope with Convenience. I am, Sir, Y^r Mo. hble Servt

P. HENRY.

Gen. Hand.

---

[71] Arkansas Post was one of the oldest in the Mississippi Valley, having been founded in 1686 by some of Henri Tonty's men. The settlement was not continuous, the fort having been permanently founded about 1718 under the regime of John Law. The official name of the post was St. Etienne, but it was commonly known as "Aux Arcs", phoneticized by Americans into Ozark. In 1748 it suffered an attack by the Chickasaw, and four years later was substantially rebuilt. The Spanish kept a garrison there throughout their possession of Louisiana, and in 1804 surrendered the fort to the Americans.—ED.

[72] For a brief sketch of Col. David Rogers and his expedition, see *Rev. Upper Ohio*, p. 232, note 75.—ED.

[General Hand to Jasper Yeates. MS. in New York Public
Library; Hand Papers—A. L. S.]

FORT PITT 17th. Jany. 1778

DEAR YEATES—Since my last nothing has Occured worth relating in the Public Way, and as to my proceedings in the private Character, I cant say how you will relish them. I have Agreed, with M^r. Ja^s. Willing for half my Concerns on Chartiers Creek,[73] the terms Kitty will communicate. M^r. Clymer begins to be uneasie at the stay of the other Gent^n. I hope I shant have Occasion to be so on Jessy's Acc^t. and that I shall See you soon

my love to every Creature of your Family, My re-

---

[73] Chartier's Creek rises in Washington County and flows north and northeast into the Ohio, a short distance below Pittsburgh. The name (which was corrupted by the early settlers into Shurtees) is an interesting reminder of early Indian occupation. A French-Canadian named Martin Chartier was one of La Salle's party, and resided at Fort St. Louis in the Illinois. Having married a Shawnee squaw he migrated south and east with a band of that tribe, finally appearing (1692) in Maryland—see Hanna, *Wilderness Trail*, i, pp. 119-135. Later, these people settled on the Susquehanna, where Chartier died in 1718. His only son Peter had great influence with the Shawnee and removed with them to the Ohio, where his village was known as Chartier's Town. Being induced to embrace the French interest he persuaded his band to remove (1745) down the Ohio, after which his history is not known. Two localities in western Pennsylvania preserve his name—Chartier's Run and Station in Westmoreland County, and Chartier's Creek. The latter is noted for the quality of its land. It was included in an Indian grant of 1749 to George Croghan, and he sold a number of locations thereon. Probably Hand's tract belonged to this number.—ED.

spects to M_r. Shippen's &c_a. Farewell D_r. Yeates
Affectionately y_rs.
M_c.Kee is Order'd down[74]
Edw_d. Hand
To Jasper Yeates Esq_r. Lancaster pr. Col: Steel

HAND'S EXPEDITION INTO THE INDIAN COUNTRY

[General Hand to Col. William Crawford. 3NN95— Transcript.]

YOHIOGANIA COT'Y, 5th Feb. 1778.

D_r SIR—As I am credibly informed that the English have lodged a quantity of arms, ammunition, provision & clothing at a small Indian town about 100 miles from Fort Pitt, to support the savages in their excursions against the inhabitants of this and the adjacent counties, I ardently wish to collect as many brave active lads as are willing to turn out, to destroy this magazine. Every man must be provided with a horse, & every article necessary to equip them for the expedition, except amunition, which, with some arms, I can furnish.

It may not be unnecessary to assure them, that everything they are able to bring away shall be sold at public vendue for the sole benefit of the captors, & the money equally distributed. tho' I am certain that a sense of the service they will render to their country

---

[74] The expression "down the country" was used as an equivalent for return to the East. February 7, 1778, General Hand wrote to Alexander McKee: "SIR—I am sorry to be under the necessity of repeating my desire of the 29th Dec. last, viz. that you may immediately repair to Yorktown, in Penn., on your parole, there to receive the further directions of the Hon. Continental Board of War." See C. W. Butterfield, *History of the Girtys* (Cincinnati, 1800), p. 40.—ED.

will operate more strongly than the expectation of gain. I therefore expect you will use your influence on this occasion, & bring all the volunteers you can raise to Fort Pitt by the 15th of this month. I am, dear Sir, Yr. obed^t huble Servt

EDW^d HAND.

Col. Wm Crawford.

N. B. The horses shall be appraised, & paid for if lost.

SUPPLIES FOR WESTERN EXPEDITIONS

[Gen. Edward Hand to Gen. Horatio Gates. 3NN98—
Transcript.]

FORT PITT, 12th Feby 1778.

SIR—I do myself the honor to enclose you the Copy of a letter I yesterday rec^d from his Exc^y Govr Henry. I can't doubt but Congress will direct an immediate compliance with the demands he makes, & would not myself hesitate to grant them, yet as time will admit of consulting your Honb^{le} Board, I think it my duty so to do. I request your instructions how to act by return of the express.

On the 17th ult^o I wrote to the Honb^{le} the Commercial Committee Enclosing a demand made on me by Capt. James Willing of the armed boat Rattle Trap, & Col. George Morgan's Estimate for provisions to be sent to the Arkansas.

It will be very necessary that their determination be immediately communicated, as the protection Major Clark's party can afford the provision boats as far as the Cherokee fort, which is within 40 miles of the mouth of the Ohio,[75] will save an expense of men, (a Matter of Consequence in this quarter.)

It is to be lamented that Govr. Henry had not recollected that the three tons of lead ordered from Virginia by Congress in April last, never reached this place, which leaves it in a deplorable Situation, & such as deserves your early attention. The whole stock now in store amounts to no more than 508 ^{lbs}—vide last return; but hope to draw from the out-posts what will serve Major Clark. The intent of the expedition is to seize upon the British post & stores at Kaskasquias in the Illinois Country, of which it is likely you are apprized. I wish you every happiness, & am, Sir, Very respectfully Y^r obed^t hble Servt.

EDW^d HAND.

P. S. An officer & private were killed within 300 yards of Fort Randolph since I left it.

To the Honb^{le} Maj. Gen. Gates, Presid^t of Board of War.

OATHS OF ALLEGIANCE

[Capt. Thomas Burk to Col. William Preston. 4QQ158— A. L. S.]

DEAR S^r—I have Call^d the men to Gather A greeable to your orders and am sorry that I Cannot Sattisfy my own Concience so far as to Cumply and take

---

[75] The Cherokee fort was that known to the French as Fort Massiac (Massac), built by them in 1757 to check the incursions of Cherokee Indians. It was garrisoned throughout the French regime. British engineers recommended it as an important site, but it was allowed to fall into ruins. At this site began Clark's overland march to Kaskaskia. In 1794 the United States rebuilt the post, which was garrisoned until after 1812. The site has recently been purchased for a state park, to be under the direction of the Historical Society of Illinois.—ED.

Oath prescribed by law and I Render^d my Reason to you When we held a Coversation at your own house & Neighther Do I through stubburnness Refuse But Ever look^d Upon it my Duty When I took an oath on any occation their should be Noo doubt of Concience I Never flew in the face of authority Neither shall I, and stand not In Defyence of Goverment But Know Very wel that I must be under the law of men and am not against any thing in Reason and stand in reasonable fear of My fellow man But must think that I have A god to fear as he is the Creator of us all and says the Rather fear him who is able to Destroy both soul and body in hell I think it Requisit at all times to take sum thought of an Eternal state as well as all for temporal I do not hint on any man that has takun it But only in vindication of my own Concience as I think the apostle Paul says What shall it profit a man if he gain the whole World and loos his own soul. I Declare my selfe a rail friend to my Country Nither have I Ever don any thing Against it and as to the Resolveing any thing of rebeling against the Country I Never thought of any such thing Neighther have I Ever heard Mankind in my own Cumpany or any other person What Ever speake or Motion the like. it is not in my thought to teach any thing Concerning scripture But Know you able to Be my Guide and am With grate Respect your Most obedient Humble servant

THO^s BURK

And I hear in Close the Commition Deliverd to me and Must Resine

febry 18th 1778.

DEFENSE OF VIRGINIA

[Gov. Patrick Henry to Col. William Fleming. 15ZZ17—
A. L. S.]

WILLIAMSBURG, Feby 19th 1778.

SIR—The Murder of the Shawanese Indians will no doubt bring on Hostilities with that People. In order to ward off the Stroke which may be expected it is necessary to have every Gun in your County put into good order & got ready for Action. Lead may be had from the Mines. An order for one pound for each Man of your Militia accompany's this. Powder it is said is plenty among you. If it cant be had otherwise send to Richmond for it. Let trusty Scouts be kept in constant Action towards the Enemys Country to discover their Movements & give Information of approaching Danger. Proper Stockades or Defences to receive the more helpless part of the People should be provided in time and fixed at Places judiciously chosen, that the able Men may be at liberty to assail the Enemy & range the Frontiers as occasion may require. These Stockades should be provided at the Expence of your People & are not meant to be garrisoned only as particular Exigencies may make necessary. I think no Neighbourhood ought to be without one where the Enemy can possibly penetrate. In case of Attack you are to draw out such Force from the Militia as you judge sufficient to chastise the Invaders. Let the pursuit of Scalping Parties, be close, hot and determined, for if Vengeance is taken on the foremost Partys, others will be intimidated. I wish to reinforce Capt. Arbuckles Garrison with a Company of fifty Men officered in the usual manner from your

County and that they should march thither without delay. Volunteers enlisted for this Business to serve six Months in it, I would prefer, but if they are not to be got without loss of Time let the Militia be drafted. For I expect the Indians very shortly on the Frontiers. I beg the favour of you to confer with Col. Preston on the propriety of establishing a Post to preserve the Communication with Fort Randolph, perhaps some Place near the mouth of Elk River might answer this purpose and also check the Inroads of the Savages if the Garrison was alert and diligent to intercept their Parties.

I am at a loss for Officers in Green Bryar and wish for a recommendation from your County Court of such as are proper; That Place will be attacked tis likely and if no other Expedient can be found I must fill up the Commisisons in Council, where the Individuals cannot be known. Rockbridge is in the same situation. Will you please to assist with such Information as you can give in finding fit Persons for Officers. I wish the Lead to be carefully preserved for the purpose of Defence & not given to the men but as Occasions call for it, except in exposed Places, where the People must be trusted with it. I think the Garrison proposed near Elk need not consist of more than sixty Men, but I submit it to you and Col. Preston to do for the best being on the Spot.

You will perceive my Views go no further than defensive Operations. I know how impossible it is to render them completely effectual against the Enemies you have to oppose. But offensive Measures set on foot against these Indians at this time after their late

Treatment, would be too full of Injustice to escape general Execration. Policy & even Self preservation may ere long call for such Measures. But even then it may be doubted if provisions purchased in your parts would answer the Design.

Having now done every thing which I can foresee to be necessary for protecting the Frontiers, I must tell you Sir that I really blush for the occasion of this War with the Shawanese. I doubt not but you detest the vile assassins who have brought it on us at this critical Time when our whole Force was wanted in another Quarter. But why are they not brought to Justice? Shall this Precedent establish the Right of involving Virginia in War whenever any one in the back Country shall please? I need not argue to shew you Sir the fatal tendency of such Conduct. You see it & I fear your County will feel indiscriminately that Misery which ought to visit only the guilty Authors of the Mischief. Some say the People of your Country will not suffer the Apprehension of the Murderers. I desire it may be remembered, that if the frontier people will not submit to the Laws, but thus set them at Defiance, they will not be considered as entitled to the protection of Government, and were it not for the miserable Condition of many with you, I should demand the Offenders previous to every other Step. For where is this wretched Business to end? The Cherokees, the Delawares and every other Tribe may be set on us in this manner this Spring for what I know. Is not this the work of Tories? No Man but an Enemy to American Independance will do it, and thus oblige our People to be hunting after Indians in the Woods, instead of facing Gen[l] Howe in the field, search into the Matter and depend upon it the Murderers are Tories. the Honor of your Country is at stake and it is time to decide whether these Villains are to meet with punishment or whether the greater Number will espouse their Interests. I desire you to the utmost, at all hazards & to the last Extremity to support and assist the civil Magistrate in apprehending and bringing these offenders to Justice.

If the Shawenese deserved Death, because their Countrymen committed Hostilities, a Jury from the Vicinage will say so and acquit the accused who must be judged by his Neighbours feeling the same Resentments and Passions with themselves. But they are Traytors I suspect and Agents for the Enemy, who have taken this method to find employment for the brave back Woodsmen at home, and prevent their joining Gen[l] Washington to strike a decisive stroke for Independency at this critical time.

Urge these things Sir with that Spirit and Warmth the Subject demands, prepare your People for their own Defence against the Indians to vindicate their Honor from the rude attack now made on it, and let them be shewn to the World as possessing the other virtues which usually accompany Courage.

In the Confidence that what I now press, I mean the bringing the Murderers of the Indians to Justice, will be done, Government will loose no Time in lending its best Aids to protect your Country. I fear something essential for the frontier Defence, may have escaped me, But your part must be in concert with your Neighbours to point out what yet remains to be done for your safety. If a Reinforcement of fifty Men more is necessary at Fort Randolph they will be sent on your and Col. Preston's writing to me.

I have it much at Heart to bring the Indians to treat on the subject of our Difference with them, perhaps the Grenadier Sqaw may be usefull in this Business, please to confer on this matter with Col. Preston and let every possible Effort be made to bring on a Treaty. the Expences necessary for the Attempt I will pay on Demand. I forbear to mention particulars for beginning this Work as they must be better judged of on the spot, but at all Events try it vigorously.

Wishing safety to you & your people I am Sir Y^r Mo. h^{ble} Servt

P. HENRY

Col^o Fleming Botetourt   The County Lieutenant of Botetourt.

NEWS FROM THE FRONT

[Col. William Russell to Col. William Fleming.   2U6— A. L. S.]

CAMP VALLEY FORGE March 1^t 1778.

D^r SIR—Having a few moments leasure, and being favoured with this opportunity by Col^o Gist;[76] I set

---

[76] Col. Nathaniel Gist was the son of Christopher Gist, scout and explorer, who accompanied Washington on his perilous journey (1753) to Venango, and saved the life of the young Virginian envoy. Nathaniel was scout under his father in Braddock's campaign, and next year (1756) lieutenant of the company of scouts in Washington's Virginia regiment. By 1762 Nathaniel had the rank of captain. At the outbreak of the Revolution he undertook a perilous journey to the Cherokee country in order to secure their neutrality. In January, 1777, he was commissioned colonel of an additional Continental regiment, raised by order of Congress, which command was known as Gist's regiment. He

down to remind you, that through mercy, I am still in existence; and tho' I have not been so happy to hear from you either by Letter or otherwise, since I left your House; yet, I flatter myselfe, you have not forgot your promise of writting to me at convenient times such news as your quarter afford. I had to go by Fort Pitt when I left you, on my way to head Quarters, which obliged me to have the small Pox till the month of July, a very hot season, but, I weather'd it with a good deal of ease, however my conflict with the measles was very severe, of which, I have but lately recovered, tho' I underwent constant Duty within a few Days after it seized me. I make no doubt but you have long since been acquainted with the news of the summer, and fall, since which, little has transpired. We have taken up winter quarters at this place, and, having erected a small city of Cabbins for the troops to live in, it is likely we shall remain here till summer, unless drove from it by Mr How; which I doubt of, as we are at present fortifying round our camp. A committee of congress is now setting near us, to regulate our army, and I expect will new model in particu-

---

served directly under Washington during 1777, but in the spring of 1778 was commissioned to undertake a second journey to the Cherokee. In that capacity he left the army, and passed through southwestern Virginia. The summer found him again with the army, and the next year he was ordered to reinforce Charleston, where Gist was one of the prisoners captured in May, 1780. Released upon parole, he returned home and resigned January 1, 1781. Later in life, after marriage to Judith Cary Bell of Virginia, Colonel Gist removed (1793) to Kentucky, where he died early in the nineteenth century, leaving several descendants, some of whom obtained prominence in the country's service. An autograph letter may be found in Draper MSS., 2L10.—ED.

lar, the present arrangement of officers. It is reported that some Regiments will be diminished, if so, it is probable some of us Field officers of the last six [Virginia regiments] will be reduced. Our lite infantry is to consi[s]t of eighteen Companies Commanded by Major General Arnold & two Brigadiers, of whom Genl Scott is to be one; the other unknown; and our officers will hereafter be on a more respectable footing. Marquis De Lafayette, Genl Conway and Genl McCalb [De Kalb] are ordered to Canada, and will command in that quarter the next campaign; their influence will undoubtedly be considerable among the Canadians it is said they are coming over fast to our interest already. The detention of Genl Burgoin and army, I expect gives great satisfaction to the People of Virginia. We have just heard that the news of his defeat occasion'd great commotions in England. The Parliament was sitting at the time, and, when the accounts reached the House; Col^o Barre asked leave to speak on the occasion; he was ordered to silence, but a great majority crying out leave leave, he was permitted together with Mr Burke; they spoke in a most copious manner, it is said much to the satisfaction of great part of the House: we daily expect the acc^{ts} in Print: if it comes shortly I will send it to you. Genl Muhlenburg[77] being gone

---

[77] Gen. John Peter Gabriel Muhlenberg, the famous "fighting parson", was born in Pennsylvania in 1746, the son of the founder of the Lutheran church in America. Peter was sent for education to Germany, where he had a brief military experience. Returning home he took orders, and settled (1772) as the pastor of Woodstock, Va., where he at once engaged in the Revolutionary movement, serving on the committees

Home, the command of the Brigade devolved on me till his return, which gives me great trouble, and have had ever since his absence, in discharging the soldiers who's times have expired, which happens almost every Day more or less. There is strong reasons to believe, that my Regiment will be ordered to Fort Pitt very soon, If so, and I continue to Command it; I shall try to get leave of absance to visit my family and friends before I go there, but if I should be continued here, I am doubtful whether I can be spared: but his Excellency General Washington has assured me he will indulge me if possible. I should be exceeding happy to spend an evening or two with you, I have much more to communicate to you than I wood chuse to do by Letter, for seldom any passes now without being opened, and too commonly lost altogether. No doubt

---

of correspondence and safety, in the state convention, and as a trusted counsellor of Henry and Washington. In 1776 he was commissioned colonel of the 8th Virginia, and stepping from the pulpit to the door of his church, he enrolled among his parishioners his famous German regiment. Muhlenberg's first operations were in Virginia, but in 1777 he joined the main army after being commissioned (February 21) brigadier-general. Here he was one of Washington's most trusted generals, partaking in all the battles and campaigns of 1777-78. The short furlough mentioned by Russell was almost his only visit to his Woodstock home during the first three years of the war. In 1779-83 he served in Virginia, receiving the rank of major-general (September, 1783). At the close of the war he made a journey to the West to locate his own and other officers' lands, intending to make his home in Kentucky. But events decided his return to Pennsylvania, where he thereafter chiefly made his home. He was one of the supreme executive council of Pennsylvania, member of the first Congress under the constitution, and U. S. senator; he was then collector of the port of Philadelphia (1801) until his death in 1807.—ED.

but you have long since heard of General Stephen[78] loseing his Post in the Army. your old acquaintances Woodford, Scott, and Weedon[79] still continue, the latter gone Home on Furloe. Discontents have much prevail'd among the officers, but, I hope the present regulations will give general satisfaction: the officers wait with great impatience to know them. I have long

---

[78] For this officer, see *Dunmore's War*, p. 191, note 35.—ED.

[79] William Woodford was the son of a militia officer in Caroline County, where he was born Oct. 6, 1734. He was first-lieutenant and then captain in the Virginia regiment during the French and Indian War, and he married a near relative of Washington. On the arming for the Revolution, Woodford was chosen colonel of the 2nd Virginia regiment, took command against Lord Dunmore, and won the engagement at Great Bridge (Dec. 9, 1775). Having resigned his rank upon entering the Continental establishment, he was, until made brigadier-general in 1777, placed below those whom he had previously ranked. His resignation was only avoided through the personal solicitation of the commander-in-chief, who had a marked regard for his abilities. At the battle of Brandywine he was wounded, but continued with the main army until (1779) he was detached to the relief of Charleston. There he was captured, taken to New York, and died while still a prisoner, Nov. 13, 1780.

Gen. Charles Scott was born in Cumberland County, Va. At the age of seventeen he was enlisted in the Virginia regiment and was at Braddock's defeat. He was appointed first sergeant, then ensign of the regiment. On the outbreak of the Revolution, Scott was recommended by Washington for a commission, and made lieutenant-colonel of the 5th Virginia. He served with the main army, commanding a brigade at Brandywine and being with Wayne at the capture of Stony Point. He was in Charleston at the time of its surrender, and did not thereafter take active part in the army. In 1787 Scott removed with his family to Kentucky, where he settled in Woodford County, near Versailles, and there his son Samuel was killed in 1789 by lurking Indians. In 1791 Scott headed a successful expedition against the Wea Indians on the Wabash, when the old Ouiatanon settlement was totally destroyed. One of his sons was out with Wayne in 1794. General Scott was very popular with his neighbors, and in 1808 he was chosen governor of Kentucky, in which office he

wished to hear the news from your Quarter, but not one old acquaintance will favour me therewith; anything from that Quarter wood be most agreeable. I am sorry to hear my old acquaintance Cornstalk is killed, am much afraid that will set on the Shawanees to War against our frontier in conjunction with the other northen tribes; which will greatly distress our People. I understand an expedition is intended against Detroyat from Fort Pitt, it is likely I shall be ordered on that service with my Regiment: I hope the Militia will be forward shou'd they be calld upon for that purpose; the reduction of that Post will secure our Frontier.

Tho' I have been frequently hindered, while writting this, by giving discharges to soldiers, yet I have persevered, till I fear it may tire your patience, but relying on your goodness to accept of what the Camp at present affords, shall after tendering my best compliments to your Lady, and all enquireing Friends, subscribe myselfe D^r Si^r, Yours most affectionately.

WM. RUSSELL.

To Col^o William Fleming. Botetourt County, Virginia.
Fav^d by Col^o Gist.

---

served for four years. He died at his home in October, 1813.
Gen. George Weedon was born in Fredericksburg, Va., about 1830. A neighbor and friend of Gen. Hugh Mercer, he was (1758) an officer in the Virginia regiment. After the war he became an innkeeper at his native place, and was an active and zealous Whig. In 1776, Weedon was commissioned lieutenant-colonel of the 3d Virginia, being transferred in August of the same year to the 1st. In February, 1777, he was appointed brigadier-general, and commanded a brigade at Brandywine and Germantown. In 1780 he was assigned to duty in Virginia, and took part in the siege of Yorktown. At the close of the war he was breveted major-general. In 1774 General Weedon married Catherine Gordon of Freder-

ACCOUNT OF HAND'S EXPEDITION

[Gen. Edward Hand to Jasper Ewing. MS. in New York Public Library; Hand Papers—A. L. S.]

FORT PITT 7th March 1778

DEAR YEATES—I omitted writing to you by the last Opertunity Because I had nothing material then to Communicate, & Expected by this to have Mighty feats to declare, having rec^d. intelligence that a Quantity of Stores were lodged at Cayahaga, I formed a Project of Seizing them by Surprise, during the Season in which the Savages might Suppose us to be inactive. A party nearly Amounting to 500 Chiefly Westmoreland Militia Offerd themselves for this Service, but unluckily the heavy Rains that fell soon after we set Out, together with the Melting of the snow raised the Waters to such a degree, that after Swiming Some Creek's & going round the heads of others we were obliged to relinquish our Design. about 40 miles up Beaver Creek we discoverd Indian Tracts & Sent out reconnoitring Parties some of them returnd & Informd they had found a Camp Containing between 50 & 60 Indians, I conjectured they were Warriors coming into Our Settlements & proceeded to Attack them But to my great Mortification found only one Man with some Women & Children. the Men were so Impetuous that I could not prevent their Killing the Man & one of the Women. another Woman was taken & with difficulty Saved. the rem^r. escaped.

The prisoner told us that ten Miles higher, Ten Moncy [Munsey] men were Making salt. I detachd

---

icksburg, and his name appears in the Spottsylvania records until after 1793, about which time he seems to have died.—ED.

a party to Secure them, they turn'd out to be 4 Women & a Boy, of these one Woman only was Saved. Notwithstanding this Savage Conduct I verily believe the Party would Behave well if they had men to contend with. You will be Surprised in performing the Above great exploits I had but one man (a Captn.) Wounded, & one Dround'd.

I cant yet give you the Information you desire of your Indian Brother but will inform myself if I can.

The Virginia Commissioners have not Arived here nor can I learn Any thing of them. I beg my Love to all Your Family. My respects to M^r. Shippens &c^a. & am Dear Yeates your Affectionate Kinsman

Edwd: Hand

To Jasper Yeates Esqr. Lancaster

[Recollections of Samuel Murphy. 3S28-32.]

General Hand's expedition. This was in the winter 1777-78 with a slight fall of fresh snow. About 400 men [went out]. Col. Providence Mounts, of Mounts Creek,[80] which empties in Youghiogheny, was out. Col. William Crawford, Major Brenton, Capt. John

---

[80] Providence Mounts was a Marylander by birth, and is said to have been with Washington at Fort Necessity. In 1768 he removed to the Youghiogheny, in what is now Connellsville township of Fayette County, where he erected a mill on a creek which there emptied into the river. During the Revolution he was colonel of the 2nd battalion of Westmoreland militia, and in addition to this expedition served in the pursuit of the savage enemy after the sack of Hannastown (1782). He died at his home in 1784, and after his decease his land was patented to his descendants.—Ed.

THE SQUAW CAMPAIGN 217

Stephenson, Captain Scott,[81] etc. William Brady, a blacksmith of Pittsburgh, was chosen pilot.[82] Simon Girty was out, and wanted the appointment. On the way out, Major Brenton lost his horse, and he got Simon Girty to remain with him, they found the horse, and rejoined the army just at the close of the fight, or rather firing, on the Indian town, in the forks of Neshaneck and Shenango and on the eastern bank of the latter.[83] Orders had been given as they

---

[81] Capt. David Scott was born on the South Branch of Potomac River, but in 1770 he moved to the Monongahela, near the site of the present Granville—a town founded by his son Felix Scott—Monongalia County, West Va. Captain Scott built one or mofe mills in the vicinity, and was a prominent resident. In 1779 Indians murdered his daughters Fanny and Phebe as they were taking dinner to men in the hayfield. Later, a son named James barely escaped capture. An old house said to have been built by Captain Scott in 1776, was lately standing on the farm of the Gapen family, who descended from Captain Scott's youngest daughter.—ED.

[82] Nothing more appears in reference to this guide. According to Samuel Murphy's recollections, he was not of the family of Samuel Brady.—ED.

[83] The first of these two streams is usually written Neshannock. The village raided must have been on the site of the present town of Newcastle, Mercer County, Pa. This was probably part of the Kuskuskies towns (see *ante*, note 45), which originally were built by the Iroquois. These villages seem to have still been their abode when Washington visited the West in 1753. The latter did not enter Kuskuskies, but passed near it on his route from Logstown to Venango. After the opening of the French and Indian War, the Iroquois abandoned this region, which was then given over to the Delawares, who had important settlements on Beaver Creek and its branches. There the Moravian envoy Frederick Christian Post visited them in the summer of 1758. He describes Kuskuskies as composed of four towns, some distance apart, and says that at one of them the French had built houses for the Delawares; probably it was on the site of Newcastle. In the period between the English capture of Fort Duquesne (1758), and Pontiac's War (1763), the Dela-

approached the town to surround it, but Colonel Mounts did not fully accomplish his part, and left a gap, and Pipe's wife and children got off, a little fall of snow on the ground. This Pipe was a brother of Captain Pipe. The mother of the Pipes, an old squaw was pursued and shot at repeatedly, when Thomas Ravenscroft[84] ran up to the old squaw and tried to pull her away, but the bullets still flying, and had a ball through his legging; when a Major came up and put a stop to firing, when it was ascertained that the only injury she had received was the loss of an end of a little finger. An old squaw was shot by Lieut. [John] Hamilton[85] and wounded in the leg, mistaking

---

ware tribesmen withdrew in large measure to the Tuscarawas and Muskingum. The village raided by Hand's warriors would appear to have been at this time (1778) inconsiderable, with few vestiges of its former importance.—ED.

[84] Thomas Ravenscroft was born about 1750, and brought up in the family of Col. William Crawford. His first military service was in Dunmore's army in 1774; the next year (1775) he enlisted in Capt. John Stephenson's company, and later joined the 13th Virginia under Colonel Russell. Discharged at the close of 1777 or early in 1778, he was out with Hand on this expedition, and in 1781 enlisted under Clark for service in an expedition to Detroit, with a commission as lieutenant. Clark's expedition having been abandoned, Ravenscroft was employed in guarding the frontier. When out with Col. John Floyd in September, 1781, he was captured and taken prisoner to Detroit—see original letter of Floyd, relating this event, in Draper MSS., 51J89. From Detroit he was sent down to Montreal and there (June 20, 1782) made his escape, but was shortly recaptured—see *Canadian Archives*, 1887, p. 307. At the close of the Revolution, Ravenscroft was exchanged and returned to Kentucky, where he married either the widow or daughter of Col. John Hinkston. He was living in Harrison County, Ky., as late as 1823.—ED.

[85] Lieut. John Hamilton lived in what is now Washington County, Pa. In the autumn of 1775 he enlisted in the 13th Virginia and served in the Eastern army, being at the battles

THE SQUAW CAMPAIGN

her for a warrior; and a soldier ran up and tomahawked her, and a second ran up and shot her. Pipe shot and wounded Captain Scott and disabled his arm, and when nearly ready to shoot again, some one shot Pipe, and Reasin Virgin passing sunk the tomahawk in his head. Then commenced a wild yelling and shooting, without giving the least heed to the officers. A few cabins only were there, a little plunder obtained. This was about midday in February or March.

That afternoon a party started off for a small Indian settlement several miles up the Mahoning at a place called the Salt Licks.[86] Simon Girty went as pilot. They did not reach the place until in the night, found the warriors all absent hunting, found a few squaws there, and took [one] prisoner and brought her off, the others were left. A small Indian boy out with a gun shooting birds was discovered and killed, and several claimed the *honor;* and it was left to Girty to de-

---

at head of Elk River, at Brandywine, and Germantown. He would seem to have been ordered to Fort Pitt late in 1777, and to have served in the West until his discharge on Nov. 23, 1778. Ten years later he moved to Ohio with Stites and Symmes, who were settling the Miami country. Hamilton was employed as an Indian trader, and died in Ohio in 1822. For much of this information, our thanks are due to Mr. John S. Hunt of Chicago.—ED.

[86] For the location of Salt Lick Town, see *ante,* p. 178, note 45. The town at this site was, according to the testimony of John McCullough, a captive living at the place, built in 1755. During the French and Indian and Pontiac's wars it was a place of much importance, and several prisoners were brought there to be delivered to General Bouquet (1764). After that, however, the town declined, but the lick was frequented for salt-making until 1804, when a final skirmish occurred between the aborigines and the intruding white settlers.—ED.

cide, and his decision was that one Zach. Connell[87] killed the lad.

At the first town, the mother of Pipe was left in the town. An old Dutchman scalped the squaw that had been killed, and put the scalp in his wallet with his provisions, and in swimming a stream on return the Dutchman lost off his wallet, and exclaimed pathetically "O, I loss my prosock and my sculp." This was long a byword with the troops.

* * * * * * * *

This campaign of Hand's was better known as the Squaw campaign.[88] Hand was greatly displeased, and doubtless it contributed greatly towards his leaving the frontiers and rejoining the main army.

---

[87] Zachariah Connell, founder of the Pennsylvania town named Connellsville in his honor, was a native of Virginia (1741) and settled upon this site about 1770. With him came his brother James, who married Anne, daughter of Col. William Crawford. In 1776 Zachariah was appointed captain of militia for Yohogania County, and one of the justices for the same. He was very regular in attendance at county court, as the records show. Connell was a surveyor and laid out a large landed estate for himself; he acted also as business agent for prominent Eastern investors in Western lands. In 1793 he chartered the town bearing his name; and in 1800 built the first bridge over the river at this place. He died at his home in the village Aug. 26, 1813. At the time of his death he was building a large stone house, which still stands in the borough of Connellsville.—ED.

[88] The British report of this misadventure is given in *Mich. Pion. & Hist. Colls.*, ix. p. 436: "A party from Fort Pitt had fallen on a Delaware Village and killed or carried off eight persons, but unfortunately for the Rebels they have struck in the wrong place and have sent back two squaws who were prisoners to atone for their error."—ED.

THE SQUAW CAMPAIGN 221

[Gen. Edward Hand to Col. David Shepherd. 3NN100—
Transcript.]

FORT PITT, 7th March, 1778.

D^r SIR—I am just returned from a short excursion into the Indian Country, in which I was prevented of completing my views by the badness of the weather & height of the waters. Except a few gentlemen from about Stewart's Crossings,[89] & Some who accidentally happened here from the different parts of the Virginia

---

[89] Stewart's Crossings is one of the historic spots of Fayette County, Pa. In 1753 William Stewart located there, about the same time that Christopher Gist built his cabin at Mount Braddock. Stewart chose a ford on the Youghiogheny where the old Catawba Indian trail from the Iroquois country crossed that river. Erecting his cabin on the southwest bank of the stream, he lived on the site of the present village of New Haven. That autumn Maj. George Washington crossed at this place, bearing the famous message from Governor Dinwiddie of Virginia to the French officers on the upper Allegheny. The next year Washington, with his Virginia soldiers, did not advance as far as Stewart's Crossings; but his French opponent Sieur de Jumonville, must have crossed at this spot when endeavoring to gain information of the English situation. After the surrender of Fort Necessity (July 4, 1754), Coulon de Villiers, the victor, retired to Gist's place and ordered all the cabins of English settlers to be burned. William Stewart's home shared the common fate, and he retreated to the Eastern settlements, leaving his name attached to the crossing of the Youghiogheny. Braddock's Road led over this crossing; but that general himself forded the stream (1755) a mile or two below. In 1765 Col. William Crawford took possession of the place. Thither, the next year, he brought his family and established his permanent home. It is to his services that Hand here refers. On his death his son John fell heir to the Stewart Crossings estate, which in 1786 he sold to Edward Cook. The latter sold to Col. Isaac Meason, whose son built a store and in 1796 laid out the town of New Haven. The site of Stewart's Crossings is now a busy one, leading to the populous city of Connellsville on the northeast bank of the stream. William Stewart was living in 1786, and testified to his early occupation of this site.—ED.

frontiers, the party Consisted of volunteers from Westmoreland County. Many of the Virginia gentlemen seem to desire an opportunity of distinguishing themselves on a Similar occasion, which would in my opinion, render much service to the Country & should meet my hearty concurrence. I therefore request that you may request that you may endeavor to promote so laudable an Enterprise. I think that 200 men, each provided with a good horse & two bushels of grain, might in 8 or 10 days from this place make a considerable blow. If the scheme be carried into execution, the men should be punctual in rendezvousing here on the 1st of Next month. I think so short a trip would not interfere with my intention of drawing what assistance I can from the frontier counties & penetrating the enemies country in May with a design of taking a larger circuit; & beg to know your sentiments on the subject, & what men I may expect from your county on either occasion. Any grain furnished will be paid for, & also, the horses by appraisement if lost.

To Col. David Shepherd.
Edwd Hand

[Col. David Shepherd to General Hand. 2U7—A. L. S.]

Fort Henry March the 10th 1778.

Dear Sir—I Received your favour By John Green which Informed me of your Safe arrival to fort Pitt, I am glad to hear that our Neighbours is Spirited anough to turn out on the Like occation and for my part I hartily Concur with you in the Scheme perpossed and all the people I have Spoke with Concerning it Join in Sentiments in favour of the Scheme. I cannot as yet give you an Exact account what Number

Colonel Moses Shepherd
From *West Virginia Historical Magazine,* iii, p. 192

THE SQUAW CAMPAIGN 223

of men I can Furnish you with, But I have summoned all the Capts in the County to meet on Friday next in order to send men to the Stations and other purposes when I Expect to give you a better account. But at this time I Expect to furnish you with 30 Men if Possible against the Day appointed. I have sent By Leu^t Berry 53 Rifles and 8 Muskets Likewise 915^{lb} of lead and there Remains in Store 390 ^{lb}. The State of the Store I shall attend to and Do Every thing in my Power to Secure the Provisions as soon as I can collect some men. Our Brave Beefeaters time is out and they are all Returning home to tell of the great Exploits they have Done on the Ohio, But I hope they will send us Better Men the Next time. As for News I have None but the people are well pleased with our last trip. Sir I am with Respect your Humble Servant

Pray Excuse this Scrall.
DAVID SHEPHERD

To Brig^r General Edward Hand Fort Pitt.
Favour of Leut Berry.

DEFENSE OF VIRGINIA FRONTIER

[Col. William Preston and Col. William Fleming to Gov. Patrick Henry. 4QQ163—A. L. S.][90]

BOTETOURT. March 14, 1778.

SIR—We had an Opportunity this day at General Lewis' of considering the different Matters recommended to us in Your Excellency's Letter of the 19th of Feby last, and was assisted with that Gentleman's Opinion. We think it will be necessary that a Post of

---

[90] The first part of this letter is in the handwriting of Colonel Fleming; the latter part, in that of Colonel Preston. Both signatures are autograph.—ED.

Communication with F. Randolph be fixed at Kellys abt 22 Miles above the Mouth of Elk, as a place proper for Checking the Inroads of the Indians as well as inspiring the frontier Settlers with Confidence and affording them protection without which we are affraid the Inhabitants will abandon that Settlement And to answer the above Purposes we are of opinion this Garrison ought to consist of 100 Men, fifty from G. Brier & 50 from Botetourt. We offer it as our Opinion that the 50 men ordered to reinforce the Garison at F. Randolph may with safety be drawn from Rockbridge as it is an interior County not so immediately subjected to the Incursions of the Enemy.

And on considering the dangerous Situation of Montgomery County, which has a Frontier of upwards of eighty Miles, greatly exposed to the Enemy & but thinly inhabited, We Judge 50 men cannot be spared as a Reinforcement to the Garison at Fort Randolph, but that two or three Companies be immediately sent to such places, as will best secure the Inhabitants from the Enemy and Encourage them to continue which they are now ready to abandon. For the support of the men in provision at the Post of Communication as well as on the Frontiers of Montgomery County We think it will be highly Necessary Commisaries should be appointed and furnished with sums sufficient for purpose as no provision can be got otherwise. We fortunately had an Opp[y] of taking Capt Arbuckle & Col Skillerns Depositions relative to the Murder of the Indians at F. Randolph which we transmitted to y[r] Excellency by Mr Barnet. As it Appears by these Depositions the Agressors live in

Augusta, Rockbridge and Greenbrier Counties, We imagine you will send Orders to the Commanding Officers of these Counties concerning them. As we think it would be necessary to have a printed Copy of y^r Proclamation for Apprehending the Guilty & bringing them to Justice, that it may be transmitted with any Letter we send by the Grenadier Squaw to the Shawness Nation, it may tend to Convince them the Murder is had in abhorences by the Government and give an Authenticity to our Letter. We Judge it likewise necessary the state should be prepared to treat with the Indians, should a Conferrence be brought about by this Means which we are doubtful of as the Application is so late. We are y^r Excellencys most ob^t Servt

Wm Preston
Wm Fleming

[Gov. Patrick Henry to Col. William Fleming. 15ZZ21— A. L. S.]

W^{m}burgh March 14th 1778

Dear Col^o—Yours by Express came to hand yesterday, & I am much obliged by your attention to the several matters I mentioned to you. Please to use the public Amunition as you see fit, for your Defence. Draft the men from your County as divided or undivided as is most for the public service.

I am really concerned at the uneasiness you express from the Manner I mention'd the Death of the Indians. I know you too well to harbour the most distant suspicion that you ever approved what is in itself unworthy. Much less any thing glaringly wrong. Believe me I meant not the smallest censure, & I hope you will not think I did. I can give no particular Orders for Kentucki.

Please to march y^r Drafts to Alexandria Dumfries or George Town in Maryland & agree with a Victualler whom I will pay on rec'g your certificate. I refer to my proclama^n on the subject, I am Sir Y^r mo. H^{ble} Servt

Col. Wm Fleming.

P. HENRY

CLARK'S PREPARATIONS

[Col. George Rogers Clark to Capt. William Harrod. 18J69—
A. L. S.]

March 15th 1778

D^r CAP^{tn}—As the time is drawing nigh that we should start for Kentucky I think it best that we should as soon as possible get our provision Boats at Whelin up the Monongehaly in order to take in our Flour. I have Instructed the different Recruiting officers to send some of their men to whelin for that purpose and hope that you will get as many of your Company to go as you can. Mr. Richd Brashear^{91}

---

[91] Richard Brashears was a lieutenant in Capt. William Harrod's company. Having accompanied Clark on his expeditions to Kaskaskia and Vincennes, he was left at the latter place in charge of the garrison from April to August, 1779. In the latter month he returned to Kaskaskia, and early in 1780 was one of the garrison at Fort Jefferson. Returning to Kaskaskia, in the autumn of 1780 he married Ann Brocus [Brooks], and with her family emigrated to the Natchez country, for this purpose resigning from the army. Some time before his departure he was promoted to a captaincy, since in that capacity he received his share in the Illinois grant. In 1785 he was in Louisville temporarily, on business concerning his land—see Draper MSS., 1M111-117. He made his home in Mississippi, and died in the southern part of the

takes charge of the party. I propose that those that go on this Com^d shall be subject to no other duty untill they get to Kentucky.

My D^r S^r you know the necessity of bringing two or three boats up. I hope that you will get as many as you can to go. I intended to have come by your house from Court but our common interest called me another way. I am Si^r Your Hbl. Servt

GEO. R. CLARK

N. B. I shall go amediately to Pittsburgh & shant Return under eight Days. G R C

To Capt. Wm Harrod. Ten Mile. Pr Mr Brashears.

[General Hand to Col. David Shepherd. 3NN105— Transcript.]

FORT PITT, 22^d March, 1778

SIR—Please to deliver three of the Continental boats at Wheeling to the party of [whom] Col. Clark shall send to receive them, and order provision and ammunition sufficient to bring them to this place. I have ordered Lt. Berry to come up at the same time; besides the stores before called for, send by him all the powder except 200 lbs. to the left at Fort Henry. I am, sir, yr. hble. serv^t,

EDW^d. HAND

Col. David Shepherd.

state in May, 1822, leaving one daughter. The Carneys and Nicholls of Mississippi are his descendants.—ED.

MESSAGE TO WHITE EYES

[Col. George Morgan to Capt. White Eyes. MS. in Carnegie Library, Pittsburgh; George Morgan's Letter Book.]

FORT PITT March 29 1778

BROTHER CAP^t WHITE EYES—Agreeable to the letters I sent you some days ago I flatter'd myself with seeing you and some others of your Wisemen here very soon but unhappily the Messenger took sick and returned to this Place. He is now recovered and I send him to you and to call on Capt Pipe in his Way with Micheykapeecci the old Delaware Woman who was taken at Beaver Creek and also the Young Munsey Woman. I hope you will use your Interest to bring Capt Pipe and other Wisemen here that we may renew and strengthen our Ancient Friendship.

Two Wisemen are arrived from Virginia tho not the same I mentioned to you as they were detained by unavoidable Bussiness.[92] Be strong Brother and let us bear down the evil Spirit. I shall now be stronger than ever and I desire you be so too.

GEORGE MORGAN

[The Commissioners to Capt. White Eyes. Source, same as preceding document.]

PITTSBURGH March [blank in MS.] 1778.

CAPTAIN WHITE EYES—The Messenger sent by M^r: Clymer & Colonel Morgan about [blank in MS.] days

---

[92] Two of the commissioners chosen by Congress (Samuel Washington and Gabriel Jones—*ante*, p. 198, note 70) having refused to serve, Sampson Matthews and Samuel McDowell were chosen by the governor of Virginia, and accepted by Congress—see *Jour. of Cong.* (new ed.), x, p. 191. For Matthews, see *Dunmore's War*, p. 223, note 54; for McDowell, *Ibid*, p. 25, note 41.—ED.

MESSAGE TO WHITE EYES

ago falling sick upon the Road was obliged to return here, by which Accident you were unhappily prevented from hearing sooner of the good disposition of Congress towards the Delaware Nation, but as he is now well again, We who are all the Commissioners appointed by Congress send him back to your Nation with a confirmation of every thing that is said in the former Message. And to give further assurance of the good intentions of Congress he takes with him [blank in MS.] the Delaware Woman taken by our People that she may be restored to her Friends. The other Woman taken with her being a Munsey is in our possession & is well treated. We shall stay here long enough to give an opportunity for you & the other wise Men to visit us at Pittsburgh, in consequence of the invitation already given, to lay the foundation of a Treaty of Peace with your Nation & all other Indians who incline to have our Friendship & good Will, but as we wish to go home to our Wives and Children who are a great way off, we hope you will lose no time in coming with the Messenger. We are Your Friends & Serv^{ts}:

SAMP. MATHEWS
GEO. CLYMER
SAM^1: M^c: DOWELL

AMERICAN SPY AT DETROIT

[Daniel Sullivan's deposition. Source, same as preceding document.]

FORT PITT March 20th 1778.

To Colonel John Cannon[93]

SIR—Agreeable to my Contract with you in behalf of the State of Virginia, I proceeded to the Indian Country in February 1777 and return'd to this place in March when I gave you an Acc^t: of such intelligence as I had obtained. I immediately returned to the Indian Country in order to attend at all the Councils of the Different Nations, to inform myself of their dispositions and designs and to obtain the knowledge of every other Matter mention'd in my agreement.

I tarried among the Delawares and at Guyahaga untill the 19th of April. During my Stay among them the Delawares and Munsies appear'd perfectly disposed for Peace with the United States—they shew'd every good Disposition for that purpose. At Guyahaga I met with a few Chipwas, Ottawas, Wiandots and Mingoes about Twenty in Number. The white Mingoe was also there on his Way from Pluggys Town to Niagara. I could make no new Discovery here of any Consequence. A Message arrived at Kuskuskias from the Sennecas to the Delawares desiring them to sit still and plant their Corn, and informing them they should go now and then to visit their White Brethern. I could not discover that any of the other Nations had determined in Council to carry on a War against our Frontiers except the Mingoes of

---

[93] For a sketch of this officer, see *Rev. Upper Ohio*, p. 221, note 63.—ED.

Pluggys Town but I apprehended they did not appear to be over friendly.

At Guyahaga were two Traders with Stores of Indian Goods and a Cargo arrived there the 18th: of April from Detroit. the 19th I hired myself agreeable to Col. Morgans directions to James Howel to Serve as a Batteau Man to go to Detroit with Peltries and to bring away other Goods. We were eight days coasting it to Detroit. On my arrival I assisted to unload the Boat and then was conducted to Governor Hamilton in my Indian dress who enquired who I was and my Business. I inform'd him that I had been taken prisoner when young by the Delawares, that nine years afterward Viz^t in 1772 or 3. I went to live with my Relations in Virginia but the present War coming on between Britain and America and having no way but by my Gun to maintain myself I had removed back to my Delaware Relations and determined to live with them untill I could do better. That I had hired with a Trader at Guyahaga to assist him with his Peltries to Detroit in order to enable me to buy some Powder and Lead to hunt. After asking me some Questions touching the Strength of Fort Pitt and other Posts on the Ohio, the Governor dismiss'd me and told me to go where I pleased and he would be me Friend. One Mr Tucker[94] an Interpreter for Governor Hamilton of the Chipwa and Ottawa Tongues took me home to his house and treated me very kindly. And his Wife who was born in Hampshire County Virginia and had lived at my Sisters told me that Governor Hamilton did all

---

[94] For this interpreter, see *Ibid*, p. 203, note 44.—ED.

in his Power to induce all Nations of Indians to massacre the Frontier Inhabitants of Pennsylvania and Virginia and paid very high prices in Goods for the Scalps the Indians brought in. That he likewise pays for Prisoners but does not redeem them from the Savages and says he will not do it untill the Expiration of the present Warr. I Slept at Mr Tuckers and the next day went to walk through the Fort and Town and then walk'd round the Common. In this Tour Pluggys Son discover'd me and applied to the Governor to have me confined on Acco^{tt} of my having in the Fall of 1776 kill'd his Brother in law near the Kenhawa. John Montour seconded this Information and as a Proof referr'd to the wound I received in my left Arm at the time.[95] I was therefore sent for by Govr Hamilton and committed to the Guard, loaded with Irons, Hand and Feet and in seventeen days was sent to Niagara and from thence to Montreal and Quebec. At Montreal my Irons were taken off. I embark'd at Quebec about the 1st day of November for New York where I arrived the 20th of December and having given a Parole I was set at Liberty or rather sent from the 22^d to General Putnams head Quarters. I am satisfied with the truth of Mrs Tuckers Information and this is all I think myself at Liberty to say. The two Horses which I received from you together with my Gun, Paint and a Shirt which I have charged you I left with Mamaltese at the Delaware Towns to take Care of, the Tomhawk I left with Mr Tucker. I doubt not but you will think it just I should be paid for

---

[95] Possibly this is the event described by Arbuckle in his letter of Nov. 2, 1776: *Ibid*, p. 211.—ED.

them. I omitted to mention that I was hurried off from Detroit on Acc^t of the Delawares being determined to have me released. If the Honble Speaker and House of Delegates of Virginia shall think proper to make me any Compensation for my Suffering in their Service, I shall receive it with gratefull acknowledgements, and if they think proper to have me exchanged or get me released from my Parole, I shall be ready and I think I should have it in my Power to render essential Service to the States under the Direction of Col° Morgan as I think the Delawares have always been and Still are well disposed for Peace, Unless the late unfortunate affair at Beaver Creek and the other Murders Committed at Fort Pitt last Summer has sour'd their Mind. I am Sir Yours &c

DANIEL SULLIVAN[96]

YOUHIOGANIA COUNTY PITTSBURGH

Personally appear'd Daniel Sullivan this 21st day of March 1778 before me John Campbell One of the Justices of the Peace for said County who being duly sworn deposeth and saith that the forgoing Letter directed to Col° John Cannon and sign'd by the said Daniel Sullivan, contains a just and true relation of the Matters and things therin mention'd, and further saith not.

DANIEL SULLIVAN

Sworn to & subscribed by the said Daniel Sullivan the day & year above mentioned before me   JOHN CAMPBELL

---

[96] Nothing more is known of Daniel Sullivan's early life than is narrated in this document. He was at Louisville in 1780 where he platted some of its lots, and founded a station in Jefferson County. In 1782, while going as express to Fort Pitt from Kentucky, he was present at the siege of Wheeling

CONCILIATING THE SHAWNEE

[Col. George Morgan to Shawnee chiefs. Source, same as preceding document.]

PITTSBURGH March 25th 1778

Wapeymachickthe[97] *to the Chiefs & Warriors of the Shawnese Nation*

BROTHERS—When I look toward you or at the Kenawa River I am ashamed of the Conduct of our young foolish Men. formerly I was ashamed of the Conduct of your young men. Now I see there are foolish people among all Nations. Our Wise men are ashamed and sorry for what has happen'd and our Warriors declare themselves in like manner. For this Reason Brothers, I now send Swatswih[98] to tell you

---

and therein wounded. In 1785 he removed to Vincennes, and was in some way connected with Clark's expedition of 1786. In 1790 he was killed by Indians near Vincennes. He is said to have been "very stout and very brave and every inch a soldier"—Draper MSS., 13CC121.—ED.

[97] This was Col. George Morgan's Shawnee name, as Taimenend was his Delaware cognomen.—ED.

[98] The Indian name of James Girty, who was the messenger employed on this occasion. James Girty was born in 1743 in Pennsylvania, captured at the age of thirteen, and carried with all his family to the Indian town at Kittanning. During Armstrong's raid the Girty boys were removed from the vicinity, but were soon brought back and parcelled out among the tribes. While Simon went to the Seneca, and George to the Delawares, James was carried to the Shawnee towns and there resided for about three years. After the treaty of Easton (1759) he was returned to the settlements and lived in the vicinity of Fort Pitt, being employed as a laborer and occasionally getting an opportunity to interpret for traders. In March, 1778, he was employed by the commissioners then at Fort Pitt to carry a message to the Shawnee, in extenuation of the murder of their chief, and to persuade them to keep the peace. McKee and the escaping Loyalists found James Girty at Old Chillicothe, and easily persuaded him to join their party. He did not arrive at Detroit until August.

not to think hard of it. I know that the wicked Mingoes and Wiandots have occasioned the loss of your People at Kenhawa. They came and kill'd some of our People whilst yours were in the Fort on purpose to have them hurt. I therefore desire you not to think hard of the white people there. *Strings of Wampum*

Brothers Now Listen to what the great Council of the United States, say to you. Open your Ears that you may hear and your hearts that you may understand them. It is as follows

Brothers the Shawnese It gave us great joy to hear by our Agent Mr Morgan that you appear to be resolved to hold fast our Friendship. We have received all your Speeches and what you said at the Treaty last Summer. Your Words please us very much and so long as your actions correspond you may depend on

---

He was then taken into British pay, and made interpreter for the Shawnee. He led out his first party against the American settlements in Kentucky, in the autumn of 1778. Thence until the close of the Revolution he was in active service, reconnoitering (1779) toward Ouiatanon at the time of Clark's expected expedition, and accompanying that of Bird to Kentucky (1780). In the summer of the latter year he was at the Shawnee towns when they were raided by Clark. In 1782 he was among the forces that defeated Crawford, and in the Shawnee towns he informed against Slover. In the autumn of 1782, while his brothers were with Caldwell in Kentucky, James Girty was with the Indian party that besieged Wheeling. At the close of the Revolution he established a trading house at St. Mary's on the Maumee, at a place later known as Girty's Town. On the approach of Harmar (1790) he removed to Auglaize, and finally (1704) retreated before Wayne to Detroit, and then to Canada. There he had a grant of land (1807) in the township of Gosfield, whither he retired. Too infirm from rheumatism to take part in the War of 1812-15, he died at his farm, April 5, 1817.—ED.

our Friendship and we are determined to give you every Proof thereof in our Power.

Brothers We are sorry to hear what has happen'd at the Kenhawa. It has been owing to foolish wicked People and they shall suffer. We therefore desire you will not think hard of your White Brothers there on that Acco[tt]. but impute the Loss of your Friends to the Wicked Mingoes & Wiandots who came and killed some of our People near the Fort whilst yours were there on purpose to have them knock'd on the Head. You know there are foolish people among all nations.

Brothers We desire to give you full Satisfaction for the wicked Murder committed on your Chiefs and young Men at the Kenhawa. Therefore and in order to convince you that our Intentions are good and that we are resolved to clear the Road between us and to destroy all the Briars and Thorns which have grown therein, We have named three Wise Men to repair to Fort Pitt to consult with you for that purpose And we desire that you will appoint a few of your Chiefs to meet them there and whatever your Wise Men and ours agree to, let each of us resolve shall bind our People so that our Friendship may endure forever.

Brothers Consider well what we have proposed to you and let nothing Prevent your coming, even though your young Men in their Anger for the Loss of their Friends may have done us mischief. What we ask is to renew our Ancient Agreements and to put our Freindship on such a footing that our peace may never be interrupted. Tell us plainly whether you will or will not come as we desire, let us know your Minds for we shall consider your Answer as the Messenger of Peace or War and prepare ourselves accordingly. We wish to live in Peace with you and with all Indian Nations and we desire to give you satisfaction for the foolish Conduct of our young Men at the Kenhawa. Therefore Brothers if you wish for Peace as we do we desire that you will send some of your Wise Men as already mention'd that the Fears of your and our Women and Children may be done away and we promise you shall Not have reason to be sorry for their coming *Belt of Wampum*

Now Brothers You have heard the Voice of our great Council. Our three Wise men are arrived here. I therefore tell you to rise quickly and let nothing prevent your coming here. You know I never deceived you, therefore you may now beleive me. And with this Belt I clear the Road &c &c *A Road Belt.*

WAPEYMACHICKTHE

To the Chiefs and Warriers of the Shawnese Nation—

We join with Colonel Morgan in our Wishes that the antient agreement between us which we fear has been interrupted by unhappy Accidents may be renewed with Sincerity on both Sides. And we unite with him in the Invitation given in the name of Congress, who have sent us here, to come to Fort Pitt to establish a Peace, but we hope you will come quickly as we shall stay no longer than will be sufficient for you to make the Journey.[99]

Deliver'd to James Girty 1 p^r: broad Arm Bands 6 Hair Plates 6 doz: Broaches, 1 Stroud 1 p^r: Leggings 1 large Silver Cross 18 Silver Rings 1 Callico Shirt 1 Conk Shell

---

[99] This portion of the document was intended for the signature of the commissioners.—ED.

REPORT OF COMMISSIONERS

[Commissioners to Gen. Edward Hand. 3NN21-23— Transcript.]

SIR—As under the present circumstances of things, immediate recourse can be had to the Militia alone for the defence of this country against the incursions of the Indians: In the several conferences with you we have agreed to the following arrangement to take place until a plan which we shall recommend to Congress can be approved of & carried into execution.

For *Westmoreland* 150 men, that is, 30 to be added to Capt. Moorhead's company, & 120 to be disposed of for the protection of the county as shall be thought proper. This county to furnish the whole number for these Services, & also to find the necessary relief.

For *Yohogania* 150 men, that is, 30 for the town of Pittsburgh, & 120 for general service. The first draft to be made in the county.

For *Ohio* 150 men, that is, 50 for the garrison of Fort Henry, & 100 for more general Service: The 50 to be Supplied by Hampshire—20 from Yohogania & 30 from Monongolia, for the last mentioned Service; the remaining 50, to be furnished by the county of Ohio. The reliefs for the three counties of Yohogania, Monongolia & Ohio, to come from the interior counties of Berkley, Frederick, Shenandore, & Hampshire.

For the frontiers of Augusta, 150 men to be drawn from that county & Rockingham.

For *Fort Randolph* 50 men from Bottetourt & Rockbridge.

For *Greenbriar,* 150 Men, of which 100 from that county, & 50 from Bottetourt. Bottetourt to relieve its

DRAFT OF MILITIA

own Militia, but Rockbridge to relieve that of Greenbriar.

For Montgomery & Washington, a number not exceeding 300; these counties to furnish the first draughts as well as the reliefs.

Bedford being already provided for, is not included in this arrangement.

With respect to the relieving counties, we think in the requisitions made for that purpose, that regard should be had to their comparative strength as it appears in the act regulating the draughts lately passed by the Legislature of Virginia. The militia act of Pennsylvania limits the Service of its Militia to two months, but we think it would be proper your requisitions on Virginia should be for three months.

This is the general plan agreed on, but as many circumstances may arise which should occasion an alteration with regard to the force to be employed in the different counties, as well as the requisitions to be made, we do not wish you should be strictly confined to it, but think it extremely proper you should in these matters use your discretion, & deviate from it where necessity seems to require it, & the public cause served by it. We wish if practicable that instead of militia called out in the ordinary way, who are with difficulty brought to consider themselves soldiers, & will frequently abandon the most important enterprise in the moment of execution when their terms of service are about expiring, that you engage an equal number of volunteers to Serve for a longer time than can be expected or required of militia. The latter mode of protecting the country would, we believe, not only be more effectual, but more economical. We are, Sir, Your Most obed^t humble Serv^{ts},

SAM MATHEWS,
GEO. CLYMER,
SAML MCDOWELL.

Brig. Genl. Hand.

MURDERERS OF CORNSTALK

[Gov. Patrick Henry to Col. William Preston and Col. William Fleming. 15ZZ23—A. L. S.]

W^{ms}BURGH Mar 27^h 1778.

GENTLEMEN—As you prefer Kellys for the new post, please to order one hundred men officer'd in the usual Manner to do Duty there in the Way most likely to answer a good purpose, during such time as the safety of the Frontiers shall require. Fifty of these men are to be drawn from Botetourt & the other fifty from Green Bryar. I order the fifty men from Rockbridge to Fort Randolph which you advise. Montgomery need not send any if you judge it best, to that post. Let the men necessary to defend Montgomery be embodied & properly stationed. I send one thousand pounds cash by Mr Neilly to put into the Hands of such commissary as you shall Appoint. He ought to give Bond & Security to account for this or more money which may be given him to conduct that Business.

I send some printed proclamations against the Murderers of the Indians, please to distribute some to the countys most proper, & send others to the Indians, with whom I ardently wish a Treaty. Will you please to tell me what preparations you judge best to make in order to facilitate this work of peace? For indeed the Injustice of pursuing by offensive & vigorous Measures, those whom by our Injustice have been provoked to Hostility, is too striking & shocks me. I am Genl^t Y^r mo. hhble Servt

P. HENRY

To Col^{os} Wm Preston & Fleming

RELATIONS WITH DELAWARES

[Col. George Morgan to the Delaware chiefs. MS. in Carnegie Library, Pittsburgh; George Morgan's Letter Book.]

FORT PITT March 27th. 1778.

The United States of America to their wise Brethren of the Delaware Council

BROTHERS—It made my Heart glad to see your Messengers, and to receive your Letter. You have now made me stronger than I was before. All our People rejoice at this fresh testimony of your Friendship.

Brothers What you say convinces me that the great & good Spirit has directed you in your Councils. Your determinations are wise, and I desire you to continue strong in good works. The Tempest will be over in a few Months. You will then enjoy the Sweets of Peace, whilst your restless Neighbours are suffering the Punishment due to their evil Deeds. I know who they are, and every one of them shall suffer, except it be such as our wise Brethern the Delawares desire us to have pity on. I therefore hope they will bury the Hatchet and accept the friendship I still offer to them, before it be too late. The foolish Lake Indians are the Slaves of their pretended Father. they are afraid of him, or I think they would not act so foolish. for this reason and because their wicked Father at Detroit

Niagara &c, has put evil into the minds of our foolish Brethren, you will see him sunk from the place he is in, never more to be heard of. I tell you Brothers you will see this. What will then become of his foolish Children who still refuse to hearken to the wise Delaware Council. I wish to save them Brothers if it be possible. if you can assist me therein, I shall leave the method to you, and whatever the wise Delaware Council do, or whatever they agree to with the Wiandots &c, it shall bind me; provided they immediately leave off their foolish conduct, & prove themselves to be our Friends.

Brothers I am much pleased to hear that three Wise Chiefs of the Shawnese have come to live with you, and that a number of their People are inclined to sit down by their Grandfathers, and hold fast to our friendship as I desired them when I sent the Token to Coitcheleh last Fall, and in my Speeches last Summer. I desire you will encourage them all in your power to this good work, and that you may be like one strong Man in your Councils, to promote the good of your young Men, Women and Children.

Brothers I thank you for sending me the Papers which the Governor of Detroit sent to you, and your Grandchildren. He no doubt thought by his promises of Cloathing &c to make Fools of the wise Delawares—but he is mistaken.

Brothers I have no Cloathing at this present time to give to you, tho' I see you have occasion of them, but your wants shall be all supplied by and by, as they have heretofore been. I do not want you to carry Papers and to kill, Men, Women, or Children, like the

Governor of Detroit does, because he is not able to do it himself. I do not want you to get hurt in my Quarrel. What I want of you is to live in Peace and Friendship with me as Brothers ought to do, and to take care of your young Men, your Women and Children—this is what we desire of all Indian Nations. And this very Paper will be brought as a Witness against all those who may hereafter continue to act as the Servants of the Governor of Detroit.

Brothers I have already told you of the great success of our Armies toward the Sea, and of General Burgoyne, and all his Army being made Prisoners by General Gates. This I now confirm. And you may depend I shall be able to give you some more good News the ensuing summer.

Brothers I refer you for other matters to my Messages lately sent to you and to our Brothers the Shawnese. I now confirm them and I desire you will consider this as directed to you and to your Grandchildren jointly. Our wise Men wait here to see you, therefore make no delay. I have taken good care of your Messengers, but have nothing more to give them than plenty of good Victuals, Drink & Tobacco.

I desire you will aid and assist my Messenger to the Shawnese at Miami all in your power. I shall be rejoiced to have all your Grandchildren behave like wise People, and I beg you will give them good Council and assist them in taking care of their young Men, their Women and Children.

TAIMENEND

[Col. George Morgan to Zeisberger. Source, same as preceding document.]

FORT PITT March 27th. 1778.

To The Rev^d: Mr: David Zeisberger,

DEAR SIR—Just after I had sent James Girty and his Wife off with the Message to the Shawnese which he will shew to you, the Delaware Messengers arrived to my very great Joy.

I have sent your Packet down to Lancaster to Col^o: Nevill who left this yesterday. I lately forwarded to you two Letters from your Friends below. I have not heard from thence lately nor have I any News of importance to communicate to you.

General Burgoyne and all his Army are at Boston detain'd as Prisoners of War. I think our Affairs below are in a good way and hope this Summer will put an end to the Contest. We shall open the Campaign with greater advantages than ever.

It gives me great pleasure to hear you have been so quiet the last Winter and that you have hopes the ensuing Summer will not be so bad as the past.

It rejoices me exceedingly to hear that Capt. Pipe, Capt. White Eyes, Capt. Killbuck, and all the other wise Delaware Chiefs resolve to remain our Friends. Were it not from the hope of promoting Peace I would not stay here a moment.

I wish to God our mutual endeavours may be bless'd with success. For my own part I wish no other reward than to render service & to promote the Peace & happiness of the Indian Nations & the United States. Both have placed great confidence in me and I never will deceive either. I am with great respect &c

[GEORGE MORGAN]

ENGAGING VOLUNTEERS 245

REPORTS FROM FORT HENRY
[Col. David Shepherd to General Hand. 2U8--A. L. S.]
FORT HENRY March the 28th 1778.

SIR—Agreable to your order of the 22^d of this Instant I have Drafted fifty of the Militia of our County & have the most part of them on the Stations. there is some of them I am forced to use such Meashures with as is Disagrable to me, accotioned by some Disaffected people in our County. I have likewise Drafted ten Men out of our County for the Regular Service and Expect to Have them Ready in a few Days to Deliver to you or any person properly authorised for that Purpose as we are so far from the seat of Government. I would be glad to know of you what would be best to Do with them as they Might be usefull in your Department. I have Engaged some Volunteers to go on the Expedition you formerly mentioned to me against the first of aprill and have ordered them to be at Pitt against that time. But I fear the Murder Done at Dunker Creek[1] will prevent some of them and the Proper Supplies not havin Come to our assistance from the other Counties, We are Very Busy in hanging and Drying the Pork in Store, But men having such an aversion to work makes it Difficult. Every other order I shall Comply with as far as is in my power.

Any other matter that you may want to know the Barer Mr Robinson can Inform you   Sir I am with Respect your Humble Servant

DAVID SHEPHARD

To His Excelency General Hand
Pr favour of Mr Robinson.

---

[1] For Dunkard Creek, see *Rev. Upper Ohio*, p. 212, note 55. The depredations are further noted in Clark's letter of March 30, *post.*—ED.

246 FRONTIER DEFENSE ON UPPER OHIO

REPORT FROM FORT RANDOLPH
[Capt. William McKee to General Hand. 2U9—A. L. S.]

For[t] Randolph, 29th March 1778

Sir—In my Last of 29th Jan. you were Inform^d that six of the soldiers were Dead of the small Pox. There has six Died since in Garrison & one that went on Furloe with Capt Arbucle Died on the Road makes 13 on the whole 8 of my Comp'y & 5 of Capt Arbucles the Remainder that had the Disorder are all Recovered except one that is yet unfit for Duty The Garrison is now in general in good Health. The Indians have made no Attempt upon us. There was the signs of a party Discovered crossing Ohio 12 miles below this [the] 9th of this Instant I sent an express to the settlement to give notice who are Return'd and are now going to your post. I also Inform^d you our Beef wou^d be exhausted some time in April. But unfortunately above 3500 ^{lbs} was spoil^d & we have been totaly out of Beef since the 17th Inst. I expected either Pork or Bacon wou^d have been sent by Lt Gilmore[2] w^h (with the weakness of the Garrison) caused my Delaying sending on express sooner. To my Mortification was Disappointed. By yours of the 12th Instant I learn^d a supply of Pork for this place was Intended soon. But

---

[2] Lieut. James Gilmore belonged to the well-known Rockbridge County family of that name (see *ante*, p. 159, note 20), and had served under Capt. William McKee in Dunmore's War. When the Revolution began, he volunteered and as early as 1776 was a lieutenant in McKee's company on the Continental establishment. Having resigned before 1781, Gilmore raised and commanded a militia company from Rockbridge, for the relief of the Southern army, marched his troops to the aid of General Greene, and participated in the victory of the Cowpens (Feb. 17, 1781) under Gen. Daniel Morgan.—Ed.

AFFAIRS AT FORT RANDOLPH 247

from Lt Gilmore & Lt Hamilton (who is now here) I also am Inform^d that the scarcity both of Boats & hands as also your not expecting we were totaly out might Procrastinate the supply too Long. have therefore sent L^t Ja^s McNut with a party & a Boat with whom I hope you'll endeavour to send a sufficient supply of Pork or Bacon there is now about 50 Days Double Rations of flower for what men is here 20 Day's will elapse before the Boat Returns so that then there will scarce be single Rations of flower for two months. it therefore appears Necessary another Boat with an Additional supply of flower shou'^{d} be sent. I have sent with L^t Ja^s McNut an acc^t agst the United States for Cloathing Money for three of my Compy who are enlisted for three years w^c I hope your excel^y will send with him. There is a sum of the Bounty Remains in my hand and it Does not appear I shou^d have an opportunity to use it in the Recruiting way here, therefore wou^d Desire your Directions where or to whom I shall refund it. the men are giving in their Notices already that they won^t serve longer than their present term. I have learn^d from good Authority that the Indians Intend striking a severe Blow at this place some time in May next. The Money arriv^d safe. Mr Gilmore is gone Down the River after those Deserters. Mr Hamilton is here after another party it seems as if all the men wou^d Desert your post. We have not ½ bushel salt in the garrison one Battoe was cut loose at three o'c in the Morning of the 9th Ins^t either by Indians or Deserters she was pursued Directly but the Darkness of the Night and a Fogg on the River prevented her being got the other Day we Catch^d one a

Drift of the same make & size with the others supposed to come from your Garrison. I have sent a certificate of Ja^s Logan & Phill. Hamond going express to Green Briar.[3] present my Comp^{ts} to Maj^r. Ewing Col^o Mathews & McDowel. I am Your Excel^{ys} Most Ob^t Hble Servt

W^m M^{c}KEE

Edward Hand B. Genl Fort Pitt

ATTACK ON DUNKARD CREEK

[Maj. George Rogers Clark to General Hand. 18J71— A. L. S.]

MUDDY C^k. March 30th 1778

Dr GENERAL—I am much obliged to you for sending my Letters to me as for your opening them it is a matter of no importance. The hostilities commited in this part of the Country stopt the party that I had ordered to wheling [Wheeling] for the Boats as their presence was amediately nessessary in the neigherhood. I have fited of a party to Day which I hope will answer the purpose intended. The Indians have made

---

[3] James Logan of that part of Augusta now a part of Rockbridge County, was a son of the elder James, who with his brother David (father of Benjamin Logan of Kentucky) settled at an early day on Carr's Creek. James the younger was in McKee's company during Dunmore's War, and appears to have enlisted as a volunteer in the Revolution. He married Hannah Irvine, and two of his sons, Robert and Joseph D., were well-known Presbyterian ministers in the Shenandoah Valley.

Philip Hammond took part in Dunmore's War, among the Botetourt volunteers. His title to fame is his notification to the inhabitants of Donnally's Fort of the approach of the Indians (May, 1778), and his gallant defense of that fort. Particulars of his after life are not known to us. He may have descended from the Maryland family of Hammonds, among whom the patronymic Philip was frequent.—ED.

three different attacks on Dunkard C[reek] which is entirely evacuated.[4] I am Si[r] your hble. Serv[t]

G. R. CLARK

Gen[l] Edw[d] Hand   Pittsburg   Pr Express

LOYALISTS ESCAPE

[Gen. Edward Hand to Jasper Yeates. MS. in New York Public Library; Hand Papers—A. L. S.]

FORT PITT 30th. M[ch]. 1778

D[r]. YEATES—I am in such Distress on being Satisfied that M[r]. M[c].Kee has made his escape from here the night before last, Accompanied by Mat: Elliot,[5]

---

[4] For the attack on the inhabitants of Dunkard Creek, see Thwaites, *Withers's Border Warfare*, pp. 238-240. The British reports of parties sent out, are in a letter of Henry Hamilton in *Mich. Pion. & Hist. Colls.*, ix, pp. 434, 435.—ED.

[5] Matthew Elliott was born in Ireland, but removing to Pennsylvania at an early age, he settled at Carlisle. Having entered the Indian trade, he was familiar with the Shawnee and acted as their peace ambassador in Dunmore's War. At the outbreak of the Revolution he was, with his servingman Michael Herbert, taken in the Muskingum country by six Wyandot Indians and carried prisoner to Detroit. In later life he claimed to have abandoned his property and gone to Detroit because of Loyalist principles (*Mich. Pion. & Hist. Colls.*, xxv, p. 178). He was, nevertheless, regarded with suspicion at Detroit, arrested, and sent down to Quebec. There he was released upon parole, and making his way to Fort Pitt escaped to Detroit, Mar. 28, 1778. He was at once made captain in the Indian department, with a salary of ten shillings per day. His influence was great with the Shawnee, among whom he had married. Throughout the Revolution Elliott was actively engaged against the American frontier, taking off the Moravians in 1781, and aiding in Crawford's defeat (1782). After the war he settled at his home on the Canadian side of Detroit River, and in 1790 became deputy superintendent of Indian affairs, and 1795 superintendent. In 1798, through some difficulty with the military arm of the service, he was summarily dismissed from office. In 1801 he represented Essex in the parliament of Upper Canada, and was again a member in 1805 and 1809. In 1808 he was restored

Simon Girty, two others I am not Acquainted with & two negroes, that I can Say very little to you at this time—
I inclose you a coppy of the Proceedings of the Commissioners respecting Col: Morgan & Matters in Gen[l]. 5 men were lately Murdered on Dunkard Creek, two Wounded & 4 taken last week a soldier kild an Indian on the Indian Side nearly Opposite M[r]. Croghans place but did not escape himself. I hope to See you Soon Untill then Adieu D[r]. Yeates most Affectionately y[rs].

EDW[d]: HAND

Jasper Yeates Esq[r]. To the Care of Rich[d]. Peters Esq[r].

[General Hand to Gen. Horatio Gates. 3NN105, 106— Transcript.]

FORT PITT, 30th. March, 1778.

SIR—I have the mortification to inform you that last Saturday night, Alex[r]. McKee made his escape from this place, as also Mathew Elliott, a person lately from Quebec on parole, Simon Girty, Rob[t]. Surplus, and one Higgins.[6] On my arrival from Kanhawa in

---

to his office as superintendent of Indian affairs, receiving at the same time a commission as captain in the regulars. At the outbreak of the War of 1812-15 he became deputy-quartermaster-general, and leader of the Indians, and in 1814 received a medal for his efficient services. When the Kentuckians captured Amherstburg after Perry's victory on Lake Erie, they completely wrecked Elliott's house and furniture, because of his conspicuous services to the British cause. Elliott retired with the army to the Thames, and after that battle proceeded to Joseph Brant's place on Burlington Bay, where in May, 1814, he died. His descendants returned to his former home in Amherstburg, where they inherited a considerable estate, including about sixty negro slaves.—ED.

[6] Robert (called Robin) Surphlitt (Surplus) was a cousin of Alexander McKee. He was placed on the pay-roll of the

Decr last, I recd. the direction of the Board of War to send McKee to York Town on his parole, and accordingly wrote him the enclosed note the 29th Decr., which he told the messenger required no answer. Finding he did not come up from his farm (where he then was) as soon as I expected, I repeated my desire in the note dated 7th Feb'y, on which he came here immediately and apologized for his delay. When I returned here from my late excursion into the Indian country, I found him still here pretending indisposition, which with other plausible excuses detained him until the time of his escape—an event the more distressing to me as it was distant from my thoughts; nor can I help thinking that Elliott brought him despatches from Quebec which influenced him at this time. * * *

P. S. Within this month 5 men have been killed, 2 wounded, & 4 taken by the Savages on Dunkard Creek. Last week two soldiers straggled over the Alleghany and fell in with 5 Indians, the soldiers had the first fire and killed one; but afterwards suffered a like loss themselves.

Indian department and apparently was employed as a messenger to the tribesmen. After the Revolution he was reduced to half pay, and in 1796 pensioned for his services as "late lieutenant of the Western Indians." In 1803 he applied for a grant of land, and spoke of his residence as not being far from the Niagara frontier.

John Higgins appears to have been a servant of McKee. He was placed upon the pay-roll of Indian volunteers at four shillings a day. In 1779 he attempted to desert to Clark's army, but was captured at the Miami towns. In February, 1783, he was discharged, and in April of that year McKee met him at Roche de Bout.—Ed.

A report prevails that 28 men were taken by the savages at the Salt Lick near Kentucky in Feb[y].[7]

To Maj. Gen. Gates

EDW[d] HAND

[General Hand to Col. William Crawford. 3NN107— Transcript.]

FORT PITT, 30th. March, 1778.

DR. CRAWFORD—I recd yr. favor of yesterday, and am sorry for the accident that befel Mr. De Camp, and send the Doctor to his assistance.

You will no doubt be surprised to hear that Mr. McKee, Matthew Elliott, Simon Girty, one Surplus, and Higgins, with McKee's two negroes, eloped on Saturday night. This will make it improper to proceed with the intended expedition to French Creek, which I beg you may give proper notice of to the gentlemen who are preparing for it; and as your assistance may be necessary towards preventing the evils that may arise from the information of these run-

---

[7] This refers to the capture of Daniel Boone and the party from Boonesborough, who were boiling salt at the Lower Blue Licks. The captors were about 120 Shawnee Indians led by their war chief, Blackfish. They were on their way to attack Boonesborough, in revenge for the killing of Cornstalk. The Kentucky pioneers did not anticipate an attack during the winter months, hence their fort was palisaded upon only three sides. Boone was captured while bringing in supplies of meat obtained in hunting. Learning the number and purpose of the enemy, he persuaded them to be content with the capture of the salt-boilers, twenty-six in number, whom he agreed to persuade to give themselves up. They were taken to the chief Shawnee town, then on the Little Miami three miles north of the present town of Xenia. There Boone was adopted into the family of Blackfish. He made his escape the following June.—ED.

aways, I beg you may return here as soon as possible
I am, Dr. Crawford, sincerely yrs,

Edwd Hand

Col. Wm. Crawford.

[Maj. Jasper Ewing to Jasper Yeates. Reprinted from
Historical Register (Harrisburg, Pa., 1884), ii, p. 157.]

FORT PITT, Mar. 30, 1778.

HOND. SIR—Last Saturday Night Mr. McKee, Matt. Elliott, and Simon Girty, together with one Higgins ran off. McKee's Conduct on this Occasion is of so infamous a Nature, that it will forever render him odious. The General's Behaviour to him, time after time, when he was ordered below, and his Pitiful Excuses, seem to infer that his Escape was premeditated. His Intimacy with Elliott has been very great, and 'tis conjectured that Elliott brought dispatches for McKee from Quebec. As he was reputed to be a Gentn. of the Strictest Honour and Probity, no body had the least Idea of his being Capable of acting in so base a manner. A man of his Capacity, and so well acquainted with the Situation of our affairs in this department, will be no unwelcome Guest at Detroit. I am, Honerd. Sir, Yr. much obliged Nephew,

J. EWING

Jasper Yeates, Esq. To the Care. of Richd. Peters, Esq.

[Col. George Morgan to the President of Congress. MS. in Carnegie Library, Pittsburgh; George Morgan's Letter Book.]

FORT PITT March 31st. 1778.
To the Honble. Henry Laurens Esqr.

SIR—As the Commissioners & General Hand are possess'd of every information respecting the situation of affairs in this Quarter, I beg leave to refer you to their Letters & to the inclosed Message from the Delawares[8] & Governor Hamilton's new Proclamation with two of his old ones which accompany this.[9]

I only wait here in hopes of being assistant to the Commissioners during their stay at this place. As they are fully acquainted with my sentiments respect-

---

[8] The message from the Delawares stated that Killbuck made a visit to Detroit in December, and that their forces were too few to cause uneasiness at Fort Pitt. White Eyes sent word that thirty Wyandots were out on the warpath toward the Redstone settlements—probably the band that made reprisals on Dunkard Creek. White Eyes also stated that Cornstalk's tribe of the Shawnee seemed willing to accept the apologies of the whites for the murder of their chief, and would continue friendly. The Delawares do not appear to have been aware of the Shawnee raid to the Blue Licks, and the capture of Daniel Boone and his men.—ED.

[9] This refers to a circular letter written by Hamilton (Jan. 5, 1778), enclosing a statement from several American captives testifying to the kind and humane treatment they had received from both Indian and white captors. This was signed by the following persons: "George Baker for himself, Wife & five Children now here, from 5 Miles below Logs Town; James Butterworth from Bigg Kenhawa; Thomas Shoers (his mark), from Harridge [Harrod's] Town near Kentucky; Jacob Pugh, from six miles below the Fort at Wheeling; Jonathan Muchmore, from Fort Pitt; James Whitaker, from Fort Pitt, taken at Fish Creek; [blank in ·MS.] from Bedford taken at Sandy Run; John Bridges (his mark) from Fort Pitt, taken at ditto." See Bausman, *Beaver County*, i, pp. 150, 151.—ED.

ing Indian Affairs I need not repeat them to Congress.

The elopement of M^r. McKee late Crown Agent at Pittsburgh who most dishonourably broke his Parole on the 28th. inst. has somewhat check'd the pleasing expectation I entertain'd respecting the Delawares & Shawnese, tho' I think the former will not be altogether influenced by him. Four persons accompanied him viz: Matthew Elliott, Simon Girty, Robin Surplis & [blank in MS.] Higgins.

Elliott had but a few weeks ago return'd from Detroit via New York on his Parole & I am told had possess'd M^r: M^c:Kee's mind with the persuasion of his being assassinated on his Road to York. Indeed several persons had express'd the like apprehensions, and perhaps had also mention'd their fears to him which I am of opinion has occasion'd his inexcuseable Flight. It is also very probable that Elliott might have been employ'd to bring Letters from Canada which may have influenced M^r: M^c:Kee's conduct.

Girty has served as Interpreter of the Six Nation Tongue at all the public Treaties here & I apprehend will influence his Brother who is now on a Message from the Commissioners to the Shawnese to join him.

The Parties of Wiandots mention'd in the Letter from Capt: White Eyes have committed several Murders in Monongahela County. Last week two Soldiers who had cross'd into the Indian Country 4 or 5 Miles from this Post to hunt, discover'd five Indians, one of whom they shot before the Indians perceived them— the Fire was return'd, one of our Men was kill'd & the other escaped back to the Fort.

The Massacre of the Indians who were invited to a friendly Conference at Fort Randolph & the unlucky mistake at Beaver Creek[10] I doubt not Congress are fully inform'd of by General Hand to whose Letters I beg leave to refer & remain with the greatest respect

[GEORGE MORGAN]

SIR—Since writing the foregoing I have received an unexpected requisition from General Hand, a Copy of which I inclose.

I am taking the necessary measures to comply with the General's order—to enable me to do this Business I must beg the favour of Congress to send to me by the Bearer James McClelland who goes Express for the Commissioners four thousand Dollars. I am with great Respect &c.

BOAT BUILDING

[Colonel Morgan to Colonel Buchanan. MS. in Carnegie Library, Pittsburgh; George Morgan's Letter Book.]

FORT PITT March 31st. 1778

To Colonel William Buchanan
  Commissary General of Purchases.

*   *   *   *   *   *   *   *

Mr: Stewart (Father to Major Stewart[11] taken on Staten Island) proposed to me the building of arm'd

---

[10] The first reference is to Cornstalk's massacre; the second to Hand's campaign.—ED.

[11] This officer, known as Maj. Jack Stewart, belonged to the Maryland line, where he was commissioned as first lieutenant in 1776, captain in December of the same year, and major in April, 1777. In August of the last-named year, he participated in Sullivan's unsuccessful attack on Staten Island, and was captured after such a brave attack "as would honor the finest troops in the world." Having been exchanged,

BOAT BUILDING

Boats on the Ohio and I believe would undertake the six Boats now order'd that he might acquire a more perfect knowledge of the Country and form a better Judgment of his proposed private undertaking.

As he has a number of his own Workmen I think it would be well to send an Express to him on this business, requesting his attendance at York if he inclines to undertake the business.

A considerable number of other Boats will be wanted as I formerly wrote to you but I have received no orders respecting them. I am with respect &c

[GEORGE MORGAN]

For your information I inclose to you the Contract of the Carpenters who built the last thirty Boats. I could wish the article of Rum to be left out if possible in the new Contract but I would not let this delay the Business. The Workmen and Materials may be directed in case of my absence to M^r: Joseph Skelton.[12] The Materials wanted will be

Rudder Irons & Pintles; Six Pump Spears and Boxes; Six large Ring Bolts; 12 Iron Potts for Cabouses; 1 large d^o:, to boil Pitch in and two Ladles; Two thousand weight of Deck Nails and Spikes assorted; Canvas & Blocks necessary for Sails; Cordage for d^o: and for Cables; 12 Barrels of Pitch; 2 d^o: Turpentine; 600 ℔ Oakum; Sail Twine; Sail Needles; 500 ℔ largest Rod Iron;

6 Rheams of Paper; 2 doz: Ink Powder; 4 hundred Quills; 1 ℔ Sealing Wax; 1 ℔ Wafers; 2 good Penknives, for the Commissary's Department

---

Major Stewart was in Wayne's forces upon their attack on Stony Point, and was honored with a silver medal struck by order of Congress to commemorate his gallantry. He was later colonel of the 1st Maryland regiment, and is said to have been killed by a fall from his horse near Charleston, not long after the close of the Revolution.—ED.

[12] Commissary of stores at Fort Pitt.—ED.

[Gen. Edward Hand to Col. George Morgan. MS. in Carnegie Library, Pittsburgh; George Morgan's Letter Book.]

FORT PITT 21st. March 1778.

To Colonel George Morgan,

SIR—The Hon'ble the Commissioners appointed by Congress to repair to this place for various purposes, have recommended the building six Boats to carry one four Pounder each, and otherwise calculated for War, to secure the Navigation of the Ohio River from Post to Post, as you have had the direction of the Boats already built here, I beg you may take the necessary steps towards the speedy building of these arm'd Boats, the Dimensions and Construction I must leave to yourself, who are a better Judge than I can possibly be. I am Sir, Your Hble Servant

EDW^d: HAND

ADDRESS TO THE SHAWNEE

[Col. William Preston and Col. William Fleming to the Shawnee. 2ZZ44—A. L. S.[13]]

To the Chiefs & Warriors of the Shawnese Nation

BROTHERS—We are Commanded by His Excellency the Governor and Council of the State of Virginia to Address your Nation. And we request in the Name of Our Governor, that you will listen patiently to what we have to say, and that you will accept the proposals we are ordered to make to you in behalf of all the good people of Virginia.

Warriors and Chiefs—It is with the deepest Concern and sincerest Sorrow that we reflect on the Mur-

---

[13] The draft of this letter is in the handwriting of Col. William Fleming; the signatures of both Fleming and Preston are appended.——ED.

der committed by some of Our rash young People, on the Corn Stalk and three Others of your Nation. Yet this Accident we hope will not lessen the Great Council Fire, before which your Father and Ours, and Yourselves and we, have sat and smoaked the Pipe of Peace. When you consider that one of our Officers was kiled by an Indian over the Kanhaway in sight of the Fort, and our hot headed young Men, believing it was done by some of Your Nation, prompted them to commit the horrid Murder, but we are Commanded to Assure you, that the Governor and all the Great Men of Virginia detest the crime and are much concerned that the Chain of Friendship which binds us together as Neighbours, Antient Allies & Friends, should contract any Rust. And to convince you of the sincerity of Our great Men, we are ordered to send you some of the Governors Proclamations, in which a reward is offered for Apprehending the Murderers, And every method taken to bring them to Justice. You may be Assured they will be punished by our Laws, when they are taken in the same manner, as if they had kiled so many of our own People. We are Ordered to propose to you that Commissioners for Virginia, meet some of your Wise Old Men in treaty at Fort Randolph, in hopes that they can make you such reparation as will satisfy Your Nation, and convince you of the Peaceble disposition of Virginia towards you. We love you, because you are Generous & Sensible. We wish to be Friends with you. We have no desire to injure or molest you. We covet nothing you have. All we desire is Peace with you. this we are earnest to propose because Our Young

Men have done amiss & treated you ill. We Acknowledge it, and are Willing to make all the satisfaction we can. When you think seriously on the whole Affair We hope Your Wise Men will conclude to meet at Fort Randolph and hear what more the Virginia Commissioners have to say to you. If you will set a time when it will suit you to meet there, The Governor and Council will appoint Commissioners to talk with you, and endeavour to Cover the Blood that has been Spilt upon the Path of Peace, and brighten the Chain of Friendship. In order to forward this happy work, that you may be easy in Your minds, and safe in your Persons, when you come to treat an equal number of white people shall be sent over the Ohio, and put into your Peoples hands, for your sincerity and safe return. And we assure you of the most Friendly treatment, And should any Chiefs or Great Men of your Neighbouring Nations, Delawares, Mingoes, Wyandots come with you, they will be received kindly and treated as Friends. In the meantime we beg you will not hearken to the bad talks of our Enemies and Yours, they want us to destroy one another;[14] And then they they will possess Your Lands and ours enslave Our Children & Yours. Your People and Ours live in the same

---

[14] Compare with this the message sent the Shawnee by White Eyes, the Delaware chief, after McKee and the other Loyalists had passed through his village: "Grand children! ye Shawanese! some days ago a flock of birds, that had come on from the east, lit at Goschochking, imposing a song of their's upon us, which song had nigh proved our ruin! Should these birds, which on leaving us, took their flight towards Sciota, endeavor to impose a song on you likewise, do not listen to them, for they lie."—Heckewelder's *Narrative*, p. 182.—ED.

land, breath the same Air, and drink the same water. We ought to live in Peace like Friends & Brothers. And we hope you will lay down the Hatchet, and restrain your Young Men from disturbing Our Frontiers, untill you hear the good Talk from Our Governor which he will send you by his Commissioners.[15] We send this by the Grenadier Squaw, and in full Assurance that you will accept the proposals we have made and send us both a Friendly Answer to Fort Randolph, which the Officer there will forward to us, we send you this String of White Wampum, And subscribe ourselves, Your Friends & Brothers

        WM. PRESTON
        WILLIAM FLEMING

Virginia Aprile 3^d 1778

---

[15] The following "Heads of a Letter to the Shawnesse" were written out by Colonel Preston and appended to his letter to Colonel Fleming, March 14, 1778 (Draper MSS., 4QQ163): "That we are commanded to write to them by the Governor. That he and all his great men & the good Men in Virg^a are sorry for the Murder. That every method is and shall be taken to bring the Murderers to Justice. That if they are taken they shall be tryed by our Laws in the same manner as if they had murdered so many white People. That the Governor is desirous some of the Warriors would come to the point & hear & that he will send Com^s to meet them. That for their Security while they are talking of Peace an equal Number of white warriors shall be sent over the River as hostages. That the Virginians are unwilling to begin a War with them, and very desirous of Peace and want to have all difference made up that they may once more be Friends. That it will be for the Benefit of their Nation. That to convince them of the sincerity of our professions & Friendship, that should any [of] the Murderers be taken up some the Indians may be present & see it. Hot headed young Men."—ED.

DEFENSE OF THE SOUTHWESTERN FRONTIER

[Gov. Patrick Henry's circular letter. 2U12. Printed document, autograph signature.]

WILLIAMSBURG, April 12, 1778.

SIR—The season is now come when the enemy will again take the field, and perhaps, by means of an increased number of forces, may oblige the continental army to retreat, and so overrun and ravage a great extent of country. In order to check this destructive progress, it is more than probable that assistance from Virginia will be called for. As the volunteer scheme does not promise to succeed, the militia will be our only resource, and from that must be drawn so many men as the exigency may require. Added to this, our own country is liable to be invaded on all sides, and a prudent regard to our safety, nay our existence, demands that we be prepared to resist.

The design of this address is to require your most strenuous exertions to get your militia in readiness. In a particular manner, I entreat your attention to the arms and accoutrements of the men, and to see that one third part of them be put into readiness to march at a moment's warning. I desire that you will be particular in getting returns from your Captains, by which the repairs necessary to be made to the arms and accoutrements may be discovered; and, after orders are given for these repairs to be made, you will order other returns, by which you may see whether they are properly executed. Let powder horns and shot bags be provided, where cartridge boxes cannot. A particular report of the number of your men, and the condition of their arms and accoutrements, when

CLARK'S PREPARATIONS   263

you have executed these orders, will be necessary; and I shall expect it with impatience, equal to the importance of those consequences which will follow from the punctual discharge of your duty. I am, Sir, Your Most humble Servant,

P. HENRY

CLARK'S PREPARATION FOR OHIO VOYAGE

[Col. George Rogers Clark to Capt. William Harrod. 18J72— A. L. S.]

April 12th 1778.

D^r C_{AP}^{tn}—I have this Day heard of our Boats coming up the River they left Wheling last tuesday. I also hear that the companies that I expected a Cross the Mountains is now on their march out so that I hope that we shall shortly be able to imbark for Kentucky as this is the Day that your Company was to imbody, I thought it necessary to get this inteligence to you as quick as possible as the men might not be uneasy. I should be glad that you would gather the remainder of your Company (that is not on Com^d to Wheling) and keep them imbodied and ready to March at the shortest warning as we shall start as soon as possible, as you are on the frontier your company will be a guard to ye Inhabitants while you stay. (what goods belonging to you & Company that is to go down may be got ready to be put on board) Lieu^t J. Swan[16] I expect will furnish Rations for the Com-

---

[16] John Swan was one of the early settlers of Monongahela, having first visited the region in 1767 and blazed trees for a claim. In 1769 he removed his family thither from the Potomac, where they had settled after leaving the ancestral home in Loudoun County. The Swan place was contiguous to

pany while they lay their, which I shall pay him for, one of my Brothers[17] came up the other day with some Acc[ts] from the Governor to me, desireing me to be expeditious as possible as he is apprehensive that the Ind[s] will shortly make a brake on the Frontiers and our being on our station he expects will draw their attention towards us until the army can be got ready to march into the Indian Cun[y]. I have sent you part of the late Laws of Virginia in which you will see part of the Invation Act and the authority of an Officer on duty. I am Si[r] your H[bl] Serv[t]

G. R. CLARK

On publick service   To Cap[tn] W[m] Harrod Tenmile Creek.

---

that of Jacob Van Meter, in Cumberland township of Greene County; and a blockhouse built about 1770 was named Fort Swan and Van Meter. It seems probable that the Lieut. John Swan, who was in Harrod's company on Clark's expedition, was a son of the first settler. John junior was in the expedition to Kaskaskia (1778), and it is said (Draper MSS., 36J26) that he went out as captain of a company in the Shawnee expedition of 1780. After that, nothing more is known to us of this officer. A family tradition (*History of Greene County, Pa.*, p. 400) relates that while one son of the elder John Swan was emigrating with his family to Kentucky, he was shot and instantly killed on the boat while going down the Ohio River. May this not account for the disappearance of the young officer who served under Clark? Charles Swan remained on the family estate in Pennsylvania, where his descendants yet live.—ED.

[17] This was probably Richard Clark, fourth son of the family; Jonathan, the oldest, was in the Continental service; George Rogers was the second son; John, the third, was in a British prison, having been captured at Germantown. Richard Clark was born (1760) in Caroline County, Va. In March, 1779, he joined his brother George's army to the Illinois as a volunteer, receiving a commission as lieutenant in June of the same year. In May, 1780, he was at Cahokia, and served with Montgomery on the latter's Peoria expedition. Later, Richard Clark was a member of the garrison at Fort Jefferson, and in the spring of 1781 returned to Louis-

INDIAN DEPREDATIONS 265

SOUTHWEST VIRGINIA FRONTIER ATTACKED

[Col. William Preston to Col. William Fleming.[18] 3ZZ14—
A. L. S.]

My Business called me 20 miles above Fort Chiswell[19] [MS. torn] whence I returned last night much fatigued having rode great part of [the way] in the Rain and crossed the River yesterday at the Risque of my Life. This [was] occasioned by an Express from Culborsons Bottom[20] which followed me to near the head of Holston. The account was, that the scouts, on tuesday last were met by fifteen Indians who pursued them so closeley that it was supposed one [was ta]ken. However I hear he is since come to the fort. The Indians have [invested] a little Garrison about five Miles above Culbersons in such a [way] that the Officer made two or three attempts before he could send me a [message]. At length an active man brought a Letter dated the 10th. They had not heard from Culbersons for three Days. I have ordered men from several companies to the Relief of these Places but I am really affraid they will not arrive in Time as the Waters are impassable. It is supposed by the People that a large Body of Indians are come in and that a Number have passed [by] the

---

ville. In March, 1784, while travelling alone from Louisville to Vincennes, he lost his life either by an accident or an Indian ambush. As his horse was found with all his trappings and accoutrements, it was at the time surmised that he was drowned while crossing the Little Wabash.—ED.

[18] This letter is unaddressed, but its contents show that it was written to Colonel Fleming, county lieutenant for Botetourt.—ED.

[19] For account of Fort Chiswell, see *Dunmore's War*, p. 52, note 90.—ED.

[20] For this location, see *Ibid*, p. 76, note 25.—ED.

garrisons down the River to strike the Inhabitants. This supposition, I [think] is probable, and if I hear any further Accounts this Day, I shall make [use of] the kind Indulgence you gave me of calling some Men from Botetourt.

I see very little Occasion to alter the Letter to the Shawnesse, two or three alterations I have pointed out, which Letter with the Wampum [MS. torn] you will meet Capt. Arbuckle at Court and get him to forward it. Have it fairly Copied please to put my Name to it.

You were certainly right in purchasing Provisions for the Draughts and not engage a Person to Victual them on the Road, and equally so in making [use of] the Public Money for that Purpose, as it was not so immediately wanted [for the] Militia. I was obliged to advance Capt Crockett[21] £70 for the Draughts in this County.

I am sorry that the Deserter brought by R. Preston[22] does not answer the [purpose]. At that time, nor till I rec^d your Message by Mr Floyd.[23] I had not adverted [to that] Clause. Since which I have been informed that the Reg^t that Deserter belonged [to was] composed of Virg^a & Maryland Troops. Had I thought or believed that it was not legally clear, I could readily have got a Deserter for him which [MS. torn] young Man to take. But as he is now in Carolina & will not

---

[21] This officer is noted in *Ibid*, p. 44, note 79.—ED.
[22] See for Robert Preston, *Ibid*, p. 174, note 21.—ED.
[23] Capt. John Floyd must have but just returned from his captivity in England, after his disastrous privateering expedition. See sketch of his life in *Ibid*, p. 9, note 15.—ED.

[return] till June I will do all I can to have the Matter fully Settled before he [gets] in.

Col° Lynch told be last Tuesday that he had but 1500 lb. of Lead [at the] Mines,[24] & the Frontier Inhabitants were daily calling for it agreeable [to the] Governors Order; but that in 8 or ten days his Furnace would be ready [and he] hoped to be able to Supply all the Demands against him for that Article; [that the] Governor had wrote a most pressing Letter to him to send two tons to Fort [Pitt and] a large Quantity to Congress.

Before I saw the Colonel, I was informed that he makes the Inhabitants [MS. torn] for the lead ordered them by the Governor. I shall write to [MS. torn] the first opportunity & know the certainty; & Mention your [MS. torn]. At present I am sure he cannot Supply you, therefore it would [be useless to] send up for it.

Any Expence that Capt Arbuckle may be at, arid he ought [not to be] restricted, must be paid him; any Assurance you think proper to give [him on] that Head, I shall most readily Join you therein.

I cannot *perfectly agree in Sentiment with the Honble the Commissioners,* that Botetourt should send as many men out of the County as Rockbridge,[25] as [that] has a Frontier of its own to Defend, which is not the case with the latter. I am convinced the Militia of Botetourt is not near equal to that [of the lat-

---

[24] For Col. Charles Lynch, see *Rev. Upper Ohio,* p. 174, note 4.—ED.

[25] For the quotas ordered by the commissioners at Fort Pitt, see *ante,* p. 238.—ED.

ter] County, but the misfortune was, that Bo^t had no representative at Pittsburg. Upon the whole, for the above reasons and many [that will] readily Occur to you, were it my Case I would postpone that [perfect] Obedience to the Commander which is required untill the Governor, who by Law has the Command of the Militia, should be made acquainted with the Demand and the ill Consequences of a Compliance; The Situation of both Counties [he is a] Stranger to, & he may be made sensible that this County, in case of [invasion] can expect no Relief but what Botetourt can give it, & then I am sure he will let these things rest on the footing his last Letter to you [advised]. I can't See how you could send off your Militia at the call of the Gen[l] [Hand], the honble the Com[rs], or still a more hon'ble [MS. torn] unless first warranted to do so by the Commander in Chief of this State. This Warrant, I imagine, you have not yet received (but the Reverse) from him, and therefore I should believe you are Justifiable in refusing, or at least postponing a Compliance [to the] Requisition, until you have Orders from the Governor.

I am affraid I have tired you with this confus'd Letter. I am excessively uneasy about our Frontiers in general & my own exposed Family in particular. I am D[r] Sir with real esteem your most [obedient servant]

W[m] PRESTON

Ap. 13, 1778[26]

---

[26] On this same date General Hand sent a warning (Draper MSS., 30NN108) to the militia officers of Ohio and Monongalia counties, of the approach of the Wyandot bands that had been sent by White Eyes. It was too late, however,

P. S. If you see any careful Person coming this way or to Mr Madisons,[27] please to Send part of the Money to Mr Floyd, as I was obliged to advance him 305 Dollars to buy provisions & shall be in want of it soon.

DELAWARES KEEP PEACE

[MS. in Carnegie Library, Pittsburgh; George Morgan's Letter Book.]

FORT PITT April 13th. 1778.

The United American States to the wise Delaware Council

BROTHERS—We have received your Letter dated the 6th. inst. we have considered the Contents and are well pleased with your repeated professions of Friendship to the United States. It was to perpetuate our mutual happiness that we invited a few of you to meet us at our Council Fire at this place, which we are determined to rekindle sometime the ensuing Summer, for our wise Brethren the Delawares in particular and for all other Nations who incline to accept our Friendship. it was for this purpose and to give you assurances of our Friendship that we desired to consult with some of your wise Chiefs and to know what time to fix for our Meeting here with all your wise Men and principal Warriors that we may determine together what steps to pursue in order to defeat the evil intentions of the Wiandots and Mingoes.

---

to avert the murders on Dunkard's Creek. See Clark's letter of March 30, *ante,* p. 248.—ED.

[27] Probably referring to Capt. Thomas Madison, for whom see *Dunmore's War,* p. 59, note 99.—ED.

Brothers We have desired to take the Tomhawk out of your Heads and to condole with you on the unhappy affair at Beaver Creek. We sent back your Women and we are sorry you have had any occasion to reproach us. But Brothers we need not tell you what your own people did before that. We do not desire to recriminate, because that would appear as though we were in a bad Temper, and wanted to quarrel with you. Brothers we tell you that is not the intention of the United States or of any of them. We have always told you so and have never deceived you. You must not look on what has been done as intended by our wise People to injure you, and we desire that you may not think hard of it. When we say you, Brothers, we not only mean the wise Council at Coochocking, but all Capt: Pipe's old Council which we consider as the same with you.

Brothers We anxiously wait to see some of your wise Chiefs as we formerly desired, for which purpose we will continue here thirteen days from the date hereof. If they can arrive sooner it will be more agreeable to [us] as we have been greatly disappointed by being detained here so long.

Brothers Be strong, for you may depend we will convince you of our Friendship: and that if you persevere in good works your Children yet unborn will thank you for taking good Council. For this reason we desire you will not listen to the stories of Deserters or other bad People. We will convince you that it is not their Interest to tell you the truth; and you may rest assured that the United States desire Friendship and Peace and not War with our Indian Brethren.

RECRUITS FOR CLARK

[Col. George Rogers Clark to General Hand. 18J73—Transcript by Dr. Draper from "original in Dr. Tho. A. Emmet's Collection, New York City."]

REDSTONE, April 17th 1778.

SIR—As I found by express from Maj. Smith, that my recruiters on Holston River had been more successful that I expected, in raising four companies,[28] and receiving intelligence of two companies more now

---

[28] William Bailey Smith was a native (1738) of Prince William County, Va. He early migrated to North Carolina, where he was associated with the Hendersons, Harts, etc. In 1775 he was present at the Treaty of Sycamore Shoals, and went out to Boonesborough during that summer. He was likewise in Boonesborough when the Boone and Calloway girls were captured (1776), and aided in their rescue. During the summer of 1777 he returned to the Yadkin, and brought out a party for the relief of the beleaguered settlements; see *ante*, p. 103, note 63. Clark had known Smith in Kentucky and gave him a commission as major, together with an advance of £150 to recruit for his expedition in the Holston settlements. Smith's letters to Clark (Draper MSS., 48J19, 20, printed in *Amer. Hist. Review*, viii, pp. 495-497), dated March 7 and 29, were encouraging and boastful. The first reached Clark March 29, and made him relax his efforts to recruit in the Redstone region. Smith eventually sent out but one small company, part of whom deserted when the destination of the expedition was made known. Smith himself appears to have arrived at Boonesborough in June or July. He took part in the great siege of that place, which was his last military service. Having returned to North Carolina he was commissioned to extend the boundary line between that state and Virginia—now that between Tennessee and Kentucky. He was so occupied in 1779-80. He received for his services a tract of land on Green River, whither he removed in 1794, settling at a place known as Smith's Ferry, not far from the mouth of the Green. There he died Oct. 19, 1818. For these and further particulars, see Draper MSS., 4B251.—ED.

on their March from Winchester,[29] I shall not attempt to recruit any more men in this department, as I believe I shall have my full quota, but shall prepare to set out on the intended expedition as soon as possible. I shall order what recruits I have west of the Monongahela to repair to Wheeling immediately, where they may probably be of service, and shall stay here myself until ye arrival of the troops I expect across the Mt^n. I should be glad to know by an answer to this letter whether I am to receive any provisions at this place or at Pittsburgh, if at Redstone, I hope, Sir, that you will send an order for ye receipt of it. I suppose it would at any rate, be of service to take the boats that I have loaded to Pittsburgh.

I should be glad to receive my powder, &c., at this post. The provision boats that you were to send down, I expect may be ready at any time. If you will send them under my convoy, I shall take pleasure in doing that or any other piece of service that lays in my power. Be pleased to send me a few lines by y^e bearer, M^r [William] Linn, who will wait on you with this letter. I am, Sir, Your h^{bl} $Serv^t$.,

G. R. CLARK.

To Gen. Hand, Pittsburgh.   Pr. favor M^r. Linn.

---

[29] Of these two companies, that of Capt. Leonard Helm was recruited largely in Fauquier County; that of Capt. Joseph Bowman in Frederick.—ED.

ATTACK ON THE MONONGAHELA

[Col. John Evans to General Hand. 2U13—A. L. S.]

FORKS CHEAT April 18th 1778.

D^r SIR—The Indians on the 15th Instant on the Monongahale, Above the Mouth of Cheat River Killed and took ten persons belonging to Maj^r Martins Fort,[30] and took at least 20 horses, on 16th. Burned a Fort that was evacuated 3 Miles from the Magazine at my house killed Seven Sheep & skined them and took 15 horses which leaves our part of the Country in such a situation that the forts are all a Breaking the Inhabitants all seem Determined to moove to some place of Safety, for my part I shall be Oblidge to follow them, and leve the Provision to the mercy of the enemy Without some other method can Speedily take place, our Country is in such confusion, at this time that the Militia Will not be Redused to their Duty. I have made bold to Detain part of a Company of the hamshire Melitia to guard the provision till I Receive orders from your honour What is to be Done. this part of the Country is much Distresed at this time and I fear Will be more so the Enemy seems to Strike only on this Quarter for farther particulars I refer you

---

[30] Apparently this is the affair assigned to the date of June, 1779, by Withers and local historians who follow his account; see Thwaites, *Withers*, pp. 282, 283. Martin's Fort was situated on Crooked Run, a small western tributary of the Monongahela, just across the Virginia line in the present Monongalia County. Martin's church is now located near by. The fort was attacked while most of its defenders had gone to work on their farms. Three men were killed—James Stuart, James Smally, and Peter Crouse; seven were taken prisoners, including sons of the three men killed and one John Shiver and his wife.—ED.

to the Barer and am Sir Your most Obedient humb¹ Servt

JOHN EVANS

P. S. We are Distitu[t]e of Amunition and beggs your Honour to Assist us with that article if in your power, as its impossible We can Defend our Selves without Amunition.
On Public Service
To His Excellency Gener'l Hand Fort Pitt.

BRITISH WELCOME McKEE

[Henry Hamilton to Alexander McKee. MS. in Canadian Archives; Series M., vol. 105, fol. 13—A. L. S.]

DETROIT Ap¹ 23^d 1778

DEAR SIR—I congratulate you on your escape, and shall be happy to see you here where you may be sure of finding friends and sincere ones.

The sooner your convenience can admit of your coming to this place, the better, as I wish to confer with you on several points 'tis impossible to touch upon in a letter. The newspapers you sent, were very acceptable, they shall be forwarded to Gen. Carleton, whom I have made acquainted with your happy escape. The council to be held at this place and which I expect to be very full, will meet on or about the 15th of May, till when matters will remain as they are—nothing can exceed the good temper and tractable behaviour of all the Indians. The bearer is a very spirited young fellow, is trusty & I hope by good behaviour will deserve to be put on a good footing.

The Six Nations are more than ever attached to Government & zealous in the Cause against the Rebels.

McKEE CONGRATULATED

Considerable reinforcements expected to Canada this year. I am Sir your very humble Servant

HENRY HAMILTON.

[Jehu Hay to Alexander McKee. Source, same as preceding document, but fol. 15—A. L. S.]

DETROIT, April 23rd 1778

SIR—Permit me to congratulate you on your escape from Fort Pitt. I was in hopes last Fall of having the pleasure of seeing you, but your situation was such that I suppose put it out of your power to make the attempt. The bearer Edward Hazel[31] sets off immediately to meet you, he tells me you desired him to bring you some refreshment which I should have been happy to send, but he goes by Land and says he can not carry any thing not so much as a Kegg of Wine, provision I hope you will not want as there is people at Sandusky, and the Miamee [Maumee] River who can and will supply you. I have given him a little Silver Works & Vermillion[32] to purchase me a good Horse or two, but if you have the least occasion for them pray make use of them. I wait with impatience

---

[31] Edward Hazel was a Loyalist from the United States, who served for a time in Butler's rangers. After he was employed in the Indian department, he was frequently sent with messages and in 1782 visited the Cherokee to instigate them against the settlements. In 1783 he was discharged, but afterwards reemployed by the government as interpreter. He lived at Detroit until its evacuation by the British (1796), when he retired to Malden. He was out in the War of 1812-15 as leader of the Wyandot, and died in Amherstburg about 1817. See Draper MSS., 17S215, 20S217, 221.—ED.

[32] Articles much prized by the Indians, hence used as currency in dealing with them.—ED.

your arrival, and asure you I am Sir With truth Your most Humble servant

JEHU HAY

BOAT BUILDING

[Col. George Morgan to Capt. Joseph Skelton. MS. in Carnegie Library, Pittsburgh; George Morgan's Letter Book.]

FORT PITT April 24th. 1778.

To Capt: Joseph Skelton,

* * * * * * * *

What follows being out of the particular Line of your Duty I must ask of you as a favour. The Boat Carpenters are to remove to this place and build the remainder of the Boats at the Point near my Redoubt or under the Council House. I shall therefore want you to hire of Major Smallman the little House where Miller lives for the use of the Carpenters and Sawyers for whom M^{rs}. Gibson[33] will cook. She is on that acc^t: to draw Provisions with them. You can order them a Barrel of Salt Pork and Beef and a Barrel of Flour at a time and whenever there is fresh Meat you can give an order for what M^{rs}. Gibson may require of all which keep an Acc^t. that I may be enabled to settle their Ration Acc^t. on my return.

The Carpenters and Sawyers are to bring down in the Boats now preparing to be launch'd, all their Tools, Crooked Timber, Boards and Plank. The Crooked or other Timber which they may hereafter want, they

---

[33] Not the wife of Col. John Gibson, but of another John Gibson, a trader and laborer at Pittsburgh. He secured supplies at that place for George Rogers Clark, and several of his letters are among the Clark papers in the Wisconsin Historical Library.—ED.

BOAT BUILDING

must cut either toward Elliott's Bullock Pens or General Hand's place,[34] paying the Owner of the Timber a reasonable price. The Quarter Master must be applied to for Teams and for a Boat to transport 20M feet of Boards and plank (which I have purchased from Benjamin Kuykendall)[35] from the Mill to Fort Pitt which must be piled and stuck near my House to season. I would beg that this be done without delay. You must also hire a House or Boat Carpenter or two, or some other handy person to attend on the Carpenters, boil the Pitch, spin Oakum & pick up the loose Nails & Iron which may drop about the Yard.

For this necessary purpose you may give good Wages to a sober careful handy Fellow. The necessary Articles which are to come up the Country for the building of Boats will be directed in my absence to your care. Write to me by every opportunity and you will oblige yours &c

[GEORGE MORGAN]

* * * * * * * *

---

[34] On the map of original grants in Pittsburgh and environs, Col. William Elliott's "bullock pens" are located just north of the present Homewood Cemetery in Homewood addition. Hand's property was southeast of Chartier's Creek in a township of that name. This information was kindly furnished by Harrison W. Craven, librarian of Carnegie Library, Pittsburgh.—ED.

[35] Benjamin Kuykendall was an early resident of Pittsburgh. In 1775 he was ordered by the county court to view a road; and the next year was chosen as one of the justices of the court, which he frequently attended. In 1780 he was sworn in as sheriff, and on Feb. 28 signed the record of the court—"Minute book of Yohogania County," in Carnegie Museum *Annals*, ii, no. 2, p. 401.—ED.

WESTERN EXPEDITIONS

[General Hand to Gen. Horatio Gates. 3NN109, 110—
Transcript.]

FORT PITT, 24th April, 1778.

SIR—Some time ago I did myself the honor to inclose you a letter from his Exc^y Govr Henry, Containing a request to supply Col. G. R. Clark with several articles to fit him for a voyage down the Ohio river & rec^d your answer on the premises. Col. Clark has rec^d from me everything he has yet desired—the remainder is ready at his call.

I yesterday rec^d a letter from his Exc^y Making a Similar demand in favor of Col. David Rogers—a Copy of which I inclose. I make no doubt but Congress will think proper to direct that Col. Rogers may be furnished agreeable to the Governor's desire; tho' I can't think myself authorized to do it without their sanction. I must, however, beg leave to remark that in my present Situation, men, arms or lead cannot be Supplied. As Col. Rogers is not yet ready to proceed, there will be time sufficient for Congress to communicate their sentiments on this, or any future demands made by his Exc^y Govr Henry, without a previous application to them.

As the time of Col. Clark's departure is very uncertain, I am preparing to send Capt. O'Hara[36] with a detachment to the Arkansas with the provisions for Capt. Willing. * * *

Desertion prevails here to a great degree. Since the 18th Jany last, 40 men have deserted from this small garrison; last night 14, the greatest number of them

---
[36] For this officer, see *Rev. Upper Ohio*, p. 253, note 1.—ED.

GENERAL JAMES O'HARA

From Mary C. Darlington, *Fort Pitt* (Pittsburgh, 1892)

DESERTIONS 279

of the guard, went off, & took with them Eleazer Davis, a prisoner formerly mentioned to the Board of War—& a party of the country people. I believe the Devil has possessed both the country and garrison. A command of 40 men & 4 officers were detached in pursuit of these deserters.

Col. Russell of the 13th Virginia regiment has arrived here. He tells me that the remainder of his reg^t are destined for this place. I think it would be prudent to accelerate their march, otherwise our magazines both here & elsewhere may fall an easey prey.

[EDWARD HAND]

P. S. Except the murder of two children & capture of another within six or seven Miles of this place, the savages have confined their visits to the settlements on Dunkard & Muddy Creeks & Tiger's Valley.[37] The militia lately abandoned one of their forts in Monongalia County, & left in it 9,000 ^{lbs} pork provided for their support, which was in a few days after the Evacuation set on fire & consumed with the provision.

---

[37] Tygart's Valley is on the east fork of the main Monongahela, chiefly in what is now Randolph County, W. Va. It received its name from its first settler, David Tygart, who was in 1753 driven from the valley by Indian depredations. This site was not permanently settled until 1772, for it was peculiarly exposed to Indian raids, the famous Shawnee and other trails passing through it. During the Revolution, it suffered several times (1777, 1779-82), also in the later Indian war (1789, 1791).—ED.

SITUATION AT DETROIT

[Gov. Henry Hamilton to Sir Guy Carleton. MS. in Canadian Archives; Series B, vol. 121, fol. 100-108—Transcript.][38]

DETROIT 25 Ap. 1778.

SIR—The last letter I had the honor of writing to your Excellency was dated January the 15th 1778.

January the 26th. Some traders to Sandooski having given room for suspecting they were carrying on a correspondence with the Rebels, I ordered a search to be made for some papers of which I had had notice; but though I was well assured that my suspicions were well grounded, they eluded the search; however, upon examining the goods carryed out and comparing them with the Invoices, a considerable quantity was found for which a pass had not been asked. The offenders were fined to the extent prescribed by the Ordinance of Quebec.

January the 30th. John Montour (formerly mentioned to Your Excellency) decoyed out of the settlement three Virginians (Prisoners) designing to have carried them to Fort Pitt. Some Indians who met them a few leagues off and suspected that they were fugitives, gave me notice of it and a party of Volunteers with an Indian Officer and some Savages were sent after them, who took and brought them all in, they had prepared arms and meant to have stood on the defensive, but were surprised and bound. Montour, at the earnest sollicitations of a number of chiefs of different nations, was set at liberty after

---

[38] A transcript of this document was made for Dr. Draper by the late Dr. Douglas Brymner, and is found in Draper MSS., 11C96.—ED.

some weeks' confinement, the others, having made so bad a use of the indulgence shown them, remain in irons. The Indians were highly pleased at their request being granted. The prisoners are to be sent down by the first vessel.

March the 7th. Lieutenant Governor Abbot with his family arrived from Ft Vincennes, from his report of the state of the post, I am humbly of opinion it must be impossible for the Ouabasha Indians to be kept in order without a vast expense in presents or the presence of some troops. Indeed in all these Posts where the French had settled a trade and intercourse with the Savages, an Officer's presence with troops is much wanted, for the minds of the Indians in remote posts are poisoned by the falsehoods and misrepresentations of the French. As to the Indians of the Ouabash, they have been out of the way of knowing the power of the English and from a presumption of their own importance will be arrogant and troublesome. Monsieur de Celoron[39] writes me word from

---

[39] One of the sons of Pierre Joseph Céloron, former commandant of Detroit; see a list of the latter's sons in *Mich. Pion. & Hist. Colls.*, xxxiv, p. 333. Céloron junior had been sent by Hamilton to command at the village known as Ouiatanon, situated on the Wabash two or three miles below the site of the present Lafayette. There had been a French fort at this place, which was destroyed in Pontiac's Conspiracy (1763). It had now grown up to be a small village. Its importance lay in the fact that it commanded the water route from Detroit to Vincennes. After the capture of the latter place in 1778, by troops sent by George Rogers Clark, a small detachment was sent to occupy Ouiatanon, whereupon its commandant, Sieur de Céloron, hastily retreated. Hamilton later claimed that Céloron was in sympathy with the American troops, and had a "brother in the Rebel service." See *Ill. Hist. Colls.*, i, pp. 336, 351-353, 359.—ED.

Ouiattanong, that some parties to the number of 50 men, partly Quigeboes, Mascoitainges & Ouiattanongs,[40] are gone to war toward the Ohio, their success is not yet known. I have sent him some ammunition and arms & to gratify those among them who behave well. All parties going to war are exhorted to act with humanity as the means of securing a sincere peace when His Majesty shall be pleased to order the Hatchet to be buried.

March 11th. One hundred and twenty five warriors, Mingoes, Shawanese & Delawares with a number of wives & children came to this place, they have accepted War Belts and I believe are too well convinced of the inability of the Virginians to do them either much good or much harm, not to be sincere. The Mingoes delivered me a young boy, whose father they had killed.

29th. John Turney arrived from Quebec. He brought a Belt sent by Colonel Butler[41] addressed to the Lake Indians and all the Western Nations from the Six Nations, by which they declare their resolution to support Government and revenge themselves, desiring all the nations of the Confederacy to act as one man—thanking them at the same time for the zeal and spirit with which they acted last year.

April the 1st. Forty Shawanese arrived having four prisoners, whom they delivered to me soon after.

---

[40] Kickapoo, Mascoutin, and Ouiatanon (Wea) Indians; see *Rev. Upper Ohio*, p. 3, note 8. These tribes all dwelt near Ouiatanon settlement.—Ed.

[41] Lieut. John Turney was in 1782 commandant at Sandusky.

For Col. John Butler, see *Ibid*, p. 152, note 67.—Ed.

AT DETROIT 283

April the 5th. Mr. Charles Baubin who acts at the Miamis[42] came in from a scout—not having been able to prevail on the Miamis to act with spirit. He with a young man named Lorimier[43] engaged four score Shawanese from Tchelacasé and Pecori[44] to go toward the Fort on Kentuck River, east of the Ohio into which it discharges directly opposite the great Mineamis or Rocky River. The Fort is about 30 miles from the mouth. The number of men in it about 80. Here they had the good fortune to make prisoners Captain Daniel Boone, with 26 of his men, whom they brought off with their arms without killing or losing a man. The savages could not be prevailed on to attempt the Fort [Boonesborough], which by means of their prisoners might have been easily done with success. These Shawanese delivered up four of their prisoners to me; but took Boone with them expecting by his means to effect something. By Boone's account, the people on the frontiers have been so incessantly harrassed by parties of Indians they have not been able to sow grain; and at Kentucke will not have a morsel of bread by the middle of June. Cloathing is not to be had, nor do they expect relief from the Congress—

---

[42] Charles Beaubien belonged to a prominent Detroit family, and was official interpreter and acting commandant at Fort Miami and the Miami village on the site of the present Fort Wayne. He was accused by Hamilton (1778-79) of collusion with the Americans, but succeeded in clearing himself. In 1780 he resisted the attack of Mottin de la Balme (see *Wis. Hist. Colls.*, xviii, p. 416, note 23). He married the widow of Chief Richardville, but left no descendants.—ED.

[43] For a sketch of this person, see *Rev. Upper Ohio*, p. 144, note 49. The given name should be Louis, not Peter.—ED.

[44] Chillicothe and Piqua Indian towns, for which see *Ibid*, pp. 15, 57, notes 30 and 87 respectively.—ED.

their dilemma will probably induce them to trust to the savages, who have shewn so much humanity to their prisoners & come to this place before winter.

The Placarts from this place having found their way among the inhabitants & one in particular signed by several Prisoners who were saved by the Indians, was seen in the hands of Mr. Morgan at Fort Pitt, who refused to let it be public; however, I believe he will [not] be able to keep up his credit much longer.

April the 20th. Edward Hazle (who had undertaken to carry a letter from me to the Moravian Minister at Kushayhking)[45] returned having executed his commission. He brought me a letter & newspaper from Mr. McKee who was Indian agent for the Crown and has been a long time in the hands of the Rebels at Fort Pitt, at length has found means to make his escape with three other men, two of the name of Girty (mentioned in Lord Dunmore's list) [an] Interpreter and Matthew Elliott, the young man who was last summer sent down from this place a prisoner. This last person I am informed has been at New York since he left Quebec, and probably finding the change in affairs unfavorable to the Rebels, has slipped away to make his peace here.

23rd. Hazle went off again to conduct them all safe thro' the village, having a letter and Wampum for that purpose. Alexander McKee is a man of good character, and has great influence with the Shawanese is well acquainted with the country & can probably give some usefull intelligence, he will probably reach this

---

[45] David Zeisberger at Coshocton; see *Ibid*, p. 45, note 71.—ED.

AT DETROIT

place in a few days. In his letter to me dated Kushayking April 4th he mentions that no expeditions of any consequence can be undertaken by the Virginians from Fort Pitt thro' the Delaware villages, hitherward; but that they meditated some attempt against the villages upon French Creek (Riviere au Boeuf) and that he had information from some Delawares that six hundred men were to set out on that design the 8th of April, but that the savages being forewarned their scheme must fail.

I have written to Col^l. Bolton[46] to acquaint him & Col^l. Butler of this as also that a party from Fort Pitt had fallen on a Delaware village & killed or carried off eight persons; but that unfortunately for the Rebels, they had struck in the wrong place & have sent back two squaws who were prisoners to atone for their error.

25th of April. Governor Abbott communicated to me the following extract of a letter from Mr.

---

[46] Lt. Col. Mason Bolton of the 34th Royal artillery had seen much service in America, having campaigned in Florida and the West Indies, and at one time been at Mackinac and the Illinois. In 1777 he was placed in charge of the important post at Niagara, being occupied not only with forwarding supplies but with controlling and propitiating the Indians, chiefly of the Six Nations. The best account of his conduct of the post at Niagara is to be found in Frank H. Severance, *Old Trails upon the Niagara Frontier* (Buffalo, 1909), pp. 63-106. Bolton was at his own request relieved of duty at Niagara, and left there late in October, 1780, on the vessel "Ontario", which foundered in the lake of the same name, all on board perishing.—ED.

de Rocheblave to one Bosseron[47] at St. Vincennes dated Feby. 28th. 78:

Par un deserteur[48] arrivé du Fort Pitt nous avons apris que le Peuple de Philadelphie ayant secoué le joug du Congrés avait levé la chaine qui empechoit les vaisseaux du Roi de venir et avoit par ce moyen rentré sous l'obeissance de sa Majesté. Que le Congrés avoit fui precipittament vers les Montagnes aprés l'entière deroute de son armée que le peuple soupirant ardemment aprés la paix pour sortir de la plus affreuse misère et que les chefs des troubles sauvoient leurs effets par la route de Fort Pitt.

Un batteau descendant de ce dit Fort a pris les Sieurs Becquets et leur pacquets. M[r] La Chence[49] a subi le meme

---

[47] Phillippe François Rastel, Sieur de Rocheblave, was born in France and served for a time in the army. Coming to New France about 1750 he entered the colonial army as a cadet, and was employed about Fort Duquesne and on the Illinois frontier. At the close of the war he retired to Kaskaskia, and was there married in 1763. Later he crossed the river, and was for a time connected with the Spanish government at Ste. Geneviève. In 1776, the last British officer who retired from Kaskaskia left Sieur de Rocheblave in command, but without a garrison or any support. July 4, 1778, he was captured by George Rogers Clark and sent a prisoner to Virginia. There he evaded his parole, and returned to the British at New York. He finally retired to Lower Canada, where he died in 1802 at Varennes.

François Bosseron was one of the most prominent citizens of Vincennes and was enrolled in the British militia forces. On the approach of the Americans he gave them his enthusiastic support and took office under Clark. He acted with Capt. Leonard Helm in the Wabash expedition (1779), and furnished ammunition for the invading army. He was later district commandant and territorial judge, dying at Vincennes in 1791 and being buried in the churchyard. A street in Vincennes still bears his name.—Ed.

[48] The name of this deserter was Henry Butler, from Pennsylvania; see his examination in *Ill. Hist. Colls.*, i, pp. 304-306.—Ed.

[49] Jean Baptiste and Charles Becquets were traders at Cahokia—see letter of Morgan, *post*. Nicolas Caillot dit Lachanse was a prominent citizen of Kaskaskia, and reputed to be an especial friend of Rocheblave. These captures were made by Willing's boat—see Chicago Historical Society *Collections*, iv, p. 402. Lachanse was absent from Kaskaskia

AT DETROIT

sort avec son eau de vie, quoique les colons n'ayent jamais reçu de deplaisir de ce pays preuve bien certaine qu'ils le menageroient peu, s'il y parvenoient en force. Certains bruits qui courent de la mauvaise disposition des sauvages m'engagent à parler au chefs des loups.

Je vous prie si vous etes a porté de les engager a me venir voir.[50]

This letter of Mr. Rocheblave explains in part the accounts given by the Delawares of parties forming for Rivière au Boeuf, which can only be calculated to draw off the attention of the Delawares from the lower part of the Ohio. I shall if possible lay a bar in the way of the communication to N. Orleans. Your Excellency's orders and instructions which I am in hourly expectation of receiving by Mr. LaMothe[51] will be my guide for my conduct.

---

at the time of its capture by Clark. He was judge in 1779 and again in 1787, retiring soon after to the Spanish side of the Mississippi. See *Ill. Hist. Colls.*, v, p. 50, note 7.—ED.

[50] Translation: By a deserter arrived from Fort Pitt we have been informed that the people of Philadelphia having shaken off the yoke of Congress had removed the chain that prevented the King's ships from getting in and had thus returned to obedience to His Majesty. But Congress had fled precipitately toward the mountains, after the complete rout of its army and that the people were sighing earnestly after peace, to escape the most frightful miseries, and that the chiefs of the troubles were saving their effects by way of Fort Pitt.

A batteau coming down from this Fort has taken the Sieurs Becquets and their peltries; Mr. La Chence has met the same fate with his brandy although the settlers [of Kentucky] never received any ill treatment from this Country. This is a very good evidence of the manner in which they would act, if they should reach there in large numbers. Certain rumours current as to the bad disposition of the Indians led me to speak to the chief (or chiefs) of the Loups [Delawares].

I request if you are in a position to do so, to induce them to come and see me.

[51] Guillaume la Mothe was a French Canadian who entered the British service. Born about 1744, he was in 1767 a trader

25th April 1778. Mr. LaMothe not yet arrived. A Huron of that band settled at Lorette named datahyjas has been lately at Fort Pitt and says Mr. Bentley[52] supplied ammunition &c. to the Rebels, he also confirms the reports of the intercourse between the Spaniards and the Virginian delegates.

---

in the neighborhood of Detroit. At the outbreak of the Revolution he was in New England; whence he retired to Quebec and soon returned to Detroit, where in 1777 he became captain of a scouting party. Apparently he was in Quebec when this letter was written. The next autumn, as captain of militia, he accompanied Hamilton to Vincennes, where he was captured (1779) and sent prisoner to Virginia. There he was kept in close confinement until exchanged (1781). The following year found him at Detroit. In 1792 he was appointed interpreter at Mackinac, until removed from that position in November, 1795. He retired with the British to St. Joseph Island (1796), where he died in 1799.—ED.

[52] Thomas Bentley was a prominent merchant of Kaskaskia during the British period, having come to that place from London and West Florida. In 1777 he married into a French family, and in the autumn of that year was arrested at Mackinac by order of Governor Hamilton, who accused him of furnishing supplies to American boats. He was detained prisoner in Canada until 1780, when he managed to escape, and by August was in the West. His letters prove his treachery and double dealing, trying to keep in touch with British and American officials at the same time—see *Ill. Hist. Colls.*, v, *passim*. In 1783 Bentley went to Virginia to settle his accounts, and appears to have died in Richmond. John Dodge was his partner, and the executor of his estate.—ED.

RELATIONS WITH SPANIARDS

[Col. George Morgan to Governor Galvez. MS. in Carnegie Library, Pittsburgh; George Morgan's Letter Book.]

FORT PITT April 26th. 1778.

To His Excellency Don Bernardo De Galvez Governor General of Louisiana[53]

SIR—On the 24th. of February I had the honor to receive your Letter dated the 9th. of August last. Not having the happiness to understand the Spanish Language I immediately transmitted your Letter by Express to Congress—but unfortunately not a Member of that Body understands it nor has any Person been yet found capable & worthy of Trust to translate it. Wherefore his Excellency the President has directed me to present his Compliments to you, he laments this disappointment and will do himself the honor to write to you the moment he can procure a translation of your Excellency's Letter.

Should you do Congress the honour to write to them, or should you again favour me, I would beg leave to solicit your Indulgence by requesting you to do it in English or in French, in which we can be at

---

[53] Bernardo de Galvez, governor-general of Louisiana, was born in Spain in 1756; his father was long viceroy of Mexico; his uncle, José de Galvez, was a minister of state. In 1777 Bernardo arrived in New Orleans. He married a French creole, and was very popular with his subjects. His sympathies with the Americans were keen, and he supplied them with munitions of war. During the war between Spain and Great Britain, Galvez energetically took the offensive and captured the English forts at Manchac, Baton Rouge, Natchez, and Mobile. In 1781 he made a brilliant campaign against Pensacola, which fell into his hands. Upon the death of his father (1785), Galvez became Mexican viceroy in his stead, which office he held until his own demise in 1794.—ED.

no loss, and least Congress may not procure an Interpreter for your late Letter, your causing it to be translated into English or French and transmitted by the first opportunity will be gratefully accepted as a very polite Condesension and particular favour.

I send this by the Boats which go to meet Capt: Willing, and as it may be acceptable to you to be inform'd of the particular occurrences of the War since the date of my Letter in April 1777, and of the present situation of our Affairs I take the liberty to give you a short detail thereof.[54]

* * * * * * * *

If I can hereafter contribute to your amusement or information, I will do myself the honor. I am with very great Respect Sir, Your very obedient & most humble serv^t:

[GEORGE MORGAN]

[Col. George Morgan to Francisco Cruzat. Source, same as preceding document.]

To Don Francisco Cruzat Esquire Commanding for his most Catholic Majesty at S^t: Louis, Illinois.[55]

SIR—The 24th. of February I had the honor to receive your Letter of the 19th. of November last, with

---

[54] The portion omitted recounts the events of the Revolution during 1777.—ED.

[55] Col. Francisco Cruzat was a Spanish army officer, who in 1775 was appointed governor of Spanish Illinois, with headquarters at St. Louis. In 1778 he was superseded by Francisco de Leyba, whom Clark (July, 1778) found in command at that place. Upon De Leyba's death (1780), Cruzat was again returned to St. Louis and remained in command until Nov. 27, 1787. He was a popular and efficient administrator, and in sympathy with the Americans.—ED.

IGNORANCE OF SPANISH

one inclosed from Don Bernardo De Galvez Governor of Louisiana.

Being ignorant of the Spanish Language I immediately transmitted his Excellency the Governor's Letter by Express to Congress—But unhappily not a Member of that Body understands it, nor has any Person been yet found capable to translate the Letter. This has been the occasion of my not having done myself the pleasure of answering your Letter till now.

As several Boats are shortly to leave this for New Orleans I shall do myself the honor to forward by them such Dispatches as may arrive for his Excellency the Governor.

During the time of waiting the orders of Congress, I had occasion to send a Messenger to the Delaware Nation—Michael the Huron, offering his services, I employ'd him, and I am sorry to inform you, that he is taken Prisoner by some of his own Nation and a Party of English who were employ'd by the Commandant of Detroit and carried to that Post. I however hope he will be very speedily released, and more especially as he is a subject of Spain, and was employ'd on a mere friendly Message to the Delawares.

I have paid to Baptist Bequette the ballance due to himself & Michael as stated in the within Account and have paid all their Expences during their detention here, which on my part was unavoidable.

You may be assured Sir, that nothing but the want of hard money has induced me to settle the account in the manner I have done. I must also make the same apology for giving Michael a Bill of Exchange last year on Messrs: Winston & Kennedy at Kaskaskias.[56] I am indeed much mortified at that Bill not having been paid, although those Gentlemen have very considerable sums of mine in their hands. I impute their conduct to their fears of Monsr: Rochblave who I am told has been too severe with others who are deemed Friends to the Americans.

This reason I expect will now be removed & I doubt not but my draft will be punctually paid.

---

[56] Winston and Kennedy were merchants at Kaskaskia, and about this time acted as Morgan's agents. Richard Winston was a Virginian, at one time sheriff of Orange County, who was trading in the Western country at the time of the French cession. When Pontiac's War broke out (1763) he was at the fort at Ouiatanon, where he was robbed of £2400 worth of goods. In compensation he was granted 1200 shares in the Indiana Company, and entered the Illinois region as soon as British traders could be protected. In 1766 he accompanied an expedition to Kaskaskia; see Jennings's "Journal", in *Pa. Hist. Magazine*, xxxi, p. 145. His sympathies were with the American cause, and Clark appointed him captain in his forces; see *Ill. Hist. Colls.*, v, p. 47. The succeeding year he was chosen sheriff by John Todd, and when the latter left the Illinois, Winston was appointed deputy lieutenant-governor. In this capacity he had difficulties both with the military authorities and with the French inhabitants, and in 1782 abolished the civic court that Todd had established. The following year he went to Richmond to have his claims settled; and after spending eighteen months in fruitlessly endeavoring to arrange with the government, he died in poverty in the autumn of 1784. The council endorsed his claims as "reasonable" (Draper MSS., 11S150), but it does not appear that they were ever paid. In 1786 his wife was reported to be reduced from affluence to indigence (*Ibid*, 4J35-38). Consult also *Ill. Hist. Colls.*, ii, v, *passim*.

Patrick Kennedy went to the Illinois country in 1766 as a batteau man. He succeeded in his business ventures and became one of the merchants of Kaskaskia. In 1773 he made a journey up the Illinois in search of copper mines. Clark appointed him deputy commissary, in which capacity he was still acting in 1781.—ED.

Notwithstanding I am so unhappy as to be totally ignorant of the Spanish Language, & my long want of Practice in the French, puts it out of my power to comply with your desire, by writing in one of those Tongues, I cannot forego the pleasure of communicating to you, in English, the very happy situation of our Affairs, compared to the state the World might have expected to have seen them by this time. Indeed our success has exceeded our most sanguine expectations; and by the blessing of God we now have the happy Certainty of securing to ourselves and to our Posterity the inestimable blessings of Peace, Liberty and Safety.[57]

* * * * * * * *

CONGRESS PLANS FOR THE WEST

[Resolutions of Congress. 4NN69, 70—Transcript.]

IN CONGRESS, May 2d, 1778

Resolved—That two Regiments be Raised in Virginia & Pennsylvania to serve for one Year unless sooner discharg'd by Congress, for the Protection & operation on the Western Frontiers, twelve Companies in Virginia and four in Pennsylvania, each Non-Commission'd Officer & Soldier to Receive twenty Dollars Bounty, and same Clothing with the Other Continental Soldiers. Every non-Commission'd Officer & Soldier who shall find his own Blanket, Musquet or Riffle & Accutrements shall have the same Allowance given by Congress to the Draughts from the Militia for filling up the Continental Regiments.

---

[57] What follows is a repetition of that written to Galvez; see *ante*, p. 290, note 54.—ED.

That Brigadier General Hand be recalled from his Command on the Western Frontier, agreeable to his request.

That a proper Officer be immediately sent to take the Command on the Western Frontier.

That a proper Person be appointed to perform the Duties of Quarter Master, Commissary & Pay Master to the Militia of Rockingham, Augusta, Rockbridge, Botetourt, Montgomery, Washington, & Green Brier in Virginia.

That the Commissioners at Fort [Pitt], or in their Absence, the Officer appointed to Command on the Western Frontiers, be Authorised to appoint a Person to perform the Duties aforesaid, & the Officers necessary for Commanding the Battalions above Mentioned.

That General Washington be desired to appoint the Officer to take the Command at Fort Pitt, and that a Copy of the Commissioner's Letter be sent to the General. *Extracts from the Minutes.*

CHARLES THOMSON Sec.

SCOUTING PARTY ON THE FRONTIER

[Andrew Robinson to Gen. Edward Hand. 2U17—A. L. S.]

FORT HENRY May the 15th 1778.

SIR—Agreeable to Order I waited on Captain Ritchey[58] who informs me that he will furnish me with

---

[58] Either Matthew or Craig Ritchie, brothers from Glasgow, Scotland, who emigrated to America in 1772 and settled in what is now Washington County.

In 1778 Matthew was chosen sheriff of Yohogania County, and in 1781 sub-lieutenant of the county. He was in the state legislature, 1782-84; and was justice and deputy-surveyor of Washington County, dying near the borough of Washington in 1798.

A FRONTIER SCOUT 295

the necessary quantities of Flour till all the wheat on hand is Ground and will deliver the Same at the Cove at any time after date. I have informed the commanding Officer at Fort Henry (Cap^{tn} Hutton) he Seems to dread Sending up the River but will I hope Comply.

a Difficulty in Kegs and bags I shall endeavour to Remedy. I have about 500 Bushels of Indian Corn on hand in this Neighbourhood which I shall have Ground this Meal with what we shall get from Mr Richey will be Sufficient till a greater Supply can be had from some other Quarter of which I shall if not Possible to furnish give timely Notice.

Sir I have Received a line from Col^o McFarland of Monongahela County desiring me to Suply a Detachment From Said County engaged for 3 Months Service having Receved a bounty of 20 dollars and upwards each 59 men of which are Now lying at the Confluence of Fish Creek and are to be Augmented to 150 in 2 weeks. They have out Spyes on both Sides of the River and observe the most Profound Silence Sending out the Spies in the Night and as they find the Place has been much frequented in the enemys Crossing they entertain hopes of intercepting them.[59] When their Number is Compleat they Purpose to Reconiture Down the River as far as Middle Island

---

Craig Ritchie was a captain of militia, and in that capacity was out with Crawford in 1782; Ritchie settled in Canonsburg and became a prominent merchant. He served in the legislature, 1793-95, and died in 1833.—ED.

[59] For the pay-roll of this company of scouts, see *post*, p. 305.—ED.

Creek[60] and Place themselves as they shall deem best either in Large or Smaller Parties as they find the disposition of the enemy and their safety may best Suit.

Sir I give this intelligence in Substance as I Received it of Mr John Maddison[61] Liu^t who Came up with Col^o McFarlands Letter. Cap^{tn} John Wheetsell commands The Party.[62]

Sir If I can Serve the Publick or your honor Please to Command me by a Line with the bearer and find a Ready Compliance from your Humble and obedient Servant

AND^w ROBINSON[63]

P. S. a party coming up from Fish Creek for meal

---

[60] For this locality, see *Rev. Upper Ohio*, p. 213, note 55.—ED.

[61] John Madison Jr. was the son of the person noted in *Dunmore's War*, p. 280, note 98. The younger John lived in Monongalia County, and was ensign of this company of scouts. In 1780 he obtained a commission as surveyor of the county, and continued his surveys until his untimely death, late in 1783 or early in 1784. See his letters and those of his brothers concerning him, in Draper MSS., 5ZZ74-79.—ED.

[62] Capt. John Wetzel was born in Switzerland, about 1733. Migrating to America with his parents when he was seven years old, he settled in Rockingham County, where were born his well-known sons, Martin, Lewis, Jacob, George, and John. About 1769 he removed to the West and settled on Wheeling Creek, nearly fourteen miles above its mouth. Probably during the Indian troubles of 1774, he removed his family to the Monongahela, while himself acting with Dunmore as a scout. At the close of this war, he returned to his home on Wheeling Creek and for some time was captain of a ranger company. In 1777 his sons Lewis and Jacob were captured, but succeeded in escaping. Martin was taken in April, 1778, and was with the Shawnee two years and four months. Capt. John Wetzel was killed in the summer of 1786 or 1787 while trapping alone near the mouth of Captina Creek; see Draper MSS., 2E8-10, 24S46, 8NN25.—ED.

[63] Andrew Robinson seems to have been a trader and officer of militia, resident in Pittsburgh during 1779-81.—ED.

Tracked two Indians but a few minutes before them as a Shower of Rain convinced them &c.

To His Excellency, General Edward Hand.

A. R.

NEWS OF THE FRENCH ALLIANCE

[George Morgan to Gen. Edward Hand. 2U18—A. L. S.]

YORK TOWN [PA.] May 16th 1778.

DEAR SIR—Long live his Most Christian Majesty. I congratulate you on the Certainty of our alliance with him, on the respective Ambassadors of Brittain & France being recalled &c &c &c. The particulars of all which the Papers I have directed Mr Boreman to deliver to you with this, will fully inform you.

The Appointment of an Officer to succeed you was referred by Congress to his Excellency General Washington who has named General McIntosh[64] who

---

[64] Gen. Lachlan McIntosh was born in 1725 in the Scotch Highlands. When he was eleven years of age his father emigrated with his family to Georgia, and became the agent of the Georgia trustees for the Highland settlement of New Inverness. In wars with the Spaniards, the elder McIntosh was captured and sent prisoner to Spain; he returned broken in health and soon died. The sons were educated by their mother. At the time of the Scotch uprising in behalf of the Pretender (1745), Lachlan and his elder brother attempted to return home; but were prevented by the authority of General Oglethorpe. Lachlan spent much of his youth in Charleston as a protegé of Henry Laurens, who had a warm friendship for him. Having married, McIntosh returned to Georgia, and on the outbreak of the Revolution was called upon to head the colony troops. Their first engagement with British men-of-war at Savannah was successful, and brought their colonel into notice, so that he was chosen (September, 1776) a brigadier-general in the Continental army, in command in Georgia. An unhappy political and personal dispute with Button Gwinnett, signer of the Declaration of Independence, led to a duel in which the latter was slain. Laurens then requested Washington to call General McIntosh to the

is expected to arrive here tomorrow on his way to Fort Pitt. Mrs Hand was well at Lancaster last Monday. I did not then know of this Opportunity or I would have informed her of it. I am Dear Sir Your very obedient hum^l Servant

GEO. MORGAN

To Genl Edward Hand

[John Campbell to Col. George Rogers Clark. 48J22—
A. L. S.]

PITTSBURGH, June 8th 1778.

GENTLEMEN—As the Opportunitys from the Seat of War and Congress into your Country is so very seldom & the late Accounts from Europe are so interesting I can not refrain from communicating them to you tho I am necessitated to be concise the bounds of a letter not admiting of any thing more.

---

main army, which he joined in the autumn of 1777 and passed the winter at Valley Forge. Washington had a high opinion of McIntosh's military ability, and he knew of his acquaintance with the Indian character from long association with the tribesmen on the Georgia frontier; he therefore chose him in May, 1778, to relieve Hand at Fort Pitt. McIntosh reached that place early in August, and took the aggressive. He moved into the Indian country with Continental troops and militia, and in October built Fort McIntosh on Beaver Creek. The same autumn, Fort Laurens was built near the Delaware towns on the Tuscarawa. The next spring McIntosh was recalled from Fort Pitt at his own request. The war in Georgia necessitated his return thither, where he participated effectively in the siege of Savannah, wherein he was wounded. Later he joined Lincoln at Charleston, and was captured when that city surrendered. At the close of the Revolution, General McIntosh returned to Georgia to find his property ruined by British incursions. He served one term in Congress (1784), but his latter years were passed in obscurity. He died at Savannah, Feb. 20, 1806.—ED.

FACSIMILE OF PORTION OF LETTER OF JOHN CAMPBELL TO GEORGE ROGERS CLARK
Photographed from original in Draper MSS., 48J22

THE FRENCH ALLIANCE

The 26th of May last we Celebrated the Joyfull News here with the Discharge of Thirteen Pieces of Canon and a Tripple discharge of Musquetry.

On or about Christmas Eve last Two Treatys were concluded between the Plenipotentiary of the United States of America & The French King whereby the French King cedes all North America & the Bermudas Islands to the United States of America and declares their Independence will Trade with them and protect their Trade. The Americans are under no restrictions whatever except they shall not return to their Dependence On Great Brittain these matters are made known to the British Court by the French Ambassador the Consequence is that Brittain has recalled her Ambassador from France and Ordered him Home. Therefore we daylay expect to hear of War being Declared between the two powers and consequently we must assist France. Lord North has moved for Conciliatory Methods with America and two Acts of Parliment are passed, one suspending several Acts of Parliment or rather explaining the right of Taxation in America & the Other Appointing Commissioners to Treat with the Americans both of which according to the way they are now understood by us will be rejected with the Comtempt they deserve.

General How is said to be on the Wing from Philadelphia and I hope to have the pleasure of informing you soon that there is not a British Soldier except Prisoners on any part of the Continent of America. Mr Wells is just waiting he can inform you of some of the particulars of these glad Tidings to whom I must refer you & am Your Hum¹ Servᵗ

JOHN CAMPBELL.

Col. George Rogers Clark In His Absence to the Inhabitans of Kentucky.

MUSTER ROLLS

[1SS67.]

A List of Effects Lost of Sundry Soldiers of Captain William Formans Company of Hampshire County Volunteers appraised by Lieutenant Anthony Miller & Ensign David Wilson officers of s^d: Company Being duely Qualify^d for that Purpose

1 Captain William Forman a Rifle Gun . . £ 11" 5"
Shotpoutch & horn 10/ pocket Compas 5/ . . 00" 15"
a Blanket . . . . 1" 17" 6

2 Edward Peterson a Rifle Gun . . . . . . 11" 5"
Shotpoutch & horn 10/ Blanket 30/ . . . . 2" 0"

3 Benjamin Powel a Rifle Gun . . . . . . 12" 10"
a Blanket 1/ 17.6 shotpoutch & horn 2/ 6 . . 3"

4 Hambleton Forman a Rifle Gun . . . . . 11" 5"
one Blanket 30/ shotpoutch & horn 10/ . . . 2" 0"

5 James Green a Rifle Gun . . . . 10" 1"
a Blanket 37/ 6 . . . . 1" 17" 6

6 John Wilsons a Rifle Gun . . . . 10" 0"
shotpoutch & horn 7/ 6 Blanket 22/ 6 . . . 1" 10"

7 Jacob Pew a Rifle Gun . . . . 8" 15"
Shotpoutch & horn 10/ Blanket 18/ 9 . . . 1" 18" 9

8 Isaac Harna a Rifle Gun . . . . 12" 10"
shotpoutch & horn 10/ Blanket 37/ 6 . . . . 2" 7" 6

9 Robert McGrew a Blanket 22/ 6 . . . . . 1" 2" 6

10 Elisha Shivers a Blanket 22/ 6 . . . . . . 1" 2" 6

MUSTER ROLLS 301

11	Henry Riser a Blanket 37/6	1" 17" 6
12	Bartholomew Niney a Blanket 22/6	1" 2" 6
13	Anthony Miller a Blanket 22/6	1" 2" 6
14	Jnº: Vincint a Blanket 30/	1" 10"
15	Soloman Jones a Dº. 30/	1" 10"
16	William Ingle a Dº: 22/6	1" 2" 6
17	Nathan Forman a Dº. 22/6	1" 2" 6
18	Abraham Powel a Dº. 37/6	1" 17" 6
19	Sam¹ Lowry a Blanket 30/	1" 10"
	Sam¹ Johnston a Rifle Gun	7" 10"
	Shotpoutch & horn 10/ Blanket 22/6	1" 12" 6

We the Subscribers do hereby Certify That the within specify^d. appraisements are Just & true to the Best of our Judgments & that the several articles were lost in the late unhappy Defeat near McMechen's Narrows on the 27th of Septemb^r: 1777 as witness hands this 3^d. of octobr^r. 1777

ANTHONY MILLER Lieut
DAVID WILSON Ensgn

Sworn Before me David Shepherd   A List of the Loses in Capt Formans Company

[Additional names of men in Foreman's company, mentioned in Draper MSS., as indicated in press-mark following each name:]

Killed: Capt. William Foreman [2S280]; Hamilton Foreman [2S280]; George Avery [37J25]; Thomas Brazier [2S97; 3S3; 37J25]; Hugh Clark [37J25]; Jacob Greathouse [3S166]; Ezekiel Hedges [2S51]; Moses Lawson [9BB58]; Jacob Ogle [2S51; 3S131]; John Polk [37J25]; William Shens [2S323]; William Williams [37J25].

Captured: Jonathan Pugh [2S97].

Escaped: Harry Castleman [37J25]; John Chambers [6ZZ16]; John Cullins [2E67]; William Engle [2S97]:

Robert Harkness [3S158, 165]; William Harrod [7NN19]; Solomon Jones [9BB58]; William Linn [6ZZ9; 9BB58]; Daniel McLain [2S280]; Joseph Ogle [6ZZ9]; John Vincent [9BB58]; Martin Wetzel [2E10].

[3NN6.]

A list of 20 officers and men under Lieut. William Cross, of Monongalia militia, under command of Major James Chew at Fort Pitt, Oct 1, 1777:

John Mills, lieut., Aug. 15, on command at Wheeling; Samuel Blackford, sergt.; Henry Yoho, Aug. 15; Stephen Gasper, Aug. 15; Peter Goosey, Aug. 15; William Hall, Aug. 16; Henry Franks, Aug. 16; Roger Barton, Aug. 19; John Yoho, Sept. 1; James Flynn, Sept. 1; Bastian Keener, Sept. 2; James Purdie, Sept. 4; Aron Flowers, Sept. 4.

[3NN6, 7.]

Capt. James O'Hara's Muster Roll of Independent company of Regulars, stationed at Fort Pitt, Oct. 1, 1777:

Thomas Gibson, 1st lieut., [with] fifty-four sergeants, corporals, and privates, of whom Samuel Fury, Charles Campbell, James Ensworth, and Thomas Robertson (enlisted Sept. 8) were on command at Wheeling. Thomas Brazee, and John Polke were killed in Foreman's defeat, Sept. 27th. Abraham Enochs (enlisted Sept. 12), James Amberson (enlisted Sept. 30), and Patrick Ryan were privates.

Capt. O'Hara's pay roll for Dec. 28, 1777, returned Bryan Burns prisoner. Thomas Hendricks deserted Oct. 20; James Ensworth, Nov. 9; Michael Dillow, after Oct. 15, and John McDonald, Sept. 1.

[3NN7.]

Return of volunteer crew of "Rattletrap," under command of Capt. James Willing, Dec. 22, 1777:

Capt. Thomas Love; Sergeant John Marney; Levin Spriggs; John Walker; Richard Murray; Mark Foley; John Ash; Daniel Whittaker; Lazarus Ryan; Philip Hupp; John Gouldin; Lawrence Kanan; Samuel Taylor; John

MUSTER ROLLS

Hanwood, and James Taylor from Captain Harrison's company of the 13th Virginia regiment.

Greenberry Shores, Nathan Henderson, Richard Rody, Henry Haut and Tobrar Haut of Captain Sullivan's company.

Thomas Beard, sergeant; Nathaniel Down; James King; Alexander Chambers; William White; and John Rowland of Captain O'Hara's company.

James Ryan, Reuben Hamilton, and James Cordonis of Captain Heth's company.

JAMES WILLING.

[3NN8.]

A general return of troops stationed at Fort Pitt under the command of General Hand, Dec. 27, 1777:

One colonel; Captain Harrison and company, 46; Captain Sullivan and company, 54; Captain Heath and company, 67; Captain O'Hara and company, 40—total 208. Captain Sullivan appears to have been absent. Included in the number were two fifers and one drummer.

[3NN8.]

Volunteer company of 52 officers and privates in Pittsburgh, under General Hand, for three months from May 1, 1778:

David Duncan, captain.
John Bradley, 1st lieutenant.
Robert McKinley, 2nd lieutenant.
Roger O'Neal
Andrew Robertson
William Evans } Sergeants.
William Dawes

Privates.

John Ormsby	Ignace Labat
James McClelland	Matthew Hayes
William Redick	Rhoderick Frazer
John Terry	William Flinn Jr.
Hugh Reed	Wyllys Pierson
Hugh Quigley	Michael Strain
William Christy	Joseph Nicholas

Hugh Smith	William Boniface
Charles Richards	Jacob Haymaker
James Robertson	Jacob Grubb
William Deal	James Fleming
John Small	Andrew Neugle
John Handlen	John Dousman
John Redick	John Truine
James Brevard	Patrick McDonald
John Girty	Philip Engle
John Hoecraft	Conrad Winbiddle
Samuel Semple	William McMaicancy
James Fernsley	Matthew Gilmore
Gasper Reel	James Ryan
William Woods	James McGouldrick
Thomas Bell	Hugh O'Hara

Jacob Wise

Endorsed: Volunteer company of the town of Pittsburgh.

[3NN9, 10.]

Abstract of Westmoreland Militia ordered out on an expedition to the Indian Country by Brigadier General Edward Hand, commanded by Col. Alexander Barr, from 10 Feb-10 March, 1778, generally credited for, some to March 8:

Alexander Barr, colonel 1st Battalion		1
John Pumroy, lieutenant colonel		1
Adam Guthrey, quarter master		1
Capt. Charles Foreman & company	1st Bat^n	28
Capt. Robert Knox & company	"	17
Capt. John Hinkson & company	"	18
Capt. Richard Williams & company	"	8
Lieut. Edward McDowell & company	"	15
Capt. Andrew Lovars & company	"	18
Capt. William Love & company	"	24
		128
Capt. John McClelland & company	2nd Bat^n	19
Capt. David Marchant & company	" "	34
Capt. Hugh Martin & company	" "	18
Capt. Christopher Truby & company	" "	20
Providence Mounts, lieutenant colonel	3d Bat^n	1
John Brannon, adjutant	" "	1
Capt. James Leetch & company	" "	13
Capt. David Vance & company	" "	25

MUSTER ROLLS

Capt. John Christy & company.................. "   "   32
Capt. William Sparks & company...............4th Batⁿ 15
Capt. John Kyle & company.................... "   "   19
Capt. James Clark & company.................2nd Batⁿ 21
Capt. Hugh Mitchell & company............... 3d Batⁿ 13

Total officers and men 362
Total pay and subsistence......................£1307. 3. 6

[From Samuel T. Wiley, *History of Monongalia County, W. Va.* (Kingswood, W. V., 1883), p. 70.]

Pay Abstract of Capt. John Whitsell's [Wetzel's] company of Rangers, Monongahala County under command of Col. Daniel McFarland. Ranging in Monongahala and Ohio Counties from the 22nd day of April to the 25th July 1778 both days included:

John Whitzell, captain
William Crawford, lieutenant
John Madison, ensign
Peter Miller, sergeant
Christian Copley, sergeant

John Six
Lewis Bonnell [Bonnet]
Joseph Morris
William Hall
John Nicholas
John Duncan
John Province Jr.
Nicholas Crousber
John Six
Conrad Hur
Enoch Enochs
Valentine Lawrence
John Smith
David Casto
Philip Catt
Joseph Coone
Jacob Spangler
Philip Barker

Samuel Brown
Jacob Teusbaugh
Benjamin Wright
Philip Nicholas
Henry Yoho
Thomas Hargis
Henry Franks
Jacob Teusbaugh
Abram Eastwood
Martin Whitzell
Jacob Riffle
John Andreuer
William Gardiner
Joseph Yeager
George Catt
Matthias Riffle
Peter Goosey

INDEX

Abbott, Gov. Edward, 281, 285; sketch, 10, 11.
Albany (N. Y.), 25, 137.
Albemarle County (Va.), 196.
Albert, George S., *Frontier Forts of Pennsylvania,* 151, 166.
Alexandria (Va.), 226.
All Face, Seneca chief, 180, 188, 189.
Almon, J., *Remembrancer,* 191.
Amberson, James, 302.
American Historical Review, 271.
American Magazine of History. 157.
Amherstburg (Ont.), 250, 275.
Amwell township, resident, 112.
Anderson, John, messenger, 128.
Anderson, Capt. John, deposition, 162, 163.
Andreuer, John, 305.
Antietam (Md.), pioneer, 40.
Arbuckle, Capt. Matthew, commandant, 5, 32, 33, 157-159, 175, 205; company, 27; nephew, 162; deposition, 224; letters from, 25-27, 80, 125-128, 149, 150, 176, 232; forwards news, 186, 266, 267; on furlough, 195, 246; tries to protect hostages, 163, 177, 189.
Argyle family, 70.
Arkansas post, supplies at, 199, 202, 278.
Armstrong, Gen. John, expedition, 43, 146, 234.
Arnold, Gen. Benedict, 139, 211.
Ash, John, 302.

Ashcraft, Richard, scout, 23.
"Augusta," British ship, 152.
Augusta County (Va.), 43, 171, 225, 294; seat, 176; pioneers, 27, 79, 123, 127, 196, 248; militia, 17, 81, 105, 126, 154, 158, 162, 171, 176; defense of, 238; county formed from, 135, 136; troops march, 149, 150, 168, 169.
Avery, George, 301.
Aylett, Col. William, 17, 43.

Bailey, John, Kentucky express, 194.
Baker, George, captured, 33, 34, 254.
Baker, Joshua, pioneer, 45.
Baker family, 34, 45.
Baldwin, Thomas, at Fort Pitt, 135.
Bane, —, Virginia loyalist, 169.
Baptists, missions, 119; in Kentucky, 184, 194.
Barker, Philip, 305.
Barnet, —, 224.
Barr, —, killed, 148.
Barr, Col. Alexander, 148, 304.
Barre, Col. Isaac, speech, 211.
Barton, Roger, 302.
Bath County (Va.), 150.
Baton Rouge (La.), captured, 289.

Battles: Blue Licks, 12. Brandywine, 114, 213, 214, 219. Captina Creek, 106. Cherry Valley, 11. Cowpens, 246. Elk River, 219.

INDEX 307

Fallen Timbers, 10, 12. Germantown, 137, 214, 219, 264. Great Bridge, 213. Guilford, 27. Lake Erie, 250. Long Island, 7. Point Pleasant, 163, 175. Sandusky, 12. Stony Point, 213. Thames, 250. Tippecanoe, 10. Wyoming, 11.
Bausman, Joseph H., *History of Beaver County, Pa.*, 34, 254.

Bays: Burlington, 250. Chesapeake, 48. Sandusky, 165.
Beard, Thomas, 303.
Beaubien, Charles, 283.
Beaver County (Pa.), 44.
Becquets, Charles, 286, 287.
Becquets, Jean Baptiste, 286, 287, 291.
Bedford County (Pa.), defense of, 239; captives from, 254; officers, 39, 133; militia, 25, 134, 147, 153, 155; pioneers, 54; raided, 151, 188.
Beech Bottom, 40, 46, 51, 62, 64, 67, 83, 130, 134, 135. See also Forts.
Bell, Judith Cary, 210.
Bell, Thomas, 304.
Bellefontaine (O.), 118.
Bellefonte (Pa.), 146.
Belmont County (O.), 106.
Bentley, Thomas, 288.
Berkeley County (W. Va.), pioneers, 15, 64, 65, 67; militia, 154, 177, 238; sketch, 135.
Berry, Lieut. —, 223, 227.
Berting, Peter, pensioner, 150.
Beverly mill, site, 176.
Big Knife, Indian term for Americans, 115, 116.
Billings, Dr. John S., aid acknowledged, 5.
Billingsport (N. J.), attacked, 152, 153.
Bird, Capt. Henry, 235.
Blackfish, Shawnee chief, 26, 252.
Blackford, Samuel, 302.
Blackford, Capt. Zephaniah, 23, 84.

Blacksnake, Seneca chief, 20, 173. 180.
Blacksville (Va.), 135.
Blue Licks (Ky.), 12, 252, 254.
Boggs, Capt. John, 65, 67, 68.
Boggs, Lydia. See Mrs. Cruger.
Boggs family, 65.
Bolton, Col. Mason, 173, 174, 285.
Boniface, William, 304.
Bonnet, Lewis, 305.
Boone, Daniel, captured, 26, 252, 254, 283.
Boone, Jemima, captured, 271.
Boonesborough (Ky.), 31, 102, 103, 182, 252, 271, 283.
Booth, James, letter from, 37.
Borden, Benjamin, land grant, 105, 170.
Boreman, —, messenger, 297.
Bosseron, François, 286.
Botetourt County (Va.), militia, 4, 17, 74, 75, 154, 158, 162, 176, 189, 224, 238, 240, 266, 267, 294; troops from, 149-151, 248; officials, 43, 123, 124, 168, 169, 265; extent, 171.
Bouquet, Col. Henry, expedition, 70, 133, 219.
Bowman, Col. John, relieves Kentucky, 31, 76; campaign, 26, 182; letter, 181-183; sketch, 183.
Bowman, Capt. Joseph, 272.
Bowyer, Capt. John, 104, 105, 122-124.
Bowyer, Capt. Michael, 105.
Boyd, John, killed, 57, 60, 63.
Braddock, Gen. Edward, 15, 209, 213, 221.
Bradley, John, 303.
Brady, Samuel, 217.
Brady, William, guide, 217.
Brannon, John, 304.
Brant, Joseph, 20, 250.
Brazier, Thomas, 301, 302.
Brenton, James, 84, 216, 217.
Brevard, James, 304.
Bridges, John, 254.
British, incite Indian raids, 7-13, 19,

20, 42, 88, 102, 137, 153, 173, 232; defeated, 136-138; supplies, 201-203.
Brock, Gen. Isaac, captures Detroit, 12.
Brocus, Ann, 226.
Brodhead, Col. Daniel, expedition, 36, 61, 147, 180.
Brooke County (Va.), 22.
Brooks. See Brocus.
Brown, Samuel, 305.
Brown, Col. Thomas, 51, 52, 93, 133.
Bryant's Station (Ky.), 12.
Buchanan, Col. William, 256.
Buckingehelas, Delaware chief, 117, 118.
Bucks County (Pa.), 198.
Buffalo Historical Society, *Publications*, 173, 180.
Bukey, Hezekiah, spy, 23.
Bukey, Mrs. Jemima, 23.
Burgoyne, Col. John, defeat, 76, 145, 146, 174, 181, 188, 243, 244, 289.
Burk, Capt. Thomas, 169, 203, 204.
Burke, Edmund, speech, 211.
Burns, Bryan, 302.
Butler, Henry, 286.
Butler, Col. John, 20, 88, 173, 174, 282, 285; rangers, 11, 275; sketch, 20.
Butterfield, C. W., *History of the Girtys*, 201; *Washington-Crawford Letters*, 193; *Irvine Correspondence*, 165.
Butterworth, James, 254.
Cahokia (Ill.), 264.
Caillot. See Lachanse.
Caldwell, Billy, Indian chief, 12.
Caldwell, James, 12.
Caldwell, John, 61, 66; sketch, 61.
Caldwell, Thomas, 12.
Caldwell, Walter, killed, 79, 80.
Caldwell, Capt. William, 11, 235.
Caldwell, William Jr., 12.
Calloway, Elizabeth, captured, 271.
Calloway, Frances, captured, 271.
Cam, Hosea, messenger, 22.
Camp Union, 81, 150.

Campbell, —, killed, 71.
Campbell, Col. Arthur, letter, 38.
Campbell, Charles, 302.
Campbell, Col. Charles, captured, 70, 152.
Campbell, Col. John, Pittsburgh resident, 32, 148, 184, 185, 233, 298-300.
Campbell, Richard, killed, 71.
Canadian Archives, 218, 274, 275, 280.
Canon, Col. John, 230, 233.
Canonsburg (Pa.), 295.
Carleton, Sir Guy, governor of Canada, 9, 14, 71, 161, 274, 280.
Carlisle (Pa.), settler, 249.
Carnahan, Adam, 41, 50.
Carnahan, James, services, 41.
Carnahan, John, killed, 42, 50.
Carney family, 227.
Caroline County (Va.), 213, 264.
Carr, Thomas, scout, 23.
Castleman, Harry, 301.
Casto, David, 305.
Catawba Indians, trail, 221.
Catfish, Delaware chief, 6.
Catfish Camp, 6, 15, 67 76, 83, 132.
Catherine. See Grenadier Squaw.
Catt, George, 305.
Catt, Philip, 305.
Céloron, —, 281.
Céloron, Pierre Joseph, 147, 281.
Centre County (Pa.), 146.
Chambers, Alexander, 303.
Chambers, James, 41, 42.
Chambers, John, 301.
Charleston (S. C.), during Revolution, 190, 210, 213, 257, 297, 298.
Charleston (Md.), 73.
Chartier, Martin, 200.
Chartier, Peter, 200.
Chartier township (Pa.), 277.
Chartier's town, 200.
Chene, Isadore, 10.
Cherokee Indians, murdered, 86; hostile, 90, 203, 207, 275; envoy to, 209, 210; treaty with, 198.
Chester (Pa.), skirmish near, 146.

INDEX

Chew, Maj. James, relieves Fort Henry, 23, 49, 120-122, 129-132; scouting, 24; in skirmish, 138, 140; at Fort Pitt, 141, 302; council, 148; letters, 134, 135, 143-145; sketch, 18.
Chicago, Indian village at, 118; Historical Society *Collections*, 286.
Chickasaw Indians, 199.
Chillicothe, Shawnee clan, 20.
Chillicothe (O.), Indian town, 25, 26, 234, 283.
Chippewa Indians, at council, 7-13; at Fort Pitt, 16; war party, 50, 102, 230; interpreter, 231.
Chisholm, Mrs. John, 184.
Christy, Capt. John, 305.
Christy, William, 303.
Cisney, Capt. —, 142.
Clark, Col. George Rogers, early life, 39, 107, 181, 182; sends spy, 184; prepares for expedition, 196, 197, 202, 203, 226, 227, 263, 264, 278; letters, 248, 249, 271, 272; message for, 46; in Illinois, 182, 235, 286, 287, 290; captures Vincennes, 7, 10, 11, 281; in 1780, 26; officers, 174, 192, 194, 218, 234, 250, 251, 292; news of French alliance, 298-300; sketch, 196.
Clark, Hugh, 301.
Clark, Capt. James, 305.
Clark, John Jr., 264.
Clark, Jonathan, 264.
Clark, Richard, 264, 265.
Clinton, Sir Henry, in New York, 192.
Cloyd, Capt. —, messenger, 171.
Clymer, George, Congressional commissioner, 198, 200, 228, 229, 240.
Coitchelah, Shawnee chief, 242.
Coleman, William, merchant, 198.
Coles, Jacob, 59, 60.
Colisqua, Shawnee chief, 114, 137.
Collinstown (Va.), rendezvous, 123.
Connell, James, 220.
Connell, Zachariah, 220.
Connellsville (Pa.), founder, 216, 220, 221.

Connolly, Col. John, 72.
Conowango (Pa.), Indian village, 180.
Continental army, 2, 104, 105, 132, 133. See also the respective regiments.
Continental Congress, seat, 133, 286, 287; appoints Hand, 1; recalls Hand, 191; petitions for, 19, 109, 110, 189; resolutions, 17, 190, 191; commissioners from, 6, 184-187, 198; relations with Indians, 92-97, 113, 117, 136, 137, 236, 237; defends West, 293, 294; Spanish message for, 289; *Journals*, 187, 198, 228.
Conway, Gen. Thomas, 211.
Conwell, Yates, 23, 107.
Cook, Col. Edward, 110, 221.
Coon, Joseph, 37, 305.
Coon, Philip, 37.
Copley, Christian, 305.
Corbly, John, letter, 23.
Cordonnis, James, 303.
Cornstalk, Shawnee chief, 26, 78, 114, 126, 254; detained as hostage, 149, 150, 167; draws map, 160; murdered, 157-163, 175-177, 214, 233-237, 256, 259; murderers, 207, 208, 224, 225, 240; effect of death, 188, 189, 252.
Coshocton (Cuchachunk), Indian town, 18, 19, 27, 29, 35, 93, 96, 100, 101, 112, 118, 136, 164, 166; trail to, 179; council at, 270; Moravians, 284; Loyalists, 260, 285; expedition against, 36, 94, 96; sketch, 18, 164.
Craig, Maj. Isaac, 165.
Craig, Rev. John, 171.
Craig, Neville B., *History of Pittsburgh*, 86.
Craven, Harrison W., aid acknowledged, 277.
Crawford, Anne, 220.
Crawford, John, 143, 221.
Crawford, Lieut. William, 305.

310 INDEX

Crawford, Col. William, 54, 190, 191, 216; letters for, 193, 201, 202, 252, 253; home, 221; defeat, 4, 12, 45, 130, 235, 249, 295; sketch, 190.
Crawford family, 218.

Creeks: Beaver (Pa.), 33-36, 178, 215, 217, 228, 233, 256, 270, 298. Big Sewickley (Pa.), 69. Big Whiteley (Pa.), 69. Blacklick (Pa.), 70, 71, 153. Booth (W. Va.), 37. Brandywine (Pa.), 114. Buffalo (W. Va.), 23, 40, 41, 47, 61, 65, 67, 130. Captina (W. Va.), 106, 296. Carr's (Va.), 105, 159. Catteraugus (N. Y.), 180. Chartier (Pa.), 67, 200, 277. Conemaugh (Pa.), 41, 71, 153. Cross (O.), 4. Decker's (Pa.), 44. Dunkard (W. Va.), 21, 24; raids on, 245, 248-251, 254, 269, 279. Elk (W. Va.), 37. Fish (W. Va.), 21, 23, 254, 295, 296. French (Pa.), 147, 252, 285. Grave (W. Va.), 21-23, 46, 106, 107, 111, 112—see also Fort Grave Creek. Indian (Va.), 80. Jacob's (Pa.), 190. Kiskiminitas (Pa.), 6, 40, 41, 82, 141, 153, 174; sketch, 40. Le Bœuf (Pa.), 147, 285, 287. Little Sewickley (Pa.), 47. Little Wheeling (W. Va.), 57. Loyalhanna (Pa.), 153, 165. Mahoning (O.), 178, 219. Middle Island (W. Va.), 295, 296. Mounts (Pa.), 216. Muddy (Va.), 81, 248, 279. Neshannock (Pa.), 217. Paint (O.), 164. Peter's (Pa.), 77. Pigeon (Pa.), 45. Raccoon (Pa.), 34, 44. Sandy (W. Va.), 38. Sewickley (Pa.), 41. Shenango (Pa.), 217. Short (W. Va.), 23, 41, 135. Shurtees,—see Chartier's. Sunfish (W. Va.), 21-23. Ten Mile (Pa.), 112, 227, 264. Tinker's (O.), 165. Wheeling (W. Va.), 3, 5, 57, 59-61, 65, 66, 106, 296—see also Fort Henry. Yellow (Pa.), 133. Yellow (W. Va.), 4.

Crockett, Capt. Walter, 266.
Croghan, George, Indian trader, 4, 30, 200; residence, 50, 250; sketch, 30.
Crooks, Capt. —, 55.
Cross, Lieut. William, 23, 302.
Crousber, Nicholas, 305.
Crouse, Peter, killed, 274.
Cruger, Gen. Daniel, 65.
Cruger, Mrs. Lydia, reminiscences, 65-68; portrait, 66.
Cruzat, Col. Francisco, 290.
Culbertson's Bottom (Va.), 265.
Cullins, John, 107, 109, 110, 301.
Culpeper County (Va.), militia, 32.
Cumberland County (Pa.), 25, 133, 146, 213.
Cuyahoga (O.), see Cuyahoga River.

Dandridge, Danske, *Historic Shepherdstown*, 135.
Dandridge family, 17.
Darlington, Mary C., *Fort Pitt and Letters from the Frontier*, 3, 24, 36, 133, 148.
Darlington, William M., *Gist's Journals* 173.
Dartmouth, Lord, papers, 161.
Datahyjas, Huron Indian, 288.
Dauphin County (Pa.), 178.
Davis, Eleazar, 279.
Dawes, William, 303.
Deal, William, 304.
Declaration of Independence, signers, 132, 198, 297.
Delaware George, chief, 117, 118.
Delaware Indians, clans, 147; villages, 164, 165, 232, 298; migrations, 217, 218; in Illinois, 287; at Fort Pitt, 35, 48, 50, 86; Detroit, 7, 233; neutral, 168, 173, 285; friendly, 28, 29, 48, 86-92, 102, 179, 255; hostile, 22, 37, 67, 207, 282; hostage, 96; messages for, 86-92, 100, 112-118, 136-138, 147, 228, 229, 241-243, 269, 270, 291; messages

INDEX   311

from, 164-167, 244, 254; fear attack, 94-96, 101; captives among, 231, 234; spy, 230; Half King, 167; messengers, 178; message to Shawnee, 126; fort to be built for, 113, 117; Loyalists among, 260.
Derry settlement, on Conemaugh, 148, 153, 178.
Deserters, from Fort Pitt, 247, 278, 279, 286.
Detroit, founded, 118; British headquarters, 128, 137, 193, 234, 241-243, 249, 252, 254, 274, 280, 288; conditions described, 103, 119; governor, 10, 102, 193; Indian council at, 7-13, 19, 25; captives, 34, 38, 41, 70, 71; Loyalists, 12, 186; raids from, 152, 164; expedition against, 214, 218; Delawares at, 115, 166; spy, 231; message from, 39; evacuated, 275; taken by Americans, 12.
Dickinson, Col. John, at Fort Randolph, 149-151, 162, 177.
Dickson, —, captured, 70.
Dillow, Michael, 302.
Dinwiddie, Gov. Robert, 221.
Doddridge, Dr. Joseph, describes siege of Fort Henry, 54-58; *Notes on the Settlements*, 54, 157.
Dodge, John, 288.
Donop, Count Carl von, Hessian officer, 152.
Dougherty, Dudley, daughter captured, 180.
Dougherty family, captives, 180.
Douglass, Alexander, 76, 77.
Dousman, John, 304.
Down, Nathaniel, 303.
Draper, Lyman C., secures manuscripts, 5, 146; interviews, 12, 107, 109, 130, 164, 173, 180; correspondence, 157; cited, 103, 151.
Drennon, Capt. Jacob, Kentucky pioneer, 62, 63.
Drennon family, 62.

Drennon's Lick, 63.
Duke, Francis, killed, 64, 67; account book, 56; estate, 66.
Duke, Francis Jr., descendants, 64.
Duke, John, 64.
Dumfries (Va.), 226.
Duncan, David, 303.
Duncan, John, 305.
Dunmore, Earl of, governor of Virginia, 2, 63; expedition, 54, 61, 181, 196, 218, 296; officers, 172, 190; sends list of Loyalists, 284; in the Revolution, 11, 136, 213.
Dunmore County (Va.), militia, 17, 128, 135, 154, 177; sketch, 136.

Eastwood, Abram, 305.
Edwards, Col. John, 164.
Eighth Pennsylvania regiment, 3, 41, 69.
Eighth Virginia regiment, 27, 190, 212.
Eighteenth British infantry, 2.
Elinipsico, killed, 159, 163, 188, 189, 259.
Elliott, James, messenger to Delawares, 87, 100, 102, 115, 117.
Elliott, Matthew, Loyalist, 12, 249-256, 284.
Elliott, Col. William, 277.
Emmet, Thomas A., 271.
Engle, Philip, 304.
Engle, William, 301.
Enoch, Capt. Henry, 52.
Enochs, Abraham, 106, 302.
Enochs, Enoch, 305.
Ensworth, James, 302.
Episcopalians, in Virginia, 54.
Equeshaway, Ottawa chief, 10.
Essex (Ont.), 249.
Evans, John, map, 164.
Evans, Col. John, letter, 273, 274; sketch, 93.
Evans, William, 303.
Ewing, Catherine, relatives, 5.
Ewing, Maj. Jasper (Jesse), 7, 20,

120, 196, 248; accompanies Hand, 156, 188; letter, 253; on furlough, 192, 197, 200.

Fairfax County (Va.), 135.
"Fairfield," Virginia estate, 17.
Falls: Great Kanawha, 151.
Fanny, Indian woman, 195.
Farmer, Jacob, 21.
Fauquier County (Va.), 272.
Fayette County (Pa.), 190, 216.
Fernsley, James, 304.
Fifth Virginia regiment, 213.
First Virginia regiment, 213.
Fleming, James, 304.
Fleming, Col. William, county lieutenant, 38, 43, 123, 154, 205-209; hears of Cornstalk's murder, 168; letters, 126, 223-225; to Shawnee, 258-261; letters for, 42, 43, 74-76, 78-82, 104, 105, 122-125, 171, 172, 209-214, 240, 241, 265-268; sketch, 38.
Fleming, Mrs. William, 123.
Fleming County (Ky.), 62.
Flinn, John, messenger, 125, 127.
Flinn, William Jr., 303.
Florida, in British regime, 285, 288.
Flowers, Aaron, 302.
Floyd, John, 218, 266, 269.
Flying Crow, Seneca chief, 180, 188, 189.
Flynn, James, 302.
Foley, Mark, 302.
Forbes, Gen. John, 6, 165.
Foreman, Capt. Charles, 304.
Foreman, Hamilton, killed, 106, 134, 300.
Foreman, Nathan, 301.
Foreman, Capt. William, defeated, 95, 106-112, 118, 120, 134, 136; causes, 129, 130; losses, 121, 122, 300, 302; men buried, 120, 122; monument, 108; sketch, 106.
Forster, Elizabeth, 178.
Fort Wayne (Ind.), site, 288.

Forts: on the Ohio, 3-5. Baker's, 106. Barr, 148. Beech Bottom, 36, 40, 51, 56, 62, 64, 67, 83, 110, 111, 130, 134, 135. Beeler's, 65. Beeson's, 67. Blackmore, 38. Cherokee—see Massac. Chiswell, 265. Coon, 37, 93. Donnally, 248. Duquesne, 2, 166, 217, 286. Dunmore —see Pitt. Garard, 23. Grave Creek, 4, 22, 61; burned, 107, 110, 111; sketch, 106. Hand, 41, 69, 82, 97-99. Henry (in Greenbrier), 79. Henry, built, 54; strengthened, 39, 47, 51; garrison, 4, 23, 135, 140, 147, 148, 238; reports from, 15, 21, 46, 47, 50, 51; siege of, 32, 36, 54-68, 72, 73; losses at, 84, 85, 95, 96; after siege, 83-85, 106, 109, 120-122, 129-132, 227; Hand visits, 146, 154; later siege, 59; commandant, 295—see also Wheeling. Jefferson, 194, 264. Kern's, 44. Kittanning, 2, 3, 15, 40, 181; attacked, 46, 50; threatened, 69; evacuated, 41, 82, 97, 98, 134. Koon— see Coon. Laurens 298; Ligonier, 165, 166. McIntosh, 165, 174, 198. Martin, 273. Massac (Cherokee), 202, 203. Mercer, 152. Miami, 283. Mingo Bottom, 4. Minor, 53. Morris, 175. Muddy Creek, 81. Necessity, 216, 221. Nelson, 194. Oriskany, 173. Palmer, 152, 166. Pitt, commandant, 1-3, 298; British garrison, 2; artillery for, 17; ammunition, 267; supplies, 74; endangered, 31, 35; skirmish near, 255; smallpox at, 210; messages for, 36, 182; route to, 176; conditions at, 14, 140, 172-174, 178-181, 188-192, 231; as a rendezvous, 49, 165, 202, 214, 245; Indians visit, 48, 62, 164, 167; Indians killed, 85, 86, 233; Loyalists at, 53, 156, 184-187; Morgan, 33, 94; commissioners, 142, 236, 294; officer's council, 145-148; cattle near, 99;

INDEX 313

celebrate French alliance, 299; sketch, 2—see also Pittsburgh. Preservation, 166. Prickett's, 24, 37. Rail's, 61. Randolph, garrison of, 5, 39, 127, 140, 177; endangered, 26; reinforced, 105, 122-128, 148, 150, 151, 205, 224, 238, 240; route to, 176; rendezvous, 42, 43; Shawnee hostages at, 149, 150; Indian massacre, 157-163, 175-177, 256, 259; conditions at, 25-27, 194-196, 246-248; officer killed, 203; Hand visits, 154, 162, 171-177, 181, 184, 186, 188-191; Shawnee invited to, 260, 261; sketch, 2, 5—see also Point Pleasant. Recovery, 10. Reardon's Bottom, 4. Sackville, 10, 194—see also Vincennes. St. Etienne—see Arkansas Post. St. Louis (Ill.), 200. Schuyler, 20. Shepherd, 57, 61, 66, 109. Stanwix, 11, 20, 116. Statler, 21, 53. Swan and Van Meter, 264. Van Bibber, 78, 80. Van Meter, 64. Venango, 217. Wallace, 148, 151-153, 166. Wayne, 118, 180. Yellow Creek, 4.
Fox Indians, on Allegheny, 147.
Franklin County (Pa.), 87.
Franks, Henry, 302, 305.
Frazer, Rhoderick, 303.
Frederick County (Va.), militia, 17, 128, 154, 177, 238; recruits from, 272; counties formed from, 136; sketch, 135.
Fredericksburg (Va.), 214.
French, forts in West, 118; alliance, 297-299.
Frontiersmen, disposition towards Indians, 119, 129.
Fury, Samuel, 302.

Gaddis, Col. Thomas, letter, 51, 52.
Galbraith, Hugh, tried for Cornstalk's murder, 178.
Galloway, Joseph, letter, 161.
Galvez, Bernardo de, 289, 291, 293.
Galvez, José de, 289.

Gapen family, homestead, 217.
Gardiner, William, 305.
Gasper, Stephen, 302.
Gates, Gen. Horatio, letter for, 202, 203, 243, 250-252, 278, 279.
George, Lieut. Robert, 192.
George, Robin, messenger to Delawares, 117.
Georgetown (Ky.), 181.
Georgetown (Md.), 226.
Georgia, during Revolution, 297, 298.
Germain, Lord George, orders, 9.
Giasodo. See Guyashusta.
Gibson, —, captured, 70.
Gibson, John, captured, 70.
Gibson, John, trader, 276.
Gibson, Mrs. John, 276.
Gibson, Col. John, at Fort Pitt, 35, 145; gives information, 73, 189, 190; at council, 148; letters, 33-36, 86, 140-142, 172-174, 178-181; sketch, 35.
Gibson, Lieut. Thomas, 302.
Gilmer, Capt. —, in Augusta militia, 122.
Gilmore, Lieut. James, 246, 247.
Gilmore, John, killed, 159.
Gilmore, Matthew, 304.
Gilmore, Ensign Robert, killed near Fort Randolph, 158-160, 163, 176, 259.
Gilmore, Thomas, killed, 159.
Gilmore, William, family attacked, 159.
Gilmore family, attacked, 159.
Girty, George, 234.
Girty, James, messenger to Shawnee, 234, 235, 237, 243, 244; deserts to British, 255, 284; sketch, 234.
Girty, John, 304.
Girty, Simon, captured when a boy, 234; wife, 106; not at siege of Fort Henry, 67; suspected Loyalist, 185; arrested, 73, 172, 185; messenger to Seneca, 172-174, 179-181; on Hand's campaign, 217,

219; deserts to British, 250-256, 284; sketch, 172.
Girty's Town (O.), 235.
Gist, Christopher, scout, 209, 221.
Gist, Col. Nathaniel, 209, 214.
Givins, Capt. George, 43.
Glenn, Thomas, killed, 58, 66.
Gnadenhütten, Moravian village, 94.
Goosey, Peter, 302, 305.
Gordon, Catherine, 214.
Gordon, Capt. Harry, 166.
Gosfield township (Ont.), 235.
Goshen church (Pa.), 23.
Gouldin, John, 302.
Graham, Elizabeth, captured, 78, 79, 127.
Graham, Col. James, home attacked, 78-80, 127.
Graham, John, killed, 79, 80.
Grant, Maj. James, defeated, 166.
Granville (W. Va.), founded, 217.
Greathouse, Jacob, 301.
Green, George, Indian trader, 59.
Green, James, 300.
Green, John, 222.
Greenbrier County (Va.), settlement, 175; pioneers, 63, 80, 163; officers, 206; defense of, 238, 239; militia, 124, 224, 225, 240, 294; raid in, 78-82, 127, 159; supplies for, 123.
Greene, Col. Christopher, at Fort Mercer, 152.
Greene, Gen. Nathaniel, 246.
Greene County (Pa.), 22, 23, 53, 264.
Greensburg (Pa.), 39, 69.
"Greenway," Pennsylvania estate, 38.
Grenadier Squaw, at Fort Randolph, 195; gives information, 26, 186, 225; messenger, 209, 261; sketch, 26.
Grigsby, Charles, 37.
Grimes. See Graham.
Grubb, Jacob, 304.
Guthrie, Adam, 304.
Guthrie, Capt. Jack, 40.

Guyashusta (Giasodo, Kyashoto), Seneca chief, 173, 188, 189.
Gwinnett, Button, 297.
Haggin, James B., aid acknowledged, 182.
Haggin, John, Kentucky pioneer, 181, 182.
Haggin's Station (Ky.), settled, 182.
Haldimand, Gen. Frederick, 11.
Half King, Wyandot chief, 28, 29, 167.
Hall, Capt. James (John), at court martial, 43; at Fort Randolph, 122, 159; tried, 177.
Hall, William, 302, 305.
Hamilton, —, at Fort Randolph, 158, 159.
Hamilton, Henry, governor of Detroit, 7, 231; holds Indian council, 7-13, 19; sends out Indian parties, 29, 88, 102, 232; welcomes Loyalists, 274, 275; suspects officer, 283; hated by Americans, 9; humane policy, 282; proclamations, 14, 39, 46, 70, 71, 143, 152, 198, 242, 254, 284; letters, 161, 249, 280-288; captured by Clark, 193, 288; Delaware message for, 115; sketch, 7.
Hamilton, Lieut. John, 218, 219, 247.
Hamilton, Reuben, 303.
Hamilton family, attacked, 159.
Hammond, Philip, messenger, 248.
Hammond family, 248.
Hampshire County (W. Va.), 135, 136, 231; militia, 17, 106, 109, 134, 154, 238, 273, 300.
Hancock County (W. Va.), 45.
Hand, Gen. Edward, appointed commandant, 1-3, 16, 55, 110; describes conditions, 19, 20, 24, 25; protects frontier, 76; popularity, 144; suspected as Loyalist, 143, 185; messages to Delawares, 86-88, 112-114, 147; orders fort evacuated, 82; summons council, 145, 147; warned of raids, 15, 21, 24, 29; warns settlements, 268; plans ex-

INDEX 315

peditions, 42-45, 48-50, 74-76, 133, 158, 193-195, 201-203; abandons expeditions, 136, 148, 154-156, 192; winter campaign, 106, 190, 215-223, 256; hears of Foreman's defeat, 106; visits Fort Henry, 138-141, 145, 146; Fort Randolph, 162, 171-177, 184, 186, 188-191; hears of American success, 136; aids Clark, 196, 197; Rogers, 199; requests recall, 189, 191; recalled, 294; property near Fort Pitt, 200, 277; papers, 5; sketch, 2; portrait, 1.
Hand, Mrs. Edward, letters for, 5, 7, 16, 49, 50, 146, 156; at Fort Pitt, 200; message, 298; sketch, 5.
Handlen. John, 304.
Hanks, John, recollections of siege of Fort Henry, 58-61.
Hanna, Charles A., *Wilderness Trail*, 165, 166, 200.
Hanna, Mrs. Robert, 71.
Hannastown (Pa.), founder, 71; recruiting at, 69; rendezvous, 39, 70; Hand visits, 82; raided, 40, 71, 216; sketch, 6.
Hanwood, John, 303.
Hardin, —, mill owner, 24.
Hardman, Shawnee chief, 126.
Hargis, Thomas, 305.
Harkness, Robert, 302.
Harmon, Gen. Josiah, 235.
Harmon, Daniel, scouting, 38.
Harmon, Peter, scouting, 38.
Harmon family, 38.
Harna, Isaac, 300.
Harness, John, 23.
Harries, Samuel, 23.
Harrison, Capt. —, 302.
Harrison County (Ky.), 62, 218.
Harrison County (W. Va.), raided, 37.
Harrod, Capt. William, at Grave Creek, 4; company, 61, 302; recruiting, 43, 44; enlists with Clark, 226, 227, 263, 264; sketch, 43.
Harrodsburg (Ky.), pioneers, 182,

194, 204; garrison, 184; attacked, 31, 183; letter from, 181-183.
Hart, Nathaniel, 271.
Hathaway, Capt. —, 55.
Haut, Henry, 303.
Haut, Tobias, 303.
Hay, Jehu, British Indian agent, 9, 12, 275, 276.
Hayes, Matthew, 303.
Haymaker, Jacob, 304.
Haymond, Henry, *Harrison County, W. V.*, 37.
Hazel, Edward, 274, 275, 284.
Hazelwood, Com. John, 152.
Heath, Capt. —, 303.
Heavins, —, Virginia Layalist, 169.
Heckewelder, John, *Narrative*, 86, 166, 167, 260.
Hedges, Ezekiel, 301.
Helm, Capt. Leonard, 194, 272, 286.
Henderson, Capt. James, 79, 80, 127.
Henderson, Col. John, 80.
Henderson, Nathan, 303.
Henderson, Col. Richard, 271.
Hendricks, Thomas, 302.
Hening, Walter, *Statutes*, 143, 170.
Henry, Patrick, governor of Virginia, 16, 79, 212; plans defense, 205-209, 262, 263; sends supplies, 203; notified of Cornstalk's murder, 175-177; sends Western expeditions, 196, 197, 199, 278; letters, 16-18, 30-33, 74-76, 202, 225, 226, 240, 241; letters for, 154, 223-225.
Herbert, Michael, 249.
Hessians, attack fort, 152; attacked, 146.
Heth. See Heath.
Hickson, —, Loyalist drowned, 142-144.
Higgins, John, deserts to British, 250-255.
Higginson. See Hickson.
Hinkston, Col. John, Kentucky pioneer, 181, 218, 304.
Historical Register, 253.

Hoagland, Capt. Henry, 45.
Hodowndaoga, Seneca chief, 180.
Hoecraft, John, 304.
Holliday's Cove, 45.
Hopkins, Capt. John, 150.
Howe, Gen. William, 73, 76, 87, 138; army, 190, 208, 210; battle with, 123; leaves Philadelphia, 299.
Howel, James, 231.
Hulbert, A. B., *Indian Thoroughfares*, 178.
Hunt, John S., aid acknowledged, 219.
Huntsville (Ala.), 184.
Hupp, Philip, 302.
Hur, Conrad, 305.
Huron Indians. See Wyandot.
Hutchins, Thomas, map, 164.
Hutton, Capt. —, at Fort Henry, 296.

Illinois, British in, 285, 292; pioneers, 36, 200; expeditions to, 203, 264; historical society, 203; *Collections*, 11, 184, 281, 286-288, 292.
Independence township (O.), 165.
Indian Territory, sites in, 119.
Indiana, Indian land cessions in, 119; land grant, 194.
Indiana Company, 292.
Indiana County (Pa.), pioneers, 70, 71.
Indians, trails, 4, 279; frontiersmen murder, 85, 86, 233; council, 7-13; method of enumeration, 13. See also respective tribes.
Ingle, William, 301.
Iowa, Indians in, 147.
Iroquois Indians. See Six Nations.
Irvine, Hannah, 248.

Islands: Bermuda, 299. Long, 192. Prison, 41. St. Joseph, 288. Staten, 256.

Jack, Capt. Matthew, 69, 71.

Jack, Lieut. William, 69, 99.
Jamestown (Va.), 105.
Jefferson, Thomas, Virginia lawyer, 170.
Jennings, John, *Journal*, 292.
Johnson, Col. Guy, British Indian agent, 8.
Johnson, Sir John, at Indian treaty, 20.
Johnson, Rachel, recollections, 107, 108.
Johnson, Sir William, 116.
Johnston, John, Indian agent, 118.
Johnston, Samuel, 301.
Jones, Rev. David, cited, 4.
Jones, Gabriel, commissioner, 198, 228.
Jones, Morgan, letter from, 23.
Jones, Solomon, 301, 302.
Jumonville, Sieur de, 221.

Kalb, Baron Johann de, 211.
Kanan, Lawrence, 302.
Kanawha County (W. Va.), 175.
Kansas, Indians in, 119.
Kaskaskia (Ill.), spies sent to, 184; expedition against, 182, 194, 203, 226, 264, 286; merchants, 288; *Papers*, 184.
Kaskaskia Indians, habitat, 119.
Katy. See Grenadier Squaw.
Kayashuta. See Guyashuta.
Keener, Bastian, 302.
Kelley, —, removes from frontier, 71.
Kelly, —, messenger, 30.
Kelly, James, messenger, 178.
Kelly, John, Indian trader, 178.
Kelly, Maj. John Jr., officer, 178.
Kelly, Walter, West Virginia pioneer, 175.
Kelly family, Pennsylvania pioneers, 178.
Kelly's, on Kanawha, 125, 127, 224, 240.
Kennedy, Patrick, 292.

INDEX 317

Kenton, Simon, 164.
Kentucky, explored, 70, 164; boundary, 271; census, 183; governor, 213; constitutional convention, 194; raided, 12, 31, 102, 103, 235, 252; destitute, 283; aid for, 76; defense, 196, 197, 226; news from, 181-183; express, 233; expedition for, 263; emigration to, 61, 106, 264; pioneers, 77, 109, 162, 174, 184, 190, 194, 210, 213, 218, 300.
Kentucky County, militia, 184.
Kickapoo Indians, neutral, 102, 119; on warpath, 282; sketch, 118.
Killbuck, Delaware chief, 15, 112, 115, 244; at Detroit, 166, 254.
Kilbuck Jr., Delaware Indian, 86.
King, James, 303.
King William County (Va.), 17.
Kinkead, Andrew, 79.
Kinkead family, Augusta County pioneers, 79.
Kiscapoo, Shawnee clan, 20.
Kittanning, Indian town, 15, 146, 234. See also Fort Kittanning.
Knox, Capt. Robert, 304.
Kushayhking. See Coshocton.
Kuskuskies, Indian town, 178, 213, 230.
Kuykendall, Benjamin, 277.
Kyle, Capt. John, 305.

La Balme, Col. Mottin de, 283.
Labat, Ignace, 303.
Lachanse, Nicolas Caillot dit, 286, 287.
Lafayette, Marquis de, 105, 211.
Lafayette (Ind.), Indian town near, 118, 281.

Lakes: Erie, 103, 164, 250. George, 31. Ontario, 285.
La Mothe, Guillaume, 287, 288.
Lancaster (Pa.), 2, 20, 103, 192, 244, 298.
Lancaster County (Pa.), 56, 139, 178.
Larue County (Ky.), 184.

La Salle, Robert Cavelier de, 200.
Laughlin, Randall, captured, 70.
Laurens, Henry, 254-256, 297.
Law, John, in Mississippi company, 199.
Law, Richard, Congressional commissioner, 187.
Lawrence, Valentine, 305.
Lawson, Moses, 301.
Leach. See Leetch.
Lee, Francis Lightfoot, 132, 133.
Lee, Richard Henry, 132, 187.
Lee family, 17.
Leetch, Capt. James, 47, 56, 304.
Lewis, Col. Andrew, 124, 125, 223.
Lewis family, residence, 176.
Lewisburg (W. Va.). See Camp Union.
Lexington (Va.), resident, 105.
Leyba, Francisco de, 270.
Ligonier (Pa.), during the Revolution, 38, 39, 151, 152; pioneer, 46; raided, 165, 173, 179, 180; sketch, 165. See also Fort Ligonier.
Limestone (Ky.), 181.
Lincoln, Gen. Benjamin, 298.
Lincoln County (Ky.), 194.
Linn, Lieut. Benjamin, 183, 184, 194.
Linn, Col. William, 106, 183, 272, 302; in Foreman's defeat, 106-112, 134; letter, 132, 133; death, 109; sketch, 106.
Linn, William, of Brownsville, 109.
Linn, William Johnson, interviewed, 109.
Little Beaver, Ouiatanon chief, 119.
Lochry, Col. Archibald, county lieutenant, 3, 70, 139, 148, 166; attacked by Indians, 71; summoned to Fort Pitt, 145; letters, 39, 40, 146, 147; expedition, 41, 46, 47, 71; sketch, 39.
Lochry, Capt. William, 139, 141.
Lockhart, Capt. Patrick, 43.
Lockridge, Capt. Andrew, 79.
Loftus, Steel, killed, 80.
Logan, Indian chief, 4.

INDEX

Logan, Col. Benjamin, 164, 182, 245.
Logan, David, 248.
Logan, James, 248.
Logan, James Jr., messenger, 248.
Logan, Joseph D., 248.
Logan County (O.), Indian town in, 118.
Logan's Station (Ky.), attacked, 31.
Logstown, fort at, 34, 35, 44, 217, 254; militia, 138, 140; skirmish near, 142, 147, 155.
Long, Gideon, 53.
Long, Jeremiah, 53.
Lorimier, Louis, 283.
Loudon, negro at Fort Henry, 60, 63.
Loudon County (Md.), 58.
Loudoun County (Va.), 135, 154, 177, 263.
Louisiana, during Spanish regime, 199, 289-293.
Louisville (Ky.), 174, 194, 226, 233, 265.
Loup Indians. See Munsee.
Lovars, Capt. Andrew, 304.
Love, Capt. Thomas, 302.
Love, Capt. William, 304.
Lower Sandusky, captives at, 47.
Lowry, Samuel, 301.
Loyalists, laws against, 169, 170; troubles with, 51-53, 142-145, 184-187, 198, 207, 208; list, 284; from New York, 173; escape to Detroit, 249-256.
Lucas, Capt. Edward, 135.
Lucas, Capt. Edward Jr., 135, 140.
Lutherans, in America, 211.
Lynch, Col. Charles, 267.

McAfee, James, Kentucky pioneer, 63.
McBride, Roger, killed, 59.
McClanahan, Maj. —, 150.
McCleary, Thomas, murdered, 5.
McClellan, —, Pittsburgh resident, 141.
McClelland, James, 256, 303.
McClelland, Capt. John, 304.
McClelland's Station (Ky.), 181, 182.
McClure, David, 76, 77, 132, 133.
McColloch, Maj. Samuel, 68.
McConnell, Hugh, 66.
McConnell, Rebecca. See Shepherd.
McCown, Malcolm, tried for Cornstalk's murder, 178.
McCullough, John, 219.
McDonald, Maj. Angus, 45, 54.
McDonald, John, 302.
McDonald, Patrick, 304.
McDowell, Lieut. Edward, 304.
McDowell, Maj. Samuel, 175, 228, 229, 240, 248; sketch, 228.
McFarland, Col. Daniel, 112, 145, 148, 295, 296, 305; sketch, 112.
McFarlane, Andrew, captured, 37.
McFarren, Capt. Martin, 43.
McGary, Hugh, Kentucky pioneer, 183.
McGouldrick, James, 304.
McGrew, Robert, 300.
McGuire, Maj. Francis, 40.
McGuire, Thomas, 40.
McIntosh, John Mor, 297.
McIntosh, Gen. Lachlan, 68, 190; appointed to Fort Pitt, 297; sketch, 297.
McKee, Alexander, Loyalist, 128, 185-187, 234; residence, 186; paroled, 156; ordered East, 201; deserts to British, 143, 249-256, 260, 284; welcomed by British, 274-276, 285; sketch, 156.
McKee, Capt. William, at Fort Randolph, 125, 127, 194-196; company, 177; letter, 246-248; sketch, 125.
McKibben, John, residence, 41, 82, 97.
Mackinac, Indians gather at, 8; British at, 285, 288.
McKinley, Robert, 303.
McLain, Daniel, 108, 302.

INDEX 319

McMahon. See McMechen.
McMaicancy, William, 304.
McMechen, Dr. James, at Fort Henry, 56, 59, 60, 63; clerk, 132.
McMechen, William, 59.
McMechen's Narrows, battle at, 106, 112, 121, 129, 130, 301. See also Foreman's defeat.
McNutt, Lieut. James, 127, 128, 247.
McNutt, John, 127.
Madison, John, 296.
Madison, Lieut. John Jr., 296, 305.
Madison, Capt. Thomas, 269.
Mahoning, Indian village, 178, 179.
Malden (Ont.), 12, 275.
Malott, Catharine, captured, 106.
Mamaltese, Delaware Indian, 232.
Manchac (La.), 192, 289.
Marchand, Capt. David, 47, 56, 304.
Marchand family, 47*r*
Marion County (W. Va.), 37.
Marney, John, 302.
Marshall County (Va.), court, 108.
Martin, Capt. Hugh, 304.
Martin's Church (W. Va.), 273.
Maryland, Indians in, 200; pioneers, 59, 248; officers, 256, 257; Howe, 87.
Mascoutin Indians, war party, 282.
Mason, Capt. Samuel, at Fort Henry, 21, 23, 39, 56, 68; Beech Bottom, 62; scouting, 21, 46; sally from fort, 60-64, 74; wounded, 58, 65.
Mason County (Ky.), pioneers, 164.
Matthews, Donelly commissary, 123.
Matthews, Sampson, 123, 228, 229, 240, 248; sketch, 228.
May, David, commissary, 124, 125.
Maysville (Ky.). See Limestone.
Meason, Col. Isaac, 221.
Mequochoke, Shawnee clan, 20.
Mercer, Gen. Hugh, 214.
Mercer County (Pa.), 217.
"Merlin," British ship, 152.
Methodists, in Virginia, 54, 175.
Meymaconon, Delaware Indian, 86.

Miami Indians, village, 283; at Detroit council, 7-13; neutral, 102, 119; sketch, 118.
Michael, Huron Indian, 291.
Micheykapeecci, captured, 228, 229.
Michigan Pioneer and Historical Collections, 11, 161, 174, 220, 249.
Miller, Lieut. Anthony, 300, 301.
Miller, Peter, 305.
Miller, Capt. Samuel, 41, 55, 69.
Mills, Edward, at Fort Henry, 62.
Mills, John, at Wheeling, 59, 60, 62.
Mills, Lieut. John, 302.
Mingo Indians, towns, 4, 165, 230; friendly, 6, 114; hostile, 19, 67, 75, 86, 112, 138, 166, 235, 236, 269; war party, 95, 96, 100, 282; conciliated, 260.
Mingo Bottom, fort at, 4, 62, 63.
Mingo Junction (O.), 4.
Minor, Capt. John, 21, 24, 53.
Mississippi, settlers in, 226, 227.
Missouri, Indians in, 119.
Mitchell, Capt. Hugh, 305.
Mobile, during the Revolution, 192, 289.
Mohawk Indians, hostile, 20.
Mohican Indians, hostile, 19, 164.
Monongahela County, 305.
Monongalia County (Va.), militia, 17, 18, 84, 112, 121, 122, 129, 140, 142, 155, 177, 238, 295, 296, 302; officers, 6, 51, 145, 148; fort in, 279; volunteers, 42; raided, 255, 268; reinforcements from, 50; Loyalists in, 143.
Monongalia County (W. Va.), site in, 21, 44, 217, 273; pioneer, 135.
Monroe County (O.), 21.
Montgomery, Col. John, 194, 264.
Montgomery County (Ky.), 58, 59.
Montgomery County (Va.), 224, 239, 240, 294.
Montour, John, Indian chief, 164, 232, 280; sketch, 19.
Montreal, captives at, 41, 71, 232.
Moore, Lieut. —, killed, 194, 203.

Moorhead, —, captured, 37.
Moorhead, Capt. Samuel, at Kittanning, 3; attacked, 46; evacuates Kittanning, 82; builds Fort Hand, 41, 97-99; company of, 238; letters, 15, 37, 38, 69, 97.
Moravians, among Delawares, 164, 217, 284; villages of, 55, 94, 165, 167; raids against, 4, 130, 249. See also Zeisberger.
Morgan, an Indian, 195.
Morgan, Gen. Daniel, 246.
Morgan, Col. George, an Illinois trader, 195, 292; acting commissary, 17, 202; Indian agent, 19, 88, 89, 91, 101, 113, 114, 126, 231, 233, 235, 236; messages to Indians, 91, 92, 115-118, 136-138, 228, 234-237, 241-243, 269, 270; goes East, 20, 94, 113, 120; returns to Fort Pitt, 33; suppresses proclamation, 284; suspected as Loyalist, 128, 184-187; arrested, 143, 184, 187; released, 185; vindicated, 187, 250; letters, 86, 244, 254-257, 276, 277, 288, 297; letters for, 18, 19, 28, 100, 101, 147, 172, 173, 188, 258; writes Spanish governor, 288-293; sends news of French alliance, 297, 298; Indian name, 92, 234; sketch, 5.
Morgan, Col. Zackwell, militia officer, 18, 37, 112, 129; defending frontier, 21, 23, 24, 47, 50, 84; active against Loyalists, 52, 53, 184, 185; arrested, 142-145; letters, 18, 43, 44, 49, 52, 93; sketch, 18.
Morgantown (W. Va.), 37.
Morris, Joseph, 305.
Morris, Robert, financier, 191.
Morris, Bishop Thomas A., 175.
Morris, William, West Virginia pioneer, 175.
Morris family, of West Virginia, 175.
Moundsville (W. Va.), 108.
Mount Braddock (Pa.), 221.

Mountains: Alleghany, 6, 136, 150, 153, 174. Blue Ridge, 135, 171. Chestnut, 153. Laurel, 25, 40, 153, 165. Sewell, 151. Shenandoah, 136.
Mounts, Col. Providence, 216, 218, 304.
Muchmore, Jonathan, 254.
Muhlenberg, Gen. John Peter Gabriel, 190, 211, 212.
Munsee Indians, messenger to, 147, 164; friendly, 230; attacked, 215, 216, 228, 229; sketch, 147.
Munter's Bottom, fort at, 31.
Murphy, Samuel, recollections, 190, 216-220.
Murray, Capt. John, 27.
Murray, Louise W., *Old Tioga Point*, 180.
Murray, Richard, 302.
Muskingum County (O.), 109.
Musquake. See Fox Indians.

Natchez (Miss.), in the Revolution, 191, 226, 289.
Neilly, —, messenger, 240.
Neugle, Andrew, 304.
Neville, Col. John, 2, 244.
New Derry (Pa.), settlement, 148.
New Haven (Pa.), 221.
New Inverness (Ga.), 297.
New Orleans, relations with, 197, 287, 291; expeditions for, 191, 197-201; Spanish govern, 289.
New York, frontier attacked, 8, 76, 173, 180; Loyalists, 173; *Colonial Documents*, 8, 20; *Journals of Provincial Council*, 20.
New York City, British hold, 192, 232; public library, 5.
Newcastle (Pa.), 217.
Newell, Samuel, residence, 142.
Newton Falls (O.), 178.
Niagara, British headquarters, 11, 153, 173, 174, 179, 230, 242, 285; commandant, 285; captives at, 37,

INDEX

180, 232; scouting toward, 128; frontier, 251; Loyalists at, 11, 12.
Nicholas, John, 305.
Nicholas, Joseph, 303.
Nicholas, Philip, 305.
Nicholls family, 227.
Nicholson (Nichols), Thomas, 147, 178.
Niles (O.), site, 178.
Niney, Bartholomew, 301.
Nonhelema, Shawnee squaw, 26.
North, Lord Frederick, 299.
North Carolina, boundary, 271.
Northumberland County (Pa.), 7.
Northumberland County (Va.), 194.

Ogle, Jacob, killed, 301.
Ogle, Capt. Joseph, at Fort Henry, 55, 56; scouting, 46, 47; at siege, 64-66; Beech Bottom, 83; with Foreman, 106, 111, 302; letter, 36; sketch, 36.
Ogle family, 36.
Oglethorpe, Gen. James, 297.
O'Hara, Hugh, 304.
O'Hara, Capt. James, 278, 302, 303; portrait, 278.
Ohio, Indian trails, 178; sites, 106; pioneers, 178; Archæological and Historical Society *Publications*, 178.
Ohio County (Va.), stations in, 33; militia, 4, 17, 18, 42, 155, 245, 305; officers, 3, 108, 130, 132, 145; scouts, 37; defense of, 177, 238, 268.
Oklahoma, residents, 119.
Old Yie (Petalla), Shawnee hostage, 149, 158; murdered, 160, 163, 188, 189, 259.
O'Neal, Roger, 303.
Oneida Indians, at Oswego treaty, 20; friendly, 87, 137.
"Ontario," foundered, 285.
Orange County (Va.), 292.
Ormsby, John, 303.

Oswego (N. Y.), treaty at, 20, 173.
Ottawa Indians, in Detroit council, 7-13; at Fort Pitt, 16; village, 164, 165, 230; interpreter, 231; war party, 102.
Ouiatanon, Indian town, 7, 119, 235, 292; British commandant, 281, 282; destroyed, 213.
Ouiatanon (Wea) Indians, neutral, 102, 119; war party, 282; campaign against, 213; sketch, 118.
Ozark. See Arkansas Post.

Page, Gov. John, letter, 85, 86; message to Indians, 88-91, 114, 118.
Parsons, Capt. James,, 135.
Patterson, Robert, 61.
Parsons, Capt. James, 135.
Pattonsburg (Va.), incorporated, 123.
Paxton, Capt. —, Augusta officer, 122.
Pennsylvania, frontier defense, 1, 8, 48, 173, 180, 232; boundary dispute, 2, 48, 72, 110, 190; troops, 5, 293; legislature, 6, 24, 168; officials, 212; Loyalists in, 143, 198; *Archives*, 5, 41, 71, 147, 166, 191; *Colonial Records*, 24; *Magazine of History*, 292.
Pensacola (Fla.), captured, 289.
Pentecost, Dorsey, 38.
Peoria (Ill.), expedition against, 264.
Peoria Indians, habitat, 119.
Perrin, Edward, 40, 41.
Perry, Capt. Oliver, 250.
Petalla. See Old Yie.
Peters, Richard, 250, 253; letters for, 155, 156, 189, 192.
Peterson, Edward, 300.
Pew. See Pugh.
Philadelphia, address from, 6; officers at, 92, 139, 192, 193; Congress leaves, 133; skirmish near, 146; British take, 286; leave, 289.

21

322　INDEX

Piankeshaw Indians, 119.
Pickaway Plains, 26.
Pickaway County (O.), 68.
Pierce, Capt. —, 45.
Pierson, Wyllis, 303.
Pigman, Capt. Jesse, 22, 49, 142.
Pipe, Delaware Indian, 218, 219.
Pipe, Captain, Delaware chief, 138, 165, 218, 228, 270; village, 179; at Detroit, 166; friendly, 244.
Piper, Col. John, 133.
Piqua, Shawnee clan, 20; village, 283.
Pittsburgh, site, 50; road to, 6; claimed by two states, 2; proposed treaty at, 19; endangered, 38; reinforced, 69; supplies for, 272; smallpox at, 141; White Eyes, 95; Girty, 67, 172; blacksmith, 217; traders, 130; officers, 7; militia, 238, 276, 277; list of, 303, 304; cemetery, 277; Carnegie Museum *Annals*, 185, 277. See also Fort Pitt.
Pluggy, hostile Indian, 30; son, 15, 232.
Pluggy's Town, hostile, 5, 6, 15, 18, 19, 48, 230, 231.
Poage, Maj. George, 43.
Poage, Maj. John, 124, 172.
Poage, Robert, Augusta pioneer, 124.
Point Pleasant (W. Va.), troops at, 33, 151, 158. See also Fort Randolph.
Polk, John, 301, 302.
Pomroy, Col. John, 153, 304.
Post, Christian Frederick, 118, 217.
Potawatomi Indians, 7-13.
Potter, Gen. James, 146.
Potter, John, 146.
Powell, Abraham, 301.
Powell, Benjamin, 300.
Presbyterians, in Virginia, 171, 248; Kentucky, 164.
Preston, Robert, 266.
Preston, Col. William, letters, 168, 223-225, 265-268; letters for, 203, 204, 206, 209, 240, 241; executes will, 271; message to Shawnee, 258-261.
Price, —, Virginia Loyalist, 169.
Prince William County (Va.), 271.
Princeton (N. J.), campaign for, 146.
Proctor, Col. John, 70, 151-153, 193.
Province, John Jr., 305.
Pugh, Jacob, 254, 300.
Pugh, Jonathan, 301.
Purdie, James, 302.
Putnam, Gen. Israel, 232.

Quakers, in New Jersey, 15.
Quebec, ordinance of, 280; captives at, 232, 249; messages from, 251, 253; attacked, 139.
Queen's Rangers, 173.
Quigley, Hugh, 303.

Rader (Roeder), Capt. Michael, 135.
Rader family, 135.
Randolph County (W. Va.), 279.
Ratchkin, Capt. James, 135.
"Rattletrap," Willing's boat, 191, 202; crew of, 302, 303.
Ravenscroft, Thomas, 218.
Ray, James, Kentucky pioneer, 182, 183.
Reardon's (Rorden) Bottom, 4, 44.
Redhawk, Shawnee hostage, 149, 157, 158; murdered, 160, 163, 176, 188, 189, 259.
Redick, John, 304.
Redick, William, 303.
Redstone (Pa.), Indian raid at, 29; refugees, 59; powder magazine, 51, 52; early settlers, 58, 133, 254; council at, 45; Hand, 73; Clark, 271, 272; sketch, 42.
Reed, Hugh, 303.
Reed, Col. Joseph, commissioner, 198.
Reed's Station, 40.

INDEX 323

Reel, Gasper, 304.
Renards. See Fox Indians.
Richards, Charles, 304.
Richardson, —, murdered, 180.
Richardville, Miami chief, 283.
Richmond (Va.), 288, 292.
Riffle, Jacob, 305.
Riffle, Matthias, 305.
Riser, Henry, 301.
Ritchie, Craig, 294, 295.
Ritchie, Matthew, 294, 295.

Rivers: Allegheny, 15, 40, 70, 82, 114, 147, 153, 173, 179, 180, 188, 193, 221, 251. Auglaize, 235. Blanche, 164, 165. Cheat, 142, 143, 273. Clinch, 38. Cuyahoga, trail to, 179; stores at, 193, 215; spy, 230, 231; sketch, 164, 165. Detroit, 249. Elk (W. Va.), 206, 224. Great Kanawha, 3, 5, 42, 74, 125, 140, 151, 155, 156, 158, 163, 167, 171, 174, 175, 178, 188, 189, 232, 234, 236, 237, 250, 254, 259. Great Miami, 39, 219, 243, 251, 283. Green (Ky.), 184, 271. Greenbrier (Va.), 79. Hinkston's (Ky.), 181. Hockhocking (O.), 126. Holston, 182, 265, 271. Jackson's (Va.), 150. Kanawha—see Great Kanawha. Kentucky, 253, 283. Licking (Ky.), 181, 190. Little Kanawha, 22. Little Miami, 26, 252. Little Wabash, 265. Maumee, 235, 275. Miami—see Great Miami. Middle (Va.), 162. Mississippi, 160, 191, 194, 287. Monongahela, 21, 23, 37, 45, 55, 56, 58, 59, 93, 143, 183, 184, 217, 226, 263, 272, 273, 279, 296. Muskingum, 4, 55, 100, 165, 178, 218, 249. Ohio, 6, 10, 21, 22, 34, 45, 55, 59, 63, 81, 107, 126, 146, 163, 172, 196, 200, 203, 231, 246, 257, 258, 264, 282, 283, 287; forts on, 3-6, 47. Potomac, 15, 34, 40, 136, 217, 263. Rock (Ill.), 194. Rocky—see Great Miami. St. Joseph, 7. Schuylkill, 123, 146.

Scioto, 4, 26, 59, 88, 126, 260. Slate, 59. Susquehanna, 20, 25, 67, 174, 200. Thames (Ont.), 250. Tuscarawas (O.), 178, 218, 298. Tygart (Va.), 279. Wabash, 10, 118, 281, 286. White (Ind.), 118. Yadkin (N. C.), 103, 271. Youghiogheny, 38, 65, 67, 120, 143, 190, 216, 221.
Roberdeau, Daniel, commissioner, 187.
Robertson, Andrew, 303.
Robertson, James, 304.
Robertson, Thomas, 302.
Robinson, —, messenger, 245.
Robinson, Andrew, letter, 294-297.
Robinson, Capt. John, 5, 72, 130.
Robinson township (Pa.), 134.
Rocheblave, François Rastel, Sieur de, 286, 287.
Roche de Bout, 251.
Rockbridge County (Va.), no exposed frontier, 224; court, 177; records, 178; pioneers, 127, 159, 206, 246, 248; militia, 105, 238-240, 267, 268, 294.
Rockingham County (Va.), militia, 238, 294, 296.
Rody, Richard, 303.
Rogers, —, loses cattle 23.
Rogers, Col. David, expedition, 199, 278.
Roeder. See Rader.
Roosevelt, Theodore, *Winning of the West*, 90.
Rordon. See Reardon.
Rowan, William, tried for Cornstalk's murder, 178.
Rowland, John, 303.
Rowland, Capt. Thomas, 43.

Runs: Beaver (Pa.), 50. Crooked (W. Va.), 273. Chartier's (Pa.), 200. McGee's (Pa.), 71. Perrin's (W. Va.), 41. Piper's (Pa.), 133. Reardon's (Pa.), 44. Sandy (W.

INDEX

Va.), 254. Twelve Mile (Pa.), 39, 151. White Pine (Pa.), 82.

Russell, Col. William, in Continental army, 209-214, 218; letter for, 134; at Fort Pitt, 279; sketch, 7, 134.

Ryan, James, 303, 304.

Ryan, Lazarus, 302.

Ryan, Patrick, 302.

St. Asaph (Ky.), founded, 182.

St. Clair, Gen. Arthur, 48, 118, 166.

St. Clair County (Ill.), 36.

Ste. Genevieve (Mo.), 286.

St. Leger, Col. Barry, expedition, 20.

St. Louis, Spanish at, 290; pioneers, 174, 175.

St. Mary's (O.), trader at, 235.

Salt Lick town, Indian village, 178, 219.

Sandusky, Indian towns, 165; British at, 275, 282; traders, 280; messengers for, 19; news from, 29, 95; supplies at, 103; expedition for, 130, 134; Crawford at, 12, 134; sketch, 134.

Saunders, John, at siege of Wheeling, 60.

Savannah (Ga.), during the Revolution, 190, 297, 298.

Scotch-Irish, in Pennsylvania, 148, 153; Virginia, 170.

Scott, Gen. Charles, 119, 211, 213.

Scott, Capt. David, 216, 217, 219.

Scott, Fanny, killed, 217.

Scott, James, escaped, 217.

Scott, Phebe, killed, 217.

Scott, Samuel, killed, 213.

Second Virginia regiment, 213.

Semple, Samuel, 304.

Seneca Indians, towns, 4; chief, 20; interpreter for, 172; captive, 234; messenger to, 179; message from, 230; friendly, 8; hostile, 172-174, 180, 188, 189; fired on, 86.

Severance, Frank H., *Old Trails on Niagara Frontier*, 173, 285. "Captives at Niagara", 180.

Shannon, Capt. Samuel, at Fort Henry, 46, 50, 56, 62; sketch, 46, 47.

Shawnee Indians, clans, 20; towns, 25, 160, 165; trail, 279; migrations, 166, 200; traders among, 249; captives, 78, 296; in French and Indian War, 159; at siege of Fort Henry, 67; messages for, 92, 114, 234-237, 242-244, 266; friendly, 25, 254; chiefs held as hostages, 126; chiefs murdered, 157-163, 169, 175-177; hostile, 22, 39, 150, 189, 205, 207, 252, 255; war parties, 282, 283; at Detroit council, 7-13; attempts to conciliate, 186, 225, 258-261; McKee's influence with, 284; expedition against, 264.

Shearer, Capt. Robert, 134, 135.

Shearer, William, 134.

Shenandoah County (Va.), militia 238. See also Dunmore County.

Shens, William, 301.

Shepherd, Col. David, commandant at Fort Henry, 22, 33, 62, 66, 76, 77, 83-85, 110, 131, 301; repairs fort, 39; describes skirmish, 37; warned, 55; during siege, 60; describes siege, 72; Foreman's defeat, 106, 107; letters, 14, 15, 46, 47, 49-51, 120, 121, 222, 223, 245; letters for, 1-3, 18, 221, 222, 227; buries dead, 122; as messenger, 133; sketch, 3.

Shepherd, Moses, 65; portrait, 222.

Shepherd, Rebecca McConnell, at siege of Fort Henry, 66.

Shepherd, Sarah, 64.

Shepherd, William, killed, 66.

Shepherd family, 46, 65; residence, 57, 59; papers, 84.

Shippen, Edward, message for, 201, 216.

Shippensburg (Pa.), resident, 133.

INDEX 325

Shirley, James, messenger, 142.
Shiver, John, captured, 273.
Shivers, Elisha, 300.
Shoers, Thomas, 254.
Shores, Greenberry, 303.
Shull, —, Virginia Loyalist, 169.
Skelton, Capt. Joseph, 257, 276.
Skillern, Col. George, at court martial, 43; commands militia, 123; at Fort Randolph, 149, 150, 158, 162, 172, 177; letter, 124, 125; deposition, 224; takes deposition, 163; sketch, 123.
Six, John, 305.
Six Nations (Iroquois) Indians, towns, 164, 178, 217; attitude, 31; hostile, 8, 11, 137, 173, 274; influence on Western tribes, 20; send war-belts, 8, 19; messages, 282; interpreter for, 255. See also Mohawk, Mingo, Oneida, Seneca, Tuscarora.
Slover, John, captive, 235.
Small, John, 304.
Smallman, Maj. Thomas, 73, 276.
Smally, James, killed, 273.
Smith, —, killed, 142.
Smith, Devereux, 70-72.
Smith, Capt. Hendry, militia officer, 81.
Smith, Hugh, 304.
Smith, Col. James, pursues Indians, 70, 71, 151; letter, 153; letter for, 193; sketch, 70.
Smith, John, 305.
Smith, William Bailey, 103, 271.
"Smithfield," Preston's residence, 168.
Smith's Ferry (Ky.), 271.
Smyth, Rev. Adam, 168, 169.
Smyth, Gen. Alexander, 169.
Smyth, Samuel, surgeon, 163.
Sovereigns, Hannah, 184.
Southern Historical Magazine, 108.
Spanish, in Louisiana, 199, 287; relations with Americans, 288-293.
Spangler, Jacob, 305.

Spark, Lieut. James, 84.
Sparks, Capt. William, 305.
Spottsylvania County (Va.), records, 215.
Spriggs, Levin, 302.
Springer, Levi, 64.
Springer, Capt. Zadoc, 37.
Stagg, Mrs. Joseph, recollections, 62-65.
Stanford (Ky.), 182.
Statler family, Virginia pioneers, 21.
Staunton, Dr. Edmund, English divine, 176.
Staunton (Va.), Augusta County seat, 72; pioneers, 162, 163, 196; a rendezvous, 150; rector of, 168; Hand visits, 156, 175, 176; sketch, 176.
Steel, —, at siege of Fort Henry, 61.
Steel, Col. Archibald, 48, 49, 77, 138, 139, 201; sketch, 139.
Stephen, Gen. Adam, 213.
Stephenson, Maj. John, 190, 216-218.
Stevens, B. J., *Facsimiles*, 161.
Stewart, —, boat-builder, 256, 257.
Stewart, Maj. Jack, 256, 257.
Stewart, William, 221.
Stewart. See also Stuart.
Stewart's Crossings (Pa.), 221.
Stiles, Benjamin, 219.
Stodgill, Joel, 78.
Stony Point, captured, 257.
Strain, Michael, 303.
Stuart, Charles A., furnishes document, 157.
Stuart, James, killed, 273.
Stuart, Capt. John, letter from, 80-82; narrative, 157-162.
Sullivan, Daniel, spy, 230-233.
Sullivan, George Rogers Clark, Kentucky pioneer, 175.
Sullivan, Capt. James, 73, 174, 303.
Sullivan, Gen. John, 256.
Sullivan, John C., at St. Louis, 174, 175.
Surphlitt (Surplus), Robert (Robin), deserts to British, 250-252, 255.

Swan, Charles, 264.
Swan, John, pioneer, 263, 264.
Swan, Lieut. John Jr., 263, 264.
Swatswih. See James Girty.
Swearingen, Col. Van, 135.
Symmes, John C., 219.

Taimenend, Morgan's Indian name, 92, 116, 118, 136, 138, 243. See also Col. George Morgan.
Tammany. See Taimenend.
Tawa Indians. See Ottawa.
Taylor, Maj. Henry, 44, 45.
Taylor, Isaac, wounded, 79.
Taylor, James, 303.
Taylor, Samuel, 302.
Taylorstown (Pa.), 130.
Tennessee, boundary, 271.
Terry, John, 303.
Teusbaugh, Jacob, 305.
Third Virginia regiment, 214.
Thirteenth Virginia (West Augusta) regiment, 7, 59, 174, 218; at Fort Pitt, 279; officers, 147, 303.
Thirty-fourth British artillery, 173, 285.
Thomas, Richard, deposition, 162, 163.
Thomson, Charles, secretary of Congress, 294.
Thwaites, R. G., *Early Western Travels*, 118; *Withers's Chronicles*, 24, 37, 62, 93, 157, 249, 273.
Tinkling Spring (Va.), church, 171.
Todd, John, in Illinois, 292.
Tonti, Henri, explorer, 199.
Tomlinson, Joseph, 21, 23.
Tomlinson, Lieut. Samuel, 21, 60, 63.

Treaties: Detroit (1777), 25. Easton (1759), 234. Franco-American (1777), 299. Fort McIntosh (1785), 165. Fort Pitt (1777), 235. Fort Stanwix (1768), 22, 116. Greenville (1795), 10, 118, 119. Niagara (1777), 25. Oswego (1777), 25, 173. Paris (1783), 71. Sycamore Shoals (1775), 271. Wea Indians, 119.
Trenton (N. J.), campaign for, 146.
Truby, Capt. Christopher, 304.
Truine, John, 304.
Trumbull, Jonathan, commissary-general, 137.
Trumbull County (O.), 178.
Tucker, William, 231, 232.
Turney, Lieut. John, 282.
Tuscarora Indians, join Americans, 87, 137.
Twigtwee Indians. See Miami.
Tygart, David, 279.
Tyler County (Va.), 150.

Uniontown (Pa.), 65, 67.
Urbana (O.), founder, 162.

Valley Forge, camp at, 209, 210, 298; officer, 69.

Valleys: Cumberland, 77, 110, 148, 153. Great Kanawha, 175. Ligonier, 166. Mississippi, 199. Path, 87. Penn's, 146. Shenandoah, 135, 248. Tygart's, 279. Virginia, 170.
Van Bibber, Capt. John, 78-81.
Van Meter, Henry, pioneer, 22.
Van Meter, Jacob, 264.
Van Meter, Capt. John, 5, 110, 111, 130, 135; sketch, 22, 23.
Van Meter, John Jr., captured, 22, 23.
Vance, Capt. David, 304.
Versailles (Ky.), 213.
Villiers, Coulon de, 221.
Vincennes (Ind.), British governor, 10, 281; settler, 234; route to, 265; expedition against, 184, 226; captured, 7, 10, 11, 194, 288.
Vincent, John, 301, 302.
Virgin, Capt. Reazin, 55, 67, 68, 219.
Virginia, frontier defense, 1, 48, 205-209, 232; boundary dispute, 2, 48, 72, 110, 190, 271; invaded, 123; militia, 5, 16, 30-32; regiments, 293; governor, 114, 118, 258; legis-

INDEX

lature, 17, 132, 142, 168; convention, 70; laws, 169, 170, 239; representative in Congress, 187; British prisoners in, 286, 288; Loyalists, 143, 198; messages to Delawares, 88; supplies lead, 203; *Historical Collections*, 157; *Historical Magazine*, 178.

Wakatomica, campaign, 45.
Walker, John, 302.
Wallace, Lieut. Andrew, 27.
Wallace, David, 196.
Wallace, Peter Jr., 27.
Wallace, Richard, 71, 148.
Wallace family, 196.
Wapeymachickthe, Morgan's Shawnee name, 234, 237.
Ward, James, killed in Dunmore's War, 162-164.
Ward, Capt. James Jr., Kentucky pioneer, 163.
Ward, John, Indian captive, 164.
Ward, J. Q. A., sculptor, 162.
Ward, William, deposition, 162, 163.
Warm Springs (Va.), 150.
Warren (Pa.), 180.

Wars: French and Indian, 4, 15, 117, 146, 165, 166, 171, 190, 213, 219. Pontiac's (1763), 119, 166, 217, 219, 281, 292. Dunmore's (1774), 2, 4, 11, 196, 246, 248, 249. Cherokee (1776), 90. Spain and Great Britain (1778), 289. 1812-15, 119, 139, 235, 250, 275. Secession, 119.
Washington, Gen. George, 17; in French and Indian War, 209, 216, 217, 221; in the West, 4, 106, 107, 190; commander in chief, 104, 105, 208, 212, 213, 297, 298; appoints officers, 190, 294; commends officer, 146; encounters Howe, 87, 123; letters for, 154, 172-174.
Washington, Col. Samuel, commissioner, 198, 228.
Washington family, 17.

Washington (D. C.), Indians at, 118.
Washington (Ky.), pioneers, 164.
Washington (Pa.), 6, 294.
Washington County (Pa.), 40, 54, 77, 112, 130, 134, 200, 218, 294.
Washington County (Va.), 38, 239, 294.
Wawiaghtana. See Ouiatanon.
Wayne, Gen. Anthony, at Stony Point, 213, 257; defeats Indians, 10, 12, 118, 164, 235.
Waynesburg (Pa.), 22.
Wea Indians. See Ouiatanon.
Weedon, Gen. George, 213, 214.
Wells, —, messenger, 299.
Wellsburg (W. Va.), 41, 54.
West Augusta, committee for, 185; regiment—see Thirteenth Virginia.
West Virginia, panhandle, 135; *Historical Magazine*, 65, 78, 149.
Western Reserve (O.), settled, 165.
Westmoreland County (Pa.), boundaries, 40, 50; seat, 6; sites in, 200; officers, 37, 39, 70, 71, 110, 139, 145, 148; militia, 1, 3, 25, 134, 141, 147, 155, 215, 216, 222, 304, 305; rangers, 22; recruits, 47; raided, 147, 155, 188; frontier defense, 69-72, 238; expedition from, 193; pioneer, 41; address to, 6; sketch, 25.
Wetzel, George, 296.
Wetzel, Jacob, 296.
Wetzel, Capt. John, 296, 305.
Wetzel, John Jr., 296.
Wetzel, Lewis, 296.
Wetzel, Martin, 296, 302.
Wharton, Thomas, 24.
Wheeling (W. Va.), commandant, 14, 110; garrison, 33, 120; skirmish near, 36; threatened, 19, 26; reinforced, 49, 106; besieged, 96, 106, 107, 118, 134; after siege, 76, 77, 83-85; losses, 95; siege of 1782, 68, 233-235; war party at, 164; Clark's expedition, 39, 272; boats, 226, 227, 263; Hand visits, 138-140;

328   INDEX

settlers, 15, 59. See also Fort Henry.
Whitaker, James, 254.
White, William, 303.
White Eyes, Delaware chief, 29; warns Americans, 62, 254, 255, 268; neutral, 173; friendly, 179, 244; messages for, 112-118, 228, 229; messages from, 93-97, 100, 101, 103; message to Shawnee, 260; in danger, 35; visits Fort Pitt, 164, 166, 167; sketch, 35.
White Mingo, on warpath, 179, 180, 188, 189; at Cuyahoga, 230.
Whittaker, Daniel, 302.
Wiley, Samuel T., *History of Monongalia County*, 44, 305.
Wilkinson, Gen. James, expedition, 119.
Williams, Capt. Richard, 304.
Williams, William, 301.
Williamsburgh (Va.), 16, 17, 142-144.
Williamson, Capt. David, 55, 130, 135.
Williamson, John, 130.
Williamson, Joseph, 130.
Willing, Anne Shippen, 191.
Willing, Charles, 191.
Willing, Capt. James, expedition, 191, 202; supplies for, 278, 290; boat crew, 302, 303; captures boat, 286; buys land, 200; letter, 198, 199; sketch, 191.
Willing, Thomas, financier, 191.
Wilmington (Del.), skirmish near, 146.
Wilson, —, mill owner, 24.
Wilson, Ensign David, 300, 301.
Wilson, James, Pennsylvania pioneer, 153.
Wilson, John, 300.
Wilson, Rev. Robert, 164.
Winbiddie, Conrad, 304.
Winchester (Va.), 181, 272.
Wingenund (Wiondoughwalind). Delaware chief, 95, 96, 101, 102, 118, 119.

Winston, Richard, 292.
Wise, Jacob, 304.
Wisconsin Historical Collections, 7-9, 29, 147.
Withers, Alexander, secures information, 61. See also, Thwaites, *Withers's Chronicles*,
Wood, James, at Indian towns, 4, 172.
Woodford, Gen. William, 213.
Woodford County (Ky.), 79, 213.
Woods, Ensign —, killed, 166.
Woods, William, 304.
Woodstock (Va.), 211, 212.
Worley, Nathan, killed, 21.
Wright, Benjamin, 305.
Wright, Capt. James, 77.
Wright, Joshua, 77.
Wyandot (Huron) Indians, at Detroit council, 7-13; friendly, 6; urged to war, 137; hostile, 19, 20, 29, 48, 86, 88, 112, 138, 154, 235, 236, 269; war parties, 35, 50, 95, 96, 100, 164, 254, 255, 268; at siege of Wheeling, 67; at Cuyahoga, 230; relations with Delawares, 28, 29, 167, 242; with Mingo, 147; chief, 25; conciliated, 260; in War of 1812-15, 275.

Xenia (O.), 26, 252.

Yeager, Joseph, 305.
Yeates, Jasper, letters for, 5, 6, 19, 20, 48, 49, 118-120, 128, 188-192, 197-201, 215, 216, 249, 250, 253; sketch, 5.
Yeates, Sarah, 5.
Yoho, Henry, 302, 305.
Yoho, John, 302.
Yohogania County (Va.), court, 190; officers, 51, 110, 145, 148, 220, 233, 294; militia, 17, 155, 177; volunteers, 42; defense of, 238; records, 185, 277.

INDEX

York (Pa.), 136, 201, 251, 255, 297.
Yorktown (Va.), siege, 214.

Zane, Andrew, early Wheeling settler, 15; at siege, 56, 57, 60, 63; sketch, 56.
Zane, Ebenezer, 15, 61, 62, 64.
Zane, Isaac, captured, 15.
Zane, Jonathan, 15.
Zane, Noah, 61.
Zane, Robert, 15.
Zane, Silas, 15, 57, 59.
Zane, William, 15.
Zeisberger, David, Moravian missionary, 244; letters, 67, 93, 94, 101, 102, 118, 164-167; warns settlers, 18, 19, 27-29; commended, 92, 115; British address, 284; sketch, 18.